REVOLUTIONARY
CHINESE COOKBOOK

REVOLUTIONARY CHINESE COOKBOOK

Recipes from Hunan Province

FUCHSIA DUNLOP

Food photography by Georgia Glynn Smith,
with additional photography by Fuchsia Dunlop

W. W. NORTON & COMPANY
NEW YORK LONDON

FOR LIU WEI AND SANSAN

Photography by Georgia Glynn Smith

First published in Great Britain in 2006 by Ebury Press,
Random House Group, 20 Vauxhall Bridge Road, London SW1V 2SA

1 3 5 7 9 10 8 6 4 2

First American edition 2007

Book design by David Fordham and Two Associates

Library of Congress Cataloging-in-Publication Data

Dunlop, Fuchsia.
Revolutionary Chinese Cookbook: recipes from Hunan province /
Fuchsia Dunlop.— 1st American ed.
p. cm.
Includes bibliographical references and index.
ISBN 0-393-06222-8
1. Cookery, Chinese. 1. Title.

W. W. Norton & Company, Inc., 500 Fifth Avenue, New York, N.Y.
10110
www.wwnorton.com

W. W. Norton & Company Ltd., Castle House, 75/76 Wells Street,
London W1T 3QT

Printed and bound in China by C&C Offset

★ CONTENTS

Hunan Province

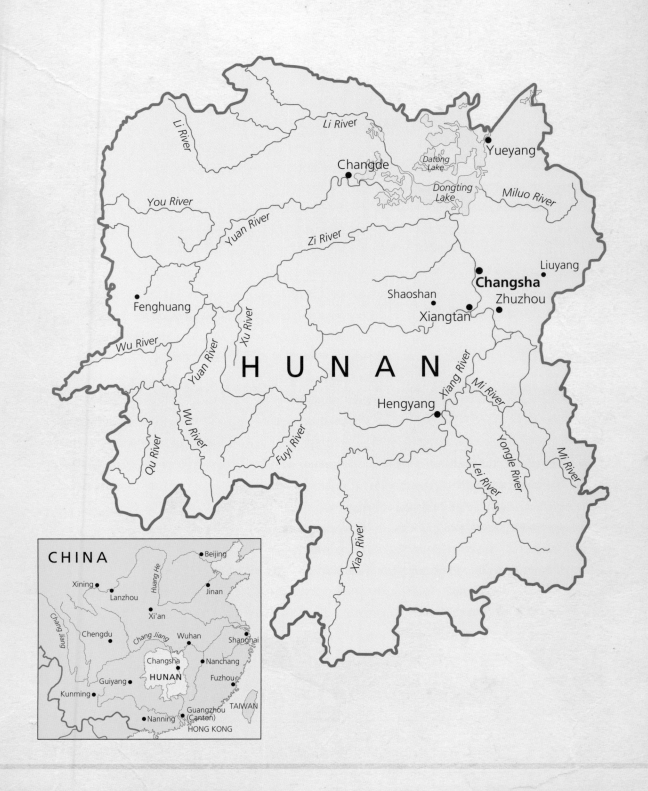

★ FOREWORD
BY KEN HOM

Fuchsia Dunlop has done it again! In *Revolutionary Chinese Cookbook*, the follow-up to her landmark *Land of Plenty*, she has brought to life a vibrant regional cuisine that is little known outside China.

Through her brilliant prose and clear recipes, Fuchsia is our guide to some of the most mouthwatering food and exciting cooking in the world. Her authoritative writing not only evokes her personal experiences, but her skilled translations of an often ambiguous language and her understanding of its exotic ingredients open the way to some of my favorite flavors in the whole of China.

Fuchsia takes the reader through the most significant dishes in Hunanese cuisine, from savory sweet-and-sour ribs to the classic Chairman Mao's red-braised pork, along with its many variations on the basic recipe. With recipes such as these she knows how to celebrate Chinese New Year, Hunan-style, as is evident from her personal observations of that important festival. Beef with cumin is a dish I have enjoyed in the past, but did not know how to make, and it, too, is here in all its glory. I was convinced Fuchsia must be at least half-Chinese when I savored her Dong'an chicken recipe, or when she so enthusiastically delves into the mystery of General Tso's chicken. Who could resist her dry-wok spicy duck? Fuchsia's version of Yueyang velveted fish is certainly the best recipe of that dish I have ever seen, and her home-style bean curd is practically the comfort food of my childhood my mother used to make. The vegetable section is full of traditional recipes little seen outside of China until now, and I can almost taste the richness and fullness of her soups. Her rice and noodle dishes will push you to your kitchen in your eagerness to make every recipe.

Fuchsia is a natural teacher: she does not give you recipes without the necessary tools. Her carefully thought through chapter on preserves, stocks, and other essentials equips you with the vital knowledge to realize the full glory of this really fabulous cuisine. And on top of all that, I love the way she has weaved in touching personal observations with a deep affection for the Chinese people and passion for their cuisine.

When I first read this book, it transported me back to China. I felt like heating up my wok and cooking every single recipe. When you, too, have read this book, you will understand what I mean.

Ken Hom
Bangkok, Thailand

湘菜

★ INTRODUCTION

★ INTRODUCTION

Chairman Mao famously said you can't be a revolutionary if you don't eat chiles (*bu chi la jiao bu ge ming*). His words were in tune with the ancient Chinese belief that you are what you eat, and that environment, diet, and human character are all intimately related. Mao himself came from the southern Chinese province of Hunan, a region famous not only for its spicy cooking, but also for the revolutionary militancy of its people. Over the past two centuries, Hunan has produced some of China's most formidable politicians and indomitable soldiers, including the nineteenth-century scholar-commander Zeng Guofan, legendary General Zuo Zongtang (the man immortalized in the name of the American-Chinese dish "General Tso's chicken"), and a whole generation of communist revolutionaries. Mao Zedong, the province's most famous son, is still remembered affectionately by local people, who say he was the product of the uniquely propitious *feng shui* of the region. Mao's home village of Shaoshan has become a shrine to the revolution, and is one of the few places in China where you still sometimes hear "Comrade" used as a form of address. Most Chinese people insist that the Hunanese have the hottest tastes in the country. As the old joke goes:

The Sichuanese are not afraid of chili heat;
No degree of hotness will affright the people of Guizhou;
But those Hunanese are terrified of food that isn't *hot.*

Their spicy diet is said to make the people of Hunan hot and fiery in nature: in fact, so renowned are they for their valor and tenacity that the Chinese say you can't have a true army without them. Hunanese women are known for their amorousness, and sometimes for being a little shrewish. I've even heard them described as *huo la la*, a phrase that literally means "fire-hot-hot," but is used admiringly to express their strength, straightforwardness, and capability.

Hunanese food, as you might expect, is as bold and colorful as its people. Picture a table set for dinner with rice bowls and chopsticks, the chatter of a family gathered around. The wooden surface is laden with dishes: a cool coriander (cilantro) salad with a hot-and-

Above: DRIED RED CHILES — THE CULINARY SYMBOL OF HUNAN PROVINCE

sour dressing; a dark, thick stew of pork belly braised to sumptuous tenderness; a wok-cooked riverfish scattered with handfuls of purple perilla; intensely smoky bacon, steamed in an earthenware bowl with dried chiles and black fermented beans; and a bamboo shoot stir-fry that dances with the fresh brightness of red peppers and Chinese leeks.

HUNAN PROVINCE

Hunan lies in southern central China, nestling at the base of the Dongting Lake, where the waters of the Yangtze gather after their thundering passage through the Three Gorges (Hunan literally means "South of the Lake"). It shares its borders with six other provinces, including Hubei to the north and Guangdong to the south. In the east of the province, where the Xiang River snakes up through hilly country to the northern plains and the great lake, the land is a patchwork of rice paddies, filling every valley like a flood of green, lapping at the feet of the hills. In the west, toward the borders with Chongqing and Guizhou, there are craggier hills and mountains, and the startling scenery of the Zhangjiajie nature reserve, with its towering peaks shrouded in mist. Once this was

Above: FENGHUANG IN WESTERN HUNAN

notorious bandit country; these days it still seems like another land, inhabited by people of the Miao, Dong and Tujia ethnic groups, with their distinctive styles of dress and architecture.

The province has a southern, subtropical climate, four distinct seasons and fertile earth, and is one of the richest agricultural regions in China. The area of the northern plains, around the shores of the Dongting Lake, has been known poetically since ancient times as "a land of fish and rice" (*yu mi zhi xiang*), and praised for the abundance of its produce, while the west of the province is famous for its edible wild animals and plants. Celebrated local products include wild turtles, citrus fruit, bamboo shoots, many varieties of fish, silver-needle tea, and lotus seeds, once sent in tribute to the imperial court, as well as the scarlet chiles, which, fresh, dried, or pickled, are brilliantly displayed in every market in the province.

The flavors of hunan

The Hunanese share with their neighbors in Sichuan and Guizhou a love of chiles, but they have their own, distinctive ways of using them. Fresh chiles and sweet bell peppers lend their bright red and green hues to all manner of stir-fries. Dried chiles, whole or pounded into flakes, spice up stews, steamed dishes, stir-fries, and salads. "White" pickled chiles are blanched in the sun and then steeped in brine, and there are also chili oils, chili pastes, and chili-laced relishes. Above all, rough-chopped salted chiles (*duo la jiao*), with their refreshing blend of sour and spicy tastes, are one of the characteristic flavors of the region. This vibrant, scarlet relish is eaten raw with

Above: PICKLED VEGETABLES

noodles, added to wok-cooked dishes as a seasoning, and used to simple but spectacular effect in steaming, where it combines with the cooking juices to make a seductive sauce.

Like people all over China, the Hunanese explain their dietary predilections in terms of the local climate. Winters are cool and damp, summers insufferably sultry, and Chinese medicine advises that these unhealthy humors should be treated with drying, heating foods like chili that drive out sweat and dampness, and restore the harmony of the body. Chiles are also thought to whet the appetite, and have a vital and almost spiritual importance for many local people. One restaurant manager confessed to me that after a few days of delicately flavored food during his travels to the south of China, he felt his spirits flagging, and began to feel sad. "It's like an opium addiction," he sighed.

But contrary to popular stereotype both in China and abroad, Hunanese cooking is not always fiendishly hot. Hunan is a region of bold spicy tastes, but also of soothing slow-cooked stews, delicate steamed vegetables, delicious smoked meats, and refreshing stir-fries. The Hunanese themselves maintain that it's their neighbors in Sichuan and Guizhou who use chiles to painful excess, while they themselves apply the spice with grace and subtlety.

The hotness of chiles is often combined with saltiness, most typically that of dark, intensely flavored black fermented soybeans. The Hunanese also love sour-and-hot (*suan la*) blends of chili with vinegar or preserved and pickled vegetables, which awake the appetite and refresh the palate. Curiously, they have a marked aversion to mixing sweet and savory tastes, which sets them apart from their spicy Sichuanese neighbors. Sugar is often absent from the *mise-en-place* of the professional Hunanese kitchen, and sweet foods play almost no part in everyday dining. Sweetmeats and sugared dumplings might be enjoyed as snacks between meals, but it is only in banquet cooking, which always involves a blurring of the boundaries of regional styles, that you commonly find sugar-sweetened dishes.

The west of Hunan is particularly known for its smoked meats, fish, and poultry, although such foods are made and eaten all over the province. In the Hunanese winter, you'll find slabs of pork belly, carp, and chickens smoking slowly over wood fires in the kitchens of most rural homes; and even in the cities, salted fish and meats hang outside apartment windows before an eventual smoking in the yard. Such meats are sometimes served on their own, perhaps after steaming with salted beans and ground chiles, but they also lend their rich, smoky flavor to all kinds of stir-fries. Another favorite winter treat in Hunan is the hotpot: a simmering pot on the table into which raw or partially cooked ingredients are dipped (see the introduction to the Soup Dishes chapter on pages 234–5).

One of the most exciting strands of Hunanese cuisine is its steamed dishes, which play a central role in the local diet. Their preparation is simplicity itself, they are nutritionally rich, and their flavors can be marvelous. Some are spicy-hot, like steamed taro with salted chiles; others have gentler tastes, like fresh peas steamed simply with slivers of ginger, a sprinkling of salt, and a drizzling of oil. And there are the subtle, comforting tonic soups and stews, such as broths of spare ribs simmered with soybeans or corn; and "Squab with five spheres," a delicate brew scattered with wolfberries, dragon-eye fruit, lychees, lotus seeds, and Chinese dates. These are dishes that exemplify the culinary principle of *yuan zhi yuan wei* ("plain, original juices and flavors"), with an emphasis on the primary tastes of raw ingredients.

The Hunanese have a strong sense of regional identity, seeing themselves as the movers and shakers of China, people who rise above petty concerns and confront the important issues of life. In local eyes, Hunan is the beating heart of China, a powerhouse of talent that has shaped the destiny of the country.

Above: HUNANESE SUPPER DISHES

Likewise, many people view Hunanese cooking as being perfectly balanced in every sense. Chefs in different parts of the province have assured me that Sichuanese food is so hot and numbing the palate is blinded to more subtle nuances of flavor; Cantonese food is too bland, and the food of the east is unspeakably sweet. Only Hunanese cuisine, they say, has what it takes to please everybody.

THE HISTORICAL ROOTS OF HUNANESE COOKING

Some of the richest information about the distant past of Chinese food culture comes from the region today known as Hunan. Some two-and-a-half millennia ago, around the time of Confucius, the area was part of the state of Chu. It was also the home in exile of the great poet Qu Yuan, who died near the Dongting Lake, and once wrote a mouthwatering description of a banquet in an invocation designed to lure back a departed soul:

> O soul, come back! Why should you go far away?
> All your household have come to do you honor; all kinds of good food are ready:
> Rice, broom-corn, early wheat, mixed all with yellow millet;
> Bitter, salt, sour, hot and sweet: there are dishes of all flavors.
> Ribs of the fattened ox cooked tender and succulent;
> Sour and bitter blended in the soup of Wu;
> Stewed turtle and roast kid, served up with yam sauce;
> Geese cooked in sour sauce, casseroled duck, fried flesh of the great crane;
> Braised chicken, seethed tortoise, high-seasoned, but not to spoil the taste;
> Fried honey-cakes of rice flour and malt-sugar sweetmeats;
> Jade-like wine, honey-flavored, fills the winged cups;
> Ice-cooled liquor, strained of impurities, clear wine, cool and refreshing;
> Here are laid out the patterned ladles, and here is sparkling wine.

FROM "THE SUMMONS OF THE SOUL," IN *THE SONGS OF THE SOUTH: AN ANCIENT CHINESE ANTHOLOGY OF POEMS BY QU YUAN AND OTHER POETS* (PENGUIN CLASSICS, LONDON, 1985, TRANSLATED BY DAVID HAWKES.)

A few hundred years later, in the second century BC, the area that is now the Hunanese provincial capital, Changsha, was the home of an astonishing culture, whose exquisite woven and embroidered textiles, painted lacquerwares and sophisticated medical and philosophical manuscripts were unearthed

Above: BAMBOO TRUNKS, NEAR YUEYANG

in a state of almost miraculous preservation in the 1970s. These treasures were found in the tombs of three Han dynasty nobles, the wealthy Marquis of Dai, his wife, and their son, who were buried at Mawangdui on the outskirts of Changsha with all they might need in the afterlife. They were accompanied by armies of wooden figurines representing domestic servants, chessboards, makeup boxes, musical instruments, and luxurious robes; and also cooking pots and steamers, extravagant serving dishes of painted lacquer, and, inevitably, plenty of food.

The Mawangdui excavations yielded a wealth of evidence of how the upper classes of this region cooked and ate some 2,000 years ago. There were many different grains; the bones of all kinds of beasts and fowl, fruits, eggshells, millet cakes, and medicinal herbs that included cassia bark and Sichuan pepper. The burial inventory, inscribed on bamboo strips, recorded flavorings such as malt sugar, salt, vinegar, pickles, fermented sauce and honey, various dishes and soups, and some ten different cooking methods, among them barbecuing, boiling, frying, steaming, salt-curing, and pickling. There was even a tray laid with a meal for the Marquis's wife: five cooked dishes, one cup each of soup and of wine, a bowl of grain, some skewers of barbecued meat, and a pair of chopsticks.

The more than 2,000 years since the Marquis and his family were buried have inevitably seen enormous changes in local cooking methods and dietary habits, most conspicuously in the adoption of the chili as the favorite local spice. Yet, what is also striking, when you survey the foods on sale in the bustling wholesale market at today's Mawangdui, and watch people cook in Hunanese kitchens, is what still remains of the cooking and eating habits of this long-lost era. Fermented black soybeans like those discovered in the tombs are still one of the most important local seasonings; lotus stem, found in slices in a painted lacquer tripod, is still a favorite vegetable; and the steaming of foods remains one of Hunan's most distinctive cooking methods.

Over the centuries, Hunan became known as one of the cultural centers of China. Great poets and essayists wrote admiringly of the sights of the region, including the famous Yueyang Pagoda with its views over the Dongting Lake to Junshan Island. Some of them mentioned the region's food in their verse.

Above: DRIED RED CHILES

Despite the remarkable threads of continuity in the history of Chinese and Hunanese food, the emergence of regional cuisines as we know them today is a comparatively recent phenomenon, dating back in many cases to the nineteenth century. The chili itself, now at the heart of Hunanese cooking, only reached China from the Americas in the late Ming, although the Hunanese were among the first in China to adopt it, in the late seventeenth century.

By the mid-nineteenth century, Changsha had become known for its flourishing catering industry. There were teahouses and noodle shops, companies that specialized in preparing banquets to order in private homes, and grand restaurants, of which the most notable became known as the "ten pillars" of the trade. Restaurateurs formed their own guild, and built a temple on Yongqing Street, where they made offerings to the mythologized founder of their profession, Yi Ya, a cook of legendary talent who worked for the Duke of Qi in the seventh century BC. (And who is said to have made his own son into a soup at the duke's request.)

The roots of modern Hunanese haute cuisine, now considered to be one of the eight regional schools of Chinese cooking, lie in the grand residences of imperial bureaucrats in the Qing period. There, private cooks created banquet delicacies for their highly educated and discriminating guests, stimulating a tradition of Epicureanism that spilled over into commercial restaurants in the civic sphere. The tradition of private cooks in official residences was still flourishing in the Republican period in the early twentieth century, when the food served in the house of one military official named Tan Yankai became so famous that it spawned its own school of Hunanese cuisine. (See page 191.)

But like haute cuisines all over China, Hunanese banquet cooking evolved to please the palates of the cosmopolitan elite and imperial and Nationalist grandees who served terms of office in many parts of the country. Incorporating influences from all over China, it relies on artful cutting, expensive ingredients, and complex cooking methods, and is far removed from the bold spiciness of everyday Hunanese food.

You can still taste some of Hunan's traditional banquet dishes at the Yuloudong restaurant in Changsha, but they have largely fallen out of fashion. Chefs regard old dishes like "Yolkless eggs with flower mushrooms" as absurdly complicated, and these days rustic cooking is all the rage. For despite the refinements that have won recognition for Hunanese cuisine as one of the "eight great culinary schools of China," the province is best known for the hearty peasant cooking that fueled a generation of revolutionary leaders, and which Mao Zedong continued to eat as the Chairman of the Communist Party in Beijing, when he had the culinary riches of the whole of China at his disposal.

Chinese food in a revolutionary century

The last century has been one of extraordinary turmoil and upheaval in China, from the overthrow of the last imperial dynasty in 1911, through republicanism, civil war, and Japanese invasion to the communist takeover in 1949. After a few years' respite in the early, optimistic days of Chinese communism, the country was torn apart again by political campaigns, economic lunacy, and the chaos of the Cultural Revolution. Now, following the economic reforms of the 1980s and 90s, China is once more in a state of radical transformation, as it undergoes a new, capitalist revolution. Food, cooking, and eating habits are the mirror of society, and no more so than in China, a country and a culture that has always had an unusual preoccupation with food. ("To the people, food is heaven," runs the ancient and oft-quoted saying.) Over the last century, Chinese and Hunanese culinary culture have also been shaped by the vicissitudes of revolution.

The late Qing dynasty and Republican periods were by all accounts the giddy heyday of Hunanese haute cuisine. But while high-ranking civil servants, and, later, Nationalist politicians, vied to outdo one another in the extravagance and sophistication of their private dinner parties, it was a different story for the poor. A recurring theme in accounts by Western visitors to China in the 1930s and 40s was the sickening contrast between the lavish banquets of the elite and the grinding poverty and hunger of those at the other end of the social scale. The Japanese invasion in the late 1930s brought widespread hardship and created floods of refugees, and in Changsha itself a botched response to the Japanese threat led to the almost total destruction of the city by fire, including its glittering restaurants and teahouses.

For the communists, food was always a political issue. In Mao's 1927 report on the Hunan peasant movement, he described how poor farmers were turning the tables on the landlords, their former oppressors. In some places women and peasants gatecrashed temple banquets, eating and drinking their fill as the "tyrants and evil gentry took flight." Peasant associations banned the recreational activities of the wealthy, including fine dining, and laid down rules on what could and could not be eaten. In Mao's own home village, Shaoshan, it was decided that guests should be served with "only

Above: REVOLUTIONARY POSTER: "WE ARE FOREVER LOYAL TO YOU, RESPECTED AND BELOVED LEADER CHAIRMAN MAO"

three kinds of animal food, namely chicken, fish, and pork," and in Hengshan county that "eight dishes and no more may be served at a banquet." In some places, the killing of oxen was prohibited because they were needed to work the land, and there were restrictions on the keeping of pigs and poultry, because they consumed grain that could otherwise feed the poor.

After their defeat by Mao Zedong's communist forces in 1949, the remnants of the Nationalist regime fled to Taiwan. Among their retinues were some of China's leading chefs, and for decades the Republic of China on Taiwan laid claim to being the custodian of Chinese gastronomy and culinary culture. On the Mainland, the communists implemented their socialist economic reforms, with devastating effects on the culture of food. In 1956, private restaurants were nationalized, an event that is now remembered as the harbinger of a long decline in incentives for chefs, and in the standard of the food they produced. Two years later, communes were set up across the country during the Great Leap Forward. Private cooking was banned, whole villages ate together in commune canteens and even their cooking pots were melted down in a futile attempt to make steel. The skewed priorities and crazy ambition of the Great Leap led to a famine that claimed an estimated thirty million lives over the next three years.

The Cultural Revolution, launched in 1966, became an all-out assault on bourgeois culture, including gastronomy and fine dining. Restaurants in Changsha were told to "cater to the needs of the masses," and serve "cheap and substantial" food. Some famous restaurants were given revolutionary names, customers had to serve themselves, and there was an attack on traditional skills and specialties.

(The architect of all this chaos, Mao Zedong, was famously rustic in his own eating habits, and had a lifelong distaste for refined and exotic food.) After the violence of the early Cultural Revolution, former Red Guards and other teenagers were sent down to the countryside to live as peasants for years. There, they scraped a living from the land, and according to many accounts were perpetually hungry.

With the implementation of economic reforms in the 1980s and 90s, Chinese culinary culture began to recover. Rationing of basic foodstuffs was gradually phased out, small restaurants and street vendors began to flourish once more, and living standards rose dramatically for many. The Hunanese catering industry now seems to have recovered something of its old vitality. Huge, slick restaurants compete with one another in design and culinary innovation; new dishes appear all the time.

I have tried in this book to include recipes that give a glimpse of this turbulent revolutionary century. So you will find a stir-fried chicken dish that was popular in restaurants in the late Qing dynasty, and a ridiculously complicated egg dish that recalls the 1930s heyday of the Changsha restaurant industry. There are recipes for some of Chairman Mao's favorite peasant dishes, which I gleaned from his nephew in Shaoshan and his Hunanese chef; recipes from restaurants that were given

Above: BEAN CURD VENDOR

revolutionary names during the Cultural Revolution, and recipes created by a famous chef who fled to Taiwan with the Nationalist army at the end of the civil war. You will also find street snacks that have been sold outside the Fire Temple in Changsha for generations; home-cooked dishes from the remote Hunanese countryside; poverty foods that were eaten out of desperation in the famine of the early 1960s, but have now come into fashion; and some tony dishes that are the product of the rampant capitalism of the past two decades.

Beyond all this, you will find echoes of Hunan's ancient past in the hotpots and chafing dishes, the *zong zi* rice parcels that are tied up with the memory of the poet Qu Yuan; and the ingredients, like black fermented soybeans, that have been eaten in this richly historical region for more than 2,000 years. For the food of Hunan, like that of China itself, embodies a narrative of a place, a tale of shifting ideologies, and the comings and goings of people, of political change and revolution, and, through all this, of the joys and sorrows of ordinary people's lives.

★ THE HUNANESE PANTRY

BEAN CURD

豆
腐 Fresh white bean curd (*bai dou fu* or *shui dou fu*), also called tofu, varies in consistency, depending on how much water has been pressed out of it. Most Chinese stores in the West sell one type of "firm" bean curd and one type of soft or "silken" bean curd (see below). Use "firm" bean curd, which holds its shape when sliced or cubed, in the recipes in this book unless otherwise specified.

BEAN CURD PUFFS

you dou fu

油
豆
腐 These chunks of golden deep-fried bean curd have a spongy consistency. They absorb the flavors of braised dishes and have a wonderful juicy mouthfeel. They are sold chilled in good Chinese food stores.

BEAN CURD SKIN ROLLS

dou sun

豆
笋 The thin, brittle sheets known in the West as "bean curd skin" (*yuba* in Japanese) are made from the protein-rich skin that forms on cooling soymilk during the preparation of bean curd. They are lifted from the surface of the soymilk on bamboo skewers and hung out to dry. Chinese supermarkets sell this product in flat sheets, or in long, crinkly rolls, which is how it is often eaten in Hunan. The Hunanese know these rolls as *dou sun*, "bean bamboo shoot."

FERMENTED BEAN CURD

dou fu ru

豆
腐
乳 Fermented bean curd has a creamy consistency and a strong, cheesy taste and smell. Most rural Hunanese households make their own (see page 282). Chunks of fermented bean curd are sold in glass jars in most Chinese supermarkets: for best results, choose one that is speckled with red chili. Aside from its use as a Chinese relish and an ingredient in sauces, it is rather good on toast— one of my regular late-night snacks.

"FLOWER" BEAN CURD

dou hua

豆
花 "Flower" bean curd, also known in Chinese as "bean curd brain," is unpressed bean curd with a light texture like crème caramel. You can make your own (see page 290), or buy it as "silken" or "soft" bean curd in Chinese or Japanese stores.

BACON

la rou

腊
肉 Hunanese bacon is sold in large pieces of dark-smoked meat, and is normally rinsed and then steamed to cook it through before it is used in recipes. In testing the recipes in this book, I have used thickly cut slices of well-smoked smoked bacon from a good butcher. You can also use the "Chinese bacon" sold in Chinese supermarkets, which is actually cured in a mixture of salt and spices, but has a similar honey color and intensity of flavor to Hunanese smoked bacon.

BLACK FERMENTED BEANS

dou chi

豆
豉

Black fermented beans are one of the most widely used seasonings in Hunanese cooking. They are made by soaking dried black or yellow soybeans in water, steaming them, and then leaving them to ferment. They have a rich savory taste, similar to soy sauce, and can be steamed with a little water to make a soy sauce substitute. In Cantonese cooking, the beans are usually mashed to a paste with garlic and other seasonings; in Hunan, they are added whole to dishes, often in conjunction with chili. Many people rinse them before use, which is what I tend to do. Fermented black beans are thought to have been invented about 2,500 years ago, and have been an important seasoning in the Hunan region for at least twenty-two centuries. They keep well: the black fermented beans with ginger that were excavated at the Han dynasty tombs at Mawangdui look a little dry, but otherwise entirely resemble the black beans you can buy in Changsha today, or indeed in any Chinese supermarket. Do buy the dried black beans rather than those preserved in brine.

CHILES

辣
椒

Chiles are vitally important in Hunanese cooking, so much so that people say you cannot have a meal without them (*mei you la jiao, chi bu xia fan*). Locals even joke that the statue of a blazing red torch that adorns the Soviet-style Changsha railway station is, in fact, meant to represent a chili. Chiles are used in various forms, and have many culinary uses.

CHILI FLAKES

gan jiao mo

干
椒
末

One of the most common seasonings is chili flakes, dried chiles (see below) that have been pounded coarsely with their seeds.

CHILI OIL

la jiao you

辣
椒
油

Chili oil is made by infusing ground chiles, sometimes mixed with other spices, in hot vegetable oil. It is mainly used in dressings for cold dishes, but can also be added to steamed and wok-cooked food. Some chefs use it for stir-frying. Chili oil can be used with or without its sediment, according to taste. (See page 284 for a recipe for chili oil.)

CHOPPED SALTED CHILES

duo la jiao

剁
辣
椒

This sour, salty preserve is one of the most distinctive Hunanese seasonings. It is made from fresh red chiles, coarsely chopped, mixed with salt, and then packed into pickle jars until they are needed. It is used in steaming, especially for fish, and also in cold-dressed and stir-fried dishes. *Duo la jiao* has a hot, sour, salty taste and is brilliantly, beautifully red in color. It is extremely easy to make (see page 283).

DRIED CHILES

gan la jiao

干
辣
椒

Small, pointed dried chiles are added whole to spiced broths, cut in half to release their fragrance, or pounded coarsely with their seeds. In markets they are laid out in sacks, some of them dark blood-red, others flamelike orange or mottled red and gold. I prefer to use chiles that are fragrant rather than fiendishly hot.

FRESH CHILES
xian hong jiao

鮮 Fresh red chiles are used to add color and heat
紅 to stir-fries and steamed dishes. The most
椒 common variety is long and pointed (4 to 6 inches in length and ¼ inch wide at the stem end), and not too hot. Fresh green chiles of varying degrees of heat are treated as a vegetable, and often stir-fried with pork or eggs.

PICKLED CHILES
pao jiao

泡 Various types of pickled chili are used in
椒 Hunanese cooking. The most essential, chopped salted chiles (see page 21), are easily made at home. There are also long green chiles that are pale green or yellow-white after pickling in brine (*suan la jiao, jiang la jiao*); pastes made from pickled red chiles (*la jiang*); small, gray-green "wild mountain chiles" pickled in brine (*ye shan jiao*); and large, very pale chiles that are blanched, dried in the sun, and then pickled in brine (*pu la jiao*). In the city of Changde, red chiles are mixed with ground rice and salted to make a local specialty, *zha la jiao* (see page 282).

CHILI BEAN PASTE
dou ban jiang

豆 Sichuan is the most famous producer of *dou*
瓣 *ban jiang*, a chunky paste made from
醬 fermented fava beans and chiles that lends a rich flavor and a deep red color to all kinds of dishes, but similar pastes, often made from soybeans rather than fava beans, are produced in other parts of the country. Hunanese cooks make regular use of *dou ban jiang*, either on its own or with the more distinctively Hunanese chopped salted chiles. The most famous Hunanese chili bean paste is Yongfeng chili paste (*yong feng la jiang*), which local historians say has been made in Shuangfeng county since the mid-seventeenth century, from fermented wheat and soybeans, glutinous rice, and red chiles. Legend has it that the great Hunanese commander Zeng Guofan, whose home was nearby, took a jar of it to the Empress Dowager Cixi in Beijing, who loved it so much it became a regular seasoning in the palace kitchens. At home, I tend to use Sichuan chili bean paste, which is often sold as Toban Djan. The best is made in the Sichuanese county of Pixian.

COOKING OILS AND FATS
CAMELLIA OIL
cha you

茶 The traditional vegetable oil of the Hunanese
油 countryside is camellia oil, made from the cold-pressed seeds of the camellia tree (*Camellia oleifera*). The tree is a botanical relative of the tea plant, and the oil it yields is known locally as "tea oil." It is a pale yellow in color, and has a delicate nutty taste and aroma. It is also extremely rich in oleic acids and comparable to olive oil in its health benefits, which is why it is sometimes known as "Chinese olive oil." Camellia oil has been used as a cooking oil in China for hundreds of years, and is mentioned in the seventeenth-century technical treatise, *The Creations of Nature and Man* (*tian gong kai wu*).

You still see orchards of camellia trees on the hillsides around Hunanese villages, but these days the harvest is often neglected because of the easy availability of cheap, processed cooking oils. It is, however, making a comeback as a gourmet food in the cities, because of its health benefits and pleasing taste. Some restaurants use it in the preparation of "rustic" dishes, naming it on their menus as a speciality ingredient, and it is thought to be particularly useful in dispelling the rank tastes of meat, fish, and poultry. (It is marketed internationally as a healthy edible oil, and is used in cosmetics that benefit the hair and skin.) If you can find a source of camellia oil, you can use it to cook any of the recipes in this book.

PEANUT OIL
hua sheng you

花生油 Peanut oil is the oil I use for cooking Chinese food at home, because it is clear, with a neutral flavor and a high burning point, and thus is extremely versatile. It also keeps well. It is not used as much in China as processed soybean oil, which is cheaper and more easily available.

LARD
zhu you

猪油 Aside from camellia oil, lard is used in traditional Hunanese cooking. Many rural families keep a pig or two and make their own (see page 289); it can also be bought in the markets. In the backstreets of Changsha, there are small lard-making workshops, with special presses to extract every last drop of molten lard from the rendered fat. Lard has a bad reputation in the West, partly because the packaged kind has an inferior flavor, but good, fresh lard adds a wonderful savor to all kinds of dishes. When I stayed with my friend Fan Qun's family in the countryside, most of our food was cooked with lard from their own, organically reared pig, and it was delicious.

COOKING WINES
FERMENTED GLUTINOUS RICE WINE
tian jiu

甜酒 This sweet, fragrant wine made from glutinous rice is often used in sweet tonic dishes, although it can also be drunk on its own. Unusually, the clear wine is used along with the rice grains, which become pulpy during fermentation. (See recipe on page 277.)

SHAOXING WINE
liao jiu

料酒 Hunanese restaurant cooks make frequent use of mild, amber-colored rice wines in marinades and stir-fries, especially where meat, fish, and poultry are involved, because they are thought to dispel "fishy tastes" (*xing wei*) and rankness. Such wines are known generically as *liao jiu*, but Shaoxing wine is the best-known example and the one most easily available in Western Chinese supermarkets. It has been produced in Shaoxing in eastern Zhejiang province since about the fifth century BC, and is about 14.5% proof. Some Chinese cooking writers recommend using medium-dry sherry as a subsitute.

CLEAR GRAIN SPIRITS

bai jiu

白酒 Clear distilled grain liquors (40–65% proof) are more common than Shaoxing wine in Hunanese home cooking. They help to preserve pickled vegetables and fermented bean curd, and are also thought to dispel rank and "fishy" tastes. I use Shaoxing wine in most of my cooking, but distilled liquors are essential for pickling.

CORIANDER (CILANTRO)

xiang cai

香菜 Coriander, also known as cilantro or Chinese parsley, is one of two herbs that are widely used in Hunanese cooking (the other is purple perilla, see page 27). It can serve as the main ingredient in a salad, a secondary ingredient in stir-fries, or a garnish, especially for beef and lamb dishes, where its strong fragrance is thought to dispel "muttony" tastes. Its common Chinese name literally means "fragrant vegetable." Coriander is native to the shores of the Mediterranean, but found its way into China some 2,000 years ago.

CRYSTAL (ROCK) SUGAR

bing tang

冰糖 Sugar is not much used in everyday Hunanese cooking, except in the form of caramel, which is added to stews and broths to give them a rich, red-brown color (see page 289). Crystal sugar (also called yellow rock sugar) is often used in sweet dishes for its pleasing taste and tonic properties. It comes in large, pale yellow crystals, and needs to be smashed with a hammer before use.

CUMIN

zi ran

孜然 Cumin is sold in Hunanese spice stores, but has only a limited use in local cooking. Street vendors sprinkle it over barbecued foods, and it is used in some spicy wok-cooked dishes. It is strongly associated with the northwestern Muslim region of Xinjiang, where it is grown, and where it is the most distinctive local seasoning. Cumin originated in the eastern Mediterranean, and its Chinese scholarly name is "Parthian fennel" (*an xi hui xiang*), a reference to its Western geographical roots.

DRIED MUSHROOMS

CLOUD EARS

yun'er

雲耳 Black cloud ear mushrooms grow in waves on decaying wood, and have a slithery texture, but very little taste. In Hunan, they are known as wood ears (*mu'er*). The black fungus sold as "wood ears" in the West, however, tends to be thick and woody, while "cloud ears" are suitably light and frilly, so I always buy the latter. Soak them in hot water from the kettle for about 30 minutes before use, pluck out the knobbly bits in the middle, and squeeze dry before cooking.

DRIED SHIITAKE MUSHROOMS

xiang gu

香菇 These dried mushrooms, commonly known in the West by their Japanese name, shiitake, have a wonderfully rich *umami* flavor, and are widely used in Hunanese and Chinese cooking. They can be found in most Chinese food stores. Superior varieties (known as "flower mushrooms," *hua gu*) have pale crisscross patterns over their brown caps. Shiitake should be soaked in hot water from the kettle for about 30 minutes before use, then squeezed dry. The stems are discarded before use.

SILVER EAR FUNGUS

yin'er

銀
耳
This pale, papery dried fungus, also known as "white wood ear," is mainly used in sweet dishes, and has tonic properties. After soaking for about 30 minutes in hot water from the kettle, it relaxes into soft, translucent waves that are simultaneously slippery and crunchy. You will find it in good Chinese supermarkets.

FRAGRANT THINGS

香
料
"Fragrant things" (*xiang liao*) is the collective name for all the dried spices used in Hunanese cooking, and particularly in aromatic broth (*lu shui*, see pages 54–5). Sometimes the spices are sold in ground blends of as many as twenty different kinds; more commonly, they are bought individually or in great bags of mixed *lu shui* spices. The following are the most important:

CAO GUO

cao guo

草
果
Cao guo, also known as "Chinese cardamom," are dark-brown, ridged seedpods the size and shape of nutmegs, and have a cardamom-like taste and fragrance. They should be bashed slightly with the flat side of a cleaver before use, to encourage them to release their flavor. (You can also use regular cardamom as an ingredient in Chinese spice blends.) They are sometimes sold as "Tsao Kuo."

CASSIA BARK

gui pi

桂
皮
This spice is the dried bark of the Chinese cassia tree, which has a cinnamon-like fragrance, but is considered inferior to true cinnamon. It comes in dark, woody strips with a pale underside. Cassia bark was one of the spices found, alongside ginger and Sichuan pepper, in the packages of medicinal herbs excavated from the Han dynasty tombs at Mawangdui.

FENNEL SEEDS

xiao hui xiang

小
茴
香
Fennel seeds have an aniseed flavor and are pale green in color. They are grown in several parts of northern China.

SICHUAN PEPPER

hua jiao

花
椒
See separate entry on page 28.

STAR ANISE

ba jiao

八
角
Star anise is the dried fruit of an evergreen tree, which, when ripe, pops open into an eight-pointed star—its Chinese name literally means "eight horns." It has a strong aniseed flavor, and should be used cautiously, as it can overwhelm other tastes.

GARLIC

da suan

大
蒜
Garlic is an essential flavoring in Hunanese cooking, and in Chinese cooking in general. The fat-cloved garlic familiar in the West is said to

have been brought into China by the Han dynasty traveler Zhang Qian, returning from one of his missions to the barbarian regions. It is still known as "big garlic," because its cloves were so much larger than those of the wild native breeds. Garlic cloves (*suan zi*) can be used whole in braised dishes, but are usually sliced or finely chopped for stir-frying. Finely chopped or puréed garlic is used in cold dishes, not only for its taste and nutritional benefits, but also for its antibacterial properties.

One of the most ubiquitous Hunanese vegetables is green garlic or "Chinese leek" (*da suan* in Hunan dialect), whose long green leaves closely resemble Chinese green onions. They are stir-fried with pork and bacon, added to red-braised dishes, and strewn onto chafing dishes as they are brought to the table. They are traditionally in season from autumn until spring, but can now be found all year-round in southern China. I occasionally find them in the winter in my local Chinese supermarkets, and snap them up, as they have a wonderfully fresh and pungent taste. My homesick Hunanese friends, missing this vegetable, leave garlic cloves to sprout in their kitchens, and add their green shoots to the wok. Delicious garlic stems (*suan miao*), which are long, green and cylindrical, are eaten as a stir-fried vegetable.

GINGER
sheng jiang

生姜 Fresh ginger root (or rhizome) is one of the most ancient Chinese flavorings, and an essential cooking ingredient, especially in the south. The Hunanese use it on a daily basis in their food, and also add it, chopped, to mugs of green tea. It is often left unpeeled in stews and braised dishes, because its skin is so flavorful, but should otherwise be peeled.

LOTUS LEAVES
he ye

荷葉 Dried lotus leaves, which are usually about 20 inches in diameter, can be found in good Chinese supermarkets. Folded in half, they are grey-green in color and resemble large fans in their size and shape. They should be soaked in hot water from the kettle for a few minutes before use until they are supple, then drained.

MONOSODIUM GLUTAMATE
wei jing

味精 Monosodium glutamate (MSG) is not a traditional ingredient in Chinese cooking, but since its discovery in the early twentieth century has become an indispensable seasoning for most Chinese cooks. It is used to enhance the *umami* tastes of food, and often as a cheap substitute for good ingredients and proper stocks. Many Hunanese cooks have told me that factory farming means food is less tasty than it used to be, and they have to use MSG to keep their customers happy. People in China also seem to have become so accustomed to the heightened *umami* tastes of food laced with MSG (as well as oyster sauce and chicken essence—two other *umami*-rich seasonings), that they find anything made without it tastes bland. Personally, I dislike this intensified, short-cut cooking, and prefer to use good ingredients and homemade stocks. I don't cook with MSG at all, so you will not find it in any of the recipes in this book.

PEPPER

hu jiao

胡椒 Pepper is still known in Chinese by a term that roughly translates as "barbarian pepper," because it was brought into China some 2,000 years ago over the land routes from Central Asia, like several other "barbarian" foodstuffs. The Chinese almost always use white pepper in their cooking. Black pepper can be used as a substitute if that is what you have, although its dark speckliness is not as attractive in pale-colored dishes.

PURPLE PERILLA

zi su

紫蘇 Purple perilla, *shiso*, or beefsteak plant is one of the two main herbs used in Hunanese cooking (the other is coriander). It has purple-and-green leaves with serrated edges, and a flavor a little reminiscent of basil. Botanically, it is related to mint. Perilla is used mainly in cooking fish and aquatic foods such as eels and frogs, because it is thought to refine their "fishy" flavors. I buy it occasionally from a Vietnamese or Japanese grocer: the Vietnamese know it as *rau tia to* and use it raw. If you can't find perilla, Asian basil is an acceptable substitute, although it is not seen as a herb that combats "fishiness."

POTATO FLOUR

dian fen

淀粉 Starches made from various foods, including peas and lily bulbs, are used in Chinese marinades and batters, and, mixed with cold water, as a thickener for sauces. At home, I use potato flour bought from any Chinese supermarket.

PRESERVED DUCK EGGS

pi dan

皮蛋 These dark, strongly flavored eggs (see page 113) can be bought in most good Chinese food stores. The best ones are still covered in their rough preserving paste, but they are often sold clean, so they just look like slightly grayish duck eggs. They are distinct from salted duck eggs (see page 286).

PRESERVED VEGETABLES

PICKLED MUSTARD GREENS

pao cai

泡菜 Brine-pickled mustard greens have thick white leaves with pale greenish-yellow edges, and add a delicate sourness to soups and stews. They are usually sold in transparent plastic packages that contain a little brine. I buy a brand made in Thailand, but sold in Chinese supermarkets.

PRESERVED MUSTARD GREENS

suan cai

酸菜 Hunanese preserved mustard greens are made by blanching the fresh leaves, plunging them into cold water, and then leaving them in the sun until they are semidry. They are then rubbed with salt and packed into clay pickle jars to ferment. The final product is dark, pleasantly sour, and salty. The preserved leaves are used in soups and stir-fries, and are particularly good steamed with belly pork (see page 83). I have never seen Hunanese *suan cai* on sale in London, but Tianjin preserved vegetable, which is made by a similar method, is an acceptable substitute. It is sold in clay jars, and should be rinsed well and squeezed dry before use.

PRESERVED MUSTARD TUBER

zha cai

榨菜 This pickle is made from the knobby stem of a type of mustard green. It is semidried, salted, and pressed to extract some of its water content, before being spiced and packed into jars to ferment. Its Chinese name literally means "pressed vegetable." *Zha cai* was originally a Sichuanese preserve, but it is now produced in other places. It has a delightful, crisp texture and a salty-sour-aromatic taste, and is often chopped and scattered over cold noodles and other snacky dishes. You will find this preserve in most Chinese food stores, where it is sold as "Sichuan preserved vegetable."

SESAME OIL

xiang you

香油 Chinese sesame oil is not cold-pressed, but is made from toasted sesame seeds, so it has a dark caramel color and a strong nutty aroma: its common Chinese name means "fragrant oil." It should always be added to dishes at the very end of cooking, or after the wok has been removed from the heat, as it loses its fragrance with long heating. It is also used in cold-dressed dishes. I only buy pure toasted sesame oil, and use it in small but potent quantities.

SICHUAN PEPPER

hua jiao

花椒 Sichuan pepper, one of the most ancient Chinese spices, plays but a minor role in Hunanese cooking, as the Hunanese don't much take to its tongue-numbing, lip-tingling effects. However, it is an important ingredient in some notable Hunanese dishes, and is also used in spice mixtures, especially in aromatic broth (*lu shui*). Some recipes require ground roasted Sichuan pepper: to make this, stir whole Sichuan pepper in a dry wok over a very gentle flame for 4 to 5 minutes, until marvelously fragrant. Use a mortar and pestle to crush it to a fine powder and then, for best results, sift through a tea strainer to remove any bits of husk.

SOY SAUCE

jiang you

醬油 Broadly speaking, there are two kinds of soy sauce: light soy sauce and dark soy sauce. Light soy sauce is saltier and less dense, and used as a flavoring; the thicker, less salty dark soy sauce is used mainly to add color to food. There are also various specialist soy sauces, including a Cantonese variety used particularly for steaming fish. (It is designed to dispel unpleasant "fishy" aspects of the natural flavors of fish and seafood.) Soy sauce traces its origins to the fermented pastes made in China from soybeans, wheat, and other grains since at least the third century BC. It remains a staple Chinese seasoning, considered to be one of the seven household essentials (along with rice, salt, vinegar, oil, tea, and firewood). Many commercial soy sauces are produced by fast, chemical fermentation: I always seek out those that are traditionally brewed.

SCALLION

cong

蔥 Chinese scallions closely resemble Western scallions, except they do not develop bulbs at their bases, and their green leaves are much longer. In Hunan there are two main varieties of scallions: regular *cong*, which are generally used to improve the flavor of meat and fish foods in stews, steamed dishes, and stir-fries; and small green onions (*xiao cong*), which are more like Western chives, and are scattered on food to add color and fragrance as a garnish. In testing the recipes in this book, I have used Western scallions, but try to find the more slender and less fibrous ones if they are to be used raw or added to dishes in the final stage of cooking.

SWEET BEAN SAUCE

tian mian jiang

甜
面
酱　Dark fermented pastes made from wheat and soybeans are common in Chinese cooking. The nearest equivalent I can find is a sweet bean sauce made in Taiwan by a company called Mong Lee, and that is what I use at home.

VINEGARS

CHINKIANG VINEGAR

chen cu

陳
醋　Brown rice vinegars are often used in Hunanese cooking. At their best they have a mellow, many-layered flavor, and are not especially sharp. Of those available in the West the best is Chinkiang vinegar, from eastern China, which is similar in character to those used in Hunan province.

CLEAR RICE VINEGAR

bai cu

白
醋　Clear vinegars made from ordinary or glutinous rice have a more invigorating sharpness than brown vinegars, and are often used to dispel the "fishiness" of strongly flavored fish, seafood, and meats. Many cooks splash a little clear vinegar around the edge of the wok while stir-frying such foods, rather than using Shaoxing wine. Clear vinegars are also used in cold dishes, and where a pale color is desired.

WINTER-SACRIFICE BEANS

la ba dou

腊
八
豆　Winter-sacrifice beans are a particularly delicious form of preserved soybean that is used in Hunanese stir-fries and steamed dishes. They are plump, glossy, and ocher yellow in color, and can be mixed with chili and other seasonings. They are made by soaking dried yellow soybeans in water and then steaming them for many hours. The cooked beans are laid out on trays and set in a warm place for several days until they sprout a delicate mold. They are then mixed with salt, wine, and ginger, sealed into clay jars and left to ferment for about ten days. Sometimes other seasonings, such as chili or various aromatics, are added. The finished beans have a rich *umami* taste, which lifts the flavor of all kinds of meaty and vegetarian dishes, and they can also be eaten as a relish with rice or noodles, or boiled into a broth reminiscent of Japanese *miso*. Try also stir-frying them with a little ground pork, some sliced red chili, and plenty of coriander stems. In Hunan these beans are often made in neighborhood workshops, and sold in big clay pots. In the West, you have to hunt them down in good Chinese supermarkets: I've been buying a Sichuanese vacuum-packed version, called in Chinese *wu xiang dou chi* (five-spice preserved soybeans), and in English, somewhat bizarrely (because they are not black), "Sichuan spicy black beans."

★ THE COOKING ARTS

One measure of the antiquity of Chinese culinary culture (and the eagerness of the Chinese to present it as one unbroken tradition) is that quite a few professional cookbooks begin their historical introductions to Chinese cooking by describing the Stone Age and the discovery of fire! This may be a little excessive, but it's certainly true that many aspects of Chinese cooking date back hundreds, even thousands of years. The following is a brief sketch of some of the fundamental arts of the Chinese kitchen.

THE ART OF CUTTING
dao gong

刀工 Look at the dishes spread on the table at any Chinese meal, and you'll notice that almost all the ingredients are cut into small, bite-size pieces. It's partly, of course, because of the use of chopsticks as serving and eating instruments, which dates back more than two and possibly even three thousand years. Chopsticks and spoons are the only implements you'll find on a typical Chinese dinner table; any cutting must be done in the kitchen. Whole fowl and larger pieces of meat are served so tender they can be torn apart with chopsticks; most other foods are finely cut before they are cooked.

Above: NEW YEAR'S EVE FEAST

Cutting is one of the fundamental arts of Chinese cooking, as central to it as the application of fire and flavor. In ancient China, cooking itself was known as *ge peng*, "to cut and to cook," and Confucius himself, who lived from the sixth to the fifth century BC, is said to have rejected food that was not properly cut. In modern China, the art of cutting remains a vital and inseparable part of the culinary arts; "knife skills" (*dao gong*) are the starting point for any aspiring chef.

At its most esoteric, the Chinese art of cutting can involve making ornate statues from carved vegetables, or assembling intricate collages in the form of auspicious symbols, using slices of multicolored meat and vegetables (the Chinese equivalent, perhaps, of the French sugar arts). Even in normal restaurant kitchens and cooking schools, chefs learn to use their cleavers in a wide variety of ways, and to cut their ingredients into a vast range of different shapes. The complex Chinese approach to cutting has spawned a highly elaborate professional vocabulary. (Readers interested in this subject might like to read the section on cutting in my first book, *Land of Plenty* (W. W. Norton & Co. 2003).

THE ART OF COMBINING FLAVORS
tiao wei

調 The roots of the modern Chinese approach to flavoring date back at least to the second century BC,
味 when Lu Buwei's astonishing gastronomic treatise, *The Root of Tastes* (*ben wei pian*), outlined some of the principles of cooking in the form of a dialogue between a Shang dynasty king and his cook. Even then, he was able to write in sophisticated terms of the alchemy of flavor: "As for the matter of harmonious blending, one must make use of the sweet, sour, bitter, pungent, and salty. But which tastes one adds first or later, and how much or how little, the balance is very subtle, for each produces its own effect. The transformation which occurs in the cauldron is wonderful and delicate…"

A few key notions of flavor are particularly useful in understanding modern Chinese and Hunanese cooking.

One is that of "fishy" tastes or odors (*xing wei, yi wei*), the unpleasant or rank aspects of the natural flavors of meat, fish, poultry and some vegetable ingredients, such as soybeans. Many Chinese culinary strategies are concerned with dispelling these "fishy tastes," by blanching, prefrying or applying refreshing ingredients such as ginger, scallions, purple perilla, vinegar, rice wine, or spices. Only then can the delicious flavor of the main ingredient be truly appreciated. Aside from the general term "fishy," cooks talk more specifically of the "muttony" (*shan*), "foul" (*sao*), and "astringent" (*se*) tastes of particular foods, all of which demand careful attention in the kitchen.

In contrast to these undesirable tastes, all that is best in the flavors of nature is represented by *xian*, the Chinese equivalent of "the fifth taste," *umami*. It is used to describe the most seductive savory tastes, the sumptuousness of dried scallops, or the soothing richness of a chicken soup. Chinese chefs traditionally use all the arts at their disposal to bring out the *xian* tastes of their raw ingredients, enhancing them with salt, sugar, and *xian*-rich foods like shiitake and chicken, and using the strategies sketched above to remove any distracting "fishiness." Sadly, in the modern Chinese kitchen, monosodium glutamate is often used as a short cut to achieving *xian*, at the expense of more subtle natural flavors.

Another constant preoccupation in the Chinese kitchen is with "sending the flavors in" (*ru wei*), or encouraging seasonings or stocks to penetrate the raw ingredients. With food that is cut into small pieces, it might be enough to marinate it for a few minutes before cooking; larger chunks of food might need a lengthy salt curing, or long simmering in a flavored broth.

THE CONTROL OF FIRE

huo hou

火 An essential skill for any Chinese chef is *huo hou*, control of the degree and duration of heating.
候 Trainee chefs will learn to recognize the properties of different types of flame: the intense heat and dazzling brightness of the hottest (*wang huo*); the bright straightness of the strong or "martial" flame (*wu huo*—the character *wu* is the same as that in *wu shu*, the martial arts); the gentle swaying of the "civil" or small flame (*wen huo*—the character *wen* carries connotations of culture and literature), and the pale blue glow of the tiny flame (*wei huo*) that might be used to coax a tough cut of meat into tenderness in a clay-pot stew. *Huo hou* is not just, however, about the quality of the fire, but also about sensitivity to the heat of the oil, and the colors and aromas of the ingredients in the pot. Awareness of *huo hou* comes with experience, and with trusting your senses. With time and practice, you'll find yourself able to sniff out the moment when garlic has released the full riches of its fragrance, and sense when a dish of stir-fried vegetables is just, perfectly done.

Above: FARMHOUSE KITCHEN FIRE, YUEYANG COUNTY

COOKING METHODS

peng tiao fang fa

烹 When people in the West think of Chinese
調 cooking, stir-frying usually springs to mind. This
方 fast, furious method of cooking is used all over
法 China, both at home and in restaurants, where the searing heat of gas or coal flames can lick a dish into shape in a matter of minutes, or even seconds. It is perfect for preserving the color and crispness of finely cut vegetables, or the silkiness of just-cooked meat. Yet, stir-frying is only one of a myriad of cooking methods routinely used in Chinese kitchens. A home-cooked meal might include a steamed dish, a slow-simmered stew, a salad with a spicy dressing, and something deep-fried. Restaurants in Hunan divide their menus according to cooking method: stir-fries are listed separately from clay-pot braises and simmering tabletop hotpots.

It's in the professional kitchen that the subtle distinctions among the different methods are most easily appreciated. For just as the French have a systematic framework of sauces, the Chinese carefully analyze their cooking methods. They can be categorized according to the cooking medium (usually oil, water, or steam, sometimes the radiated heat of a fire, or even salt or mud), the heat of the flame, the amount of liquid present, the color or flavor of the seasonings used. The choice of cooking method depends, naturally, on the kind of ingredients to be cooked, but also on the desired texture or mouthfeel (*kou gan*) of the finished dish. There are regional differences, too, in preferred cooking methods, and in their dialect names.

Above: STEAMED DISHES, LIUYANG

Stir-frying may be the most ubiquitous cooking method in modern China, but it has a comparatively recent history. Although the wok itself dates back some 2,000 years to the Han dynasty, it was at first mainly used for drying grains. The earliest extant written reference to stir-frying as we might recognize it today is in the sixth-century agricultural treatise *Essential Skills for the Life of the Common People* (*qi min yao shu*), and it only became common centuries later, in the Ming dynasty. Before then, other methods such as steaming, boiling, and roasting were the mainstays of the Chinese kitchen, along with methods of food-preservation like smoking, pickling, and fermenting.

Steaming might be considered the most characteristically Chinese cooking method, since it has such a long and continuous history in the country. Even in the New Stone Age, people living on the central Chinese plains were using steamers made from pottery; later, in the Shang and Zhou dynasties, ornate steamers cast in bronze were used as sacrificial vessels. And in Hunan, a Han dynasty steamer set made of clay was among the burial goods unearthed at Mawangdui. (One taxi driver I met on my way back from a Xi'an archaeological museum snorted in derision when I mentioned that I'd just seen a Stone Age rice steamer: "Yes," he said, "The Chinese *discovered* steaming and all they did with it was cook! And we left it to you English to invent the steam engine! If we'd thought a bit less about food, perhaps we would have been a more advanced country.")

Above: CUTTING SHEETS OF RICE
PASTA, CHANGSHA

★ BASIC KITCHEN TECHNIQUES

CUTTING
dao gong

刀 Almost all Chinese recipes are precise about the
工 shapes into which their ingredients should be cut;
chunks (*kuai*), small cubes (*ding*), slices (*pian*), strips
(*tiao*), or slivers (*si*), to name but five. This is partly for
technical reasons: if you are making a stir-fry of beef, for
example, the meat must be cut into thin slices or slivers
that will cook quickly, and a degree of evenness is vital if
some of the pieces are not to be overcooked by the time
the others are done. But harmonious cutting is also part
of the aesthetic pleasure of a dish, however simple. For a
detailed account of the Chinese art of cutting, see the
introduction to my earlier book, *Land of Plenty.*

BLANCHING
chao shui

焯 Meat and poultry are often blanched in boiling water
水 before cooking to dispel blood and "fishy" tastes.
Some root vegetables, such as the Asian radish (*daikon*), are also blanched, in that case to soften the
peppery aspects of its flavor. To blanch meats and poultry, bring a large saucepan of water to a boil over
a high flame, add the food and then return the water to a boil. Skim off and discard any scum that rises
to the surface, and then drain. With vegetables, follow the same procedure, but refresh them under cold
water immediately after blanching.

MARINATING
yan zhi

腌 Because the food is usually cut into small pieces for wok-cooked dishes, it does not require long
製 marinating, and seasonings such as salt and soy sauce are often added just before it is cooked. Large
pieces of food can be left to marinate for some time before cooking. The same term, *yan zhi*, is used by
Hunanese cooks to describe the addition of salt to crunchy vegetables such as cucumber, to draw out
some of their water content before they are served or cooked.

COATING IN STARCH OR BATTER

gua hu shang jiang

掛
糊
上
浆
Small pieces of raw meat, fish, and poultry can be coated in a very light paste of starch and water or egg white, which gives them a pleasantly silky texture after cooking. Food that is to be deep-fried can be coated in a thicker batter made from flour or starch mixed with beaten egg.

PASSING THROUGH OIL

guo you

過
油
Many Chinese recipes use this as a first stage in cooking. It is done in two very different ways, each with a different culinary function. The first method is to fry small pieces of food, usually meat or fish, lightly clothed in a starch-and-water paste, at a low temperature, not exceeding 300°F. This separates the pieces, fixes their shape, and partially cooks them, but retains their tenderness, and the starch paste gives them a wonderfully smooth and slippery mouthfeel. With this method, it is important not to overheat the oil; not to stir the pieces too much lest the starch paste disperses; and to remove them from the oil before they are fully cooked. (If you cook them through on the first frying, they won't be so beautifully soft and tender in the final dish.) The partially cooked pieces of food are then tossed briefly in a wok filled with seasonings, which finishes the cooking. This method is often referred to in English as "velveting," because of the smooth texture of the food in the finished dish. It is used more in restaurants than at home.

The second method is to fry pieces of food, usually coated in some kind of batter, in hot oil, to separate them, fix their shape, and to cook them through. For a crisp mouthfeel, they are then deep-fried a second time, when the oil has returned to its original temperature.

THICKENING SAUCES

gou qian

勾
芡
Chinese sauces are thickened by sprinkling a mixture of starch and cold water into the wok in the final stages of cooking. Where there is a lot of liquid, the starch gives it a denser consistency. Where there is very little liquid, the starch makes it cling to the surface of the food, which looks enticingly glossy and has a moist mouthfeel. Thickening sauces with starch requires a little attention: add too much and the sauce can become gloppy; and if you don't sufficiently dilute the starch, or pour it directly onto the hot surface of the wok, it can form gummy strands before it has the chance to disperse. I tend to use potato flour, but you can use cornstarch instead; just substitute 1¼ teaspoons cornstarch for every teaspoon of potato flour.

★ COOKING METHODS

The following is an outline of the principal methods used in Hunanese cooking.

EXPLOSION-FRYING

bao

爆 As its name suggests, this method involves stir-frying small pieces of food very fast, and at a very high temperature (although not actually detonating an explosion in your kitchen). It is a method particularly suitable for maintaining the delectable crispness of certain types of variety meat, such as kidney and tripe, and is more typical of restaurant than home cooking. The character *bao* literally means "burst" or "explode."

STIR-FRYING

chao

炒 Stir-frying involves cooking small, evenly cut pieces of food in a wok over a high flame, but without the speed and explosive heat of "explosion-frying." In restaurants, it is done over the ferocious flame of the professional gas burner; at home, over the more modest heat of the domestic gas stove or, in the countryside, a wood or coal fire. There are various different kinds of basic stir-frying. *Bian chao* refers to the simplest, where pieces of food, usually without any starch coating, batter, or marinade, are stirred and tossed in a wok with a little oil until just cooked (for example, Dongting stir-fried duck breast on page 141). Seasonings are added during the cooking. This is a typical domestic cooking method, and many home cooks would not bother to thicken the sauce of such dishes with starch. "Cooked stir-frying" (*shu chao*) is similar, but is used for meat and poultry that has been precooked, boned and cut into pieces before it is added to the wok. (For an example of this cooking technique, turn to Qing Qing's back-in-the-pot pork on page 81.)

LIU COOKING

liu

熘 *Liu* is just one of many Chinese culinary terms that defy direct translation into English. It involves precooking food that has been cut into small pieces and clothed in a starch paste or batter, and then marrying it with a sauce that is separately prepared. Sometimes the precooked main ingredient is returned to the wok and tossed in the sauce; sometimes it is arranged on a plate with the sauce drizzled over. There are many permutations of this method, but the most important are "crisp-*liu*" (*jiao liu*), where the food is deep-fried first until crisp; and "slippery-*liu*" (*hua liu*), where the food is coated in a light starch paste, often with the addition of egg white, and cooked at a relatively low temperature to preserve its slippery tenderness. (An example of the *jiao liu* technique is General Tso's chicken on pages 120–2; an example of *hua liu* is Beef with cumin on page 102.)

PAN-FRYING

jian

煎 This refers to frying food at medium temperature, in a
moderate amount of oil, without moving it around too much,
until it is golden on both sides. It is often done in a flat frying pan.
Most Hunanese cooks maintain that pan-frying fish brings out its
flavor and fragrance much more than deep-frying. (See Duck egg
and chive omelet on page 147.)

Above: A SIMPLE LUNCH IN A
VILLAGE NEAR YUEYANG.

DEEP-FRYING

zha

炸 Deep-frying is often used as a first stage in Chinese cooking
(see "Passing through oil" on page 35), but also as a cooking
method in its own right, and involves cooking food in plenty of oil, usually at a high temperature.
Hunanese chefs make distinctions among various types of deep-frying, including "clear" or "dry"
deep-frying (*qing zha, gan zha*), where the food is seasoned but not battered; "soft" deep-frying (*ruan
zha*), where it is clothed in batter and cooked at a relatively low temperature, so it remains tender
inside; and "crisp" deep-frying (*su zha*), where the food is marinated, steamed, and then deep-fried
until crisp. (An example of "soft" deep-frying is Lotus root "sandwich" fritters on page 48; an example
of "crisp" deep-frying is Crispy aromatic duck, Hunan-style on pages 56–7.)

STEAMING

zheng

蒸 Steaming is one of the most ancient Chinese cooking methods, used for both grains and other types
of dishes, and it is widely used in Hunanese cooking, especially in the city of Liuyang. There, many
restaurants display great towers of bamboo steamers at their entrances, billowing gentle clouds of steam.
Each layer is filled with bowls of piping-hot steamed dishes, ready to eat: meats, smoked foods,
vegetables, bean curd. It is a wonderfully easy way of cooking, and good for preserving the nutrients and
the juiciness of food. In Hunan, earthenware bowls are used to hold food for steaming, but you can use
any heatproof bowl or plate, or indeed wrap the food in lotus leaves or stuff it into a section of fresh
bamboo. Some foods are simply cut up, raw, and steamed with oil and seasonings; others are blanched
first, or stir-fried briefly to get rid of excess moisture.

The most traditional way to steam food is in a bamboo steamer. To do this, set your steamer (or stack of steamers) in a wok, and fill the bottom of the wok with water. Bring it to a boil, place your prepared dish in the steamer, and cover with a lid. Make sure you don't let the wok boil dry. You can also use a metal steamer set, with a base layer filled with boiling water and one or two perforated layers. If you don't have either of these, you can still steam food, either by setting the dish on a trivet in a saucepan above a layer of water, or by laying two chopsticks across the bottom of a wok, placing the dish on them, filling the bottom of the wok with water, and covering it with a wok lid. I have steamed a bowlful of food on a sponge-cake ring in a saucepan; and my Hunanese friends sometimes steam a couple of bowls in two layers in a tall saucepan, separating them with a pair of chopsticks. Feel free to improvise! (For an example of steamed food, see Steamed taro with chopped salted chillies on page 222.)

CLEAR-STEWING

qing dun

清 This method is commonly used to make gentle stews of fowl, flesh, or fish, usually with a little ginger
炖 to refine their flavors, and sometimes with the addition of medicinal herbs and roots with tonic properties. The main ingredient can be fried-fragrant in oil with ginger as a first stage; it is then covered generously with water, brought to a boil, and simmered until tender. The dish can be finished with a dash of oil or lard and a scattering of ground pepper and scallion greens. It is often cooked and served in a tall clay pot. (An example of this is Spare rib and corn soup on page 244.)

MEN COOKING

men

燜 *Men* involves frying food in a little oil (or sometimes blanching it), adding some stock or water, and then simmering until cooked. The wok is usually covered with a lid for *men* cooking. Hunanese cooks often refer to *men* as a stage in other cooking methods, adding a little liquid to a wok and then leaving the food to "*men* a little" (*men yi xia*). (See Chicken with ginger on pages 130–1 for an example of this cooking technique.)

HUI COOKING

hui

燴 With this method, a number of different types of food are finely cut and cooked together in plenty of liquid, over a brisk flame. (See Lily flower, cloud ear, and sliced pork soup on page 237.)

Right: CLAYPOT CHICKEN ON A
TABLETOP BURNER, CHANGDE

SLOW-COOKING
wei

煨 This method replicates the slow, gentle cooking of the
farmhouse fire. Large pieces of food are partially cooked
(perhaps by frying in oil with spicy seasonings), and then
simmered with stock or water in a clay casserole pot, very slowly
and for many hours, until the liquid is much reduced, the flavors
are rich and mellow, and the food is fall-apart tender. It is a particularly suitable method for sinewy cuts of
meat. *Wei* can also be used to refer to clay-pot soups: they are made in a similar way to clear-stewed soups
(see above), but cooked for much longer. (See Slow-braised beef with potatoes on page 106.)

BRAISING
shao

燒 Braising is a method that overlaps slightly with *men* cooking and *wei* slow-cooking. It usually involves
a first stage of frying, then stock or water is added and the food is simmered until tender. The cooking
time is shorter than for *wei* and more liquid is added; and there is usually less liquid in the final product
than for *men* dishes. Where the food is braised with dark soy sauce or caramel coloring, the method is
known as "red-braising" (*hong shao*). (For an example, see Chairman Mao's red-braised pork on page 78.)

STEWING IN AROMATIC BROTH
lu

鹵 Often referred to in English as "flavor-potting," this extremely widespread and popular Chinese
cooking method involves simmering all kinds of food in a dark broth that is richly flavored with
spices. The cooked food can be eaten hot or cold, deep-fried until crisp, or "returned to the wok" in a
stir-fry. (See Aromatic duck salad on page 56.)

HOTPOTS AND OTHER CHAFING DISHES
bo zi cai

鉢
子
菜 This refers to the Hunanese habit of serving precooked soups and dishes on a tabletop burner,
where they continue to simmer away during the meal. Sometimes raw vegetables and bean curd
are added to soups served in this way at the table. (The "Dry-wok" spicy duck on pages 139–40 is
a good example of this Hunanese technique.)

★ KITCHEN EQUIPMENT

Chinese cooking is about a way of approaching food as much as any specialist equipment or ingredients, and you don't really need any special tools to do it. Stir-frying can be done, at a pinch, in a flat-bottomed pan, you can cut your ingredients with a Western knife, and a steamer can be improvised from a saucepan and trivet. The basic equipment of the Chinese kitchen, however, is extremely simple to use, cheap to buy, and wonderfully versatile. I highly recommend it.

CLEAVER
cai dao

菜刀 The cleaver is the essential Chinese knife, and unmatched in its versatility. The basic cutting cleaver (*cai dao*) can be used for chopping all kinds of foods, from the smallest garlic clove to the largest piece of meat. The flat of the blade can be used for whacking ginger and scallions to release their fragrances, its spine for pulverizing meat to a paste, and, held horizonally, the knife is perfect for transferring cut foods to the wok or serving dish. It is also far lighter than you might imagine, and so lovely to use that, with a little practice, you will find you rarely need any other knife. Aside from the basic cutting cleaver, it is useful to have a heavier cleaver (*kan dao, zhan dao*) for chopping through poultry and spare ribs on the bone. Cleavers can be made of stainless or carbon steel: I prefer those made from carbon steel, which must be kept bone-dry and lightly oiled to prevent rusting, but are much easier to sharpen. You can buy cleavers, and the whetstones for sharpening them, in good Chinese supermarkets. I use mine on a round chopping board made from a tree-trunk section, which I bought in a Chinese store in London.

Above: A WOKFUL OF PORK, SHAOSHAN

WOK
chao guo

炒鍋 The wok is the ideal pan for stir-frying, because its curved bottom allows for even heating, and the easy movement of food around the hot metal surface. But it is also an all-purpose pot, used for boiling, steaming, braising, deep-frying, dry-roasting, and even smoking. The best woks to use are the traditional Chinese ones, made from cast iron or carbon steel, which are much cheaper than those you can buy in department stores, and last forever. Flat-bottomed woks are less effective for stir-frying than those with curved bottoms, but you will need one if you are cooking on an electric stove. Nonstick woks make life easier in some respects, but I don't like using them.

When you buy your wok, make sure you also buy a wok lid, which is essential if you wish to use it for steaming, and a wok stand, which will stabilize the wok when it is full of hot water or oil.

If you work with a traditional cast-iron or carbon-steel wok, it is best to take note of a couple of things:

SEASONING THE WOK
zhi guo

炙 Before you use a new wok for the first time, you must season the surface. Scrub it very thoroughly
鍋 with steel wool, rinse it, and then heat it over a high flame. When it is very hot, rub the interior surface all over with a thick wad of paper towels soaked in peanut oil, taking care not to burn your fingers, then leave it to cool for a few minutes. Repeat this procedure twice with fresh paper and oil. Over time, your wok will darken, and develop a rich patina that protects the metal from rusting.

People often ask me how to prevent food from sticking to the surface of the wok, particularly when stir-frying small pieces of meat or fish coated in starch. The best way to do this is to follow the method used in professional kitchens: pour a little oil into the wok and heat over a high flame until the wok smokes at the edges. Swirl the oil around the surface of the wok, and then pour it into a heatproof container. Then add cool oil, and heat it to your desired temperature for cooking. This is what I always do when cooking Chinese food (it also works for notoriously sticky Western dishes, like scrambled eggs). If you find this too troublesome, simply heat the wok until smoking before you add the oil for cooking: it is fairly effective, but not as good as the professional method for really sticky foods. In the interests of simplicity, I have specified the former method in all the recipes in this book.

TAKING CARE OF THE WOK

After cooking, a quick rinse with water and a gentle scrub with a brush is usually enough to clean the wok. If you need to use steel wool to scrape off some intractable stickiness, or boiling or steaming has stripped off its protective patina, you should repeat the initial seasoning process. Some people insist that you should never use detergent on a wok, but in my experience you can do almost anything to it without lasting damage: a neglected wok simply needs a good scrub to get rid of any rust, and re-seasoning. It is not necessary to clean the outside of the wok.

WOK SCOOP

guo chan

鍋 Restaurant chefs tend to use long-handled ladles (*piao zi*) to stir the food in the wok: they can also
鏟 be used to scoop up oil or water, to ladle food into serving bowls, or to mix seasonings together
for a sauce. At home, the wok scoop (*guo chan*) is more commonly used.

STRAINER

lou piao

漏 A perforated metal ladle (*lou piao*) or a wire mesh strainer with a bamboo handle (*zhao li*) are
瓢 useful for removing pieces of food from boiling water or deep-frying oil.

STEAMER

zheng long

蒸 Bamboo steamers can be picked up cheaply in Chinese supermarkets: buy one (or a stack of two or
籠 three) with a diameter a little less than that of your wok. The food you wish to steam should be
placed in a heatproof dish or bowl that will fit into the steamer with enough room around the edges for
the steam to circulate. Food can also be wrapped in lotus leaves that sit directly on the bamboo. Bamboo
steamers, placed on a plate, make attractive serving vessels. Metal steamers are effective, but best left in
the kitchen. And if you don't have an actual steamer, you can still steam food (see page 37).

ELECTRIC RICE COOKER

dian fan guo

電 Once you acquire an electric rice cooker, you will wonder how you survived without it. It can be set
飯 up long before dinner, produces perfect rice every time, keeps it warm until you need it, and allows
鍋 you to concentrate your energies on cooking the other dishes. Please note that most electric rice
cookers are only good for cooking Thai or Chinese-type rices, and don't work with brown rice or basmati.

OTHER BITS AND PIECES

A bamboo wok brush (*zhu shua*) is useful for scrubbing out a hot wok between dishes (it won't melt
like a plastic one). I also find an oil thermometer most useful, and a pair of long-handled chopsticks
for separating pieces of deep-frying food in the wok. A selection of small bowls and dishes are
invaluable for preparing ingredients for Chinese cooking.

SERVING DISHES

In the Hunanese farmhouse, almost all food is still served in the traditional manner, in bowls, with small plates used occasionally for dried fruits, nuts, and other snacks. Clay bowls can also be set onto tabletop burners in the winter, especially in the north of the province. At home in London, I prefer to use a variety of different dishes, including a Chinese soup pot for soups, long oval plates for whole fish, clay bowls for braised dishes, and whatever else takes my fancy. If you want to serve a soup as a hotpot, you can buy electric or gel-fueled burners in Chinese supermarkets.

Above: A BANQUET, LIUYANG

THE HUNANESE MEAL

A Hunanese meal usually consists of a number of dishes with plain steamed rice, with soup served at the end of the meal. It's best to think in terms of a dish for everyone in your party, and one extra: so three dishes for a couple, and five for a party of four. Try to prepare a selection of dishes that use different main ingredients and different cooking methods, and remember that cooking some of the food in advance will relieve you of a last-minute rush.

ALL RECIPES IN THIS BOOK SERVE TWO PEOPLE WITH ONE OR TWO OTHER DISHES AND RICE, OR FOUR WITH THREE OR FOUR OTHER DISHES AND RICE, UNLESS OTHERWISE STATED.

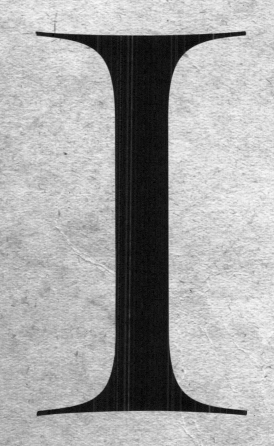

I

APPETIZERS AND STREET FOOD

開胃小吃

★ APPETIZERS AND STREET FOOD

Many Hunanese meals begin very simply, with a dish or two of relishes to awaken the appetite, rather than an appetizer course as such. These might include a pickle of sun-dried radish with chopped salted chiles, a few cubes of piquant fermented bean curd, or some fragrant peanuts. The Hunanese do, however, enjoy eating various aromatic meats, salads, and deep-fried snacks that work well as appetizers in the Western sense, and I have gathered some of these together in this chapter.

You still find snack sellers on the streets of Hunanese cities, especially during the New Year holiday season. They might be serving delicious spring rolls, with crisp and wafer-thin wrappers embracing a juicy stuffing; steamed glutinous rice dumplings, speckled dark green with wild artemisia; bowls of cool noodles or beanstarch jelly slathered in spicy seasonings; aromatic boiled peanuts, or crisp dough twists.

There are also *tang you ba ba*, squidgy, glutinous rice balls coated in golden toffee, and *san zi*, great skeins of hand-pulled dough that have been deep-fried until crisp: soaked in stock and topped with a little stewed meat and scallion, they are wonderfully savory and juicy in the mouth. Both these snacks are considered by local scholars to be descendants of the fried honey cakes and malt-sugar sweetmeats mentioned in Qu Yuan's stirring poem more than 2,000 years ago (see page 14). One Qing dynasty source mentions several snacks that are still common, including "flower" bean curd, mung bean porridge, glutinous rice balls, and stinking bean curd, which were sold by street vendors who used shoulder poles to carry their food and equipment as some still do.

Aside from the street vendors themselves, many of the traditional snacks are now sold in specialist restaurants, most famously the Fire Temple, Huogongdian (see pages 68–9). They can be eaten with early morning tea, like Cantonese *dim sum*, as late-night snacks while watching a performance of Hunan opera, or as a casual meal on the hoof. They also work well as a Western-style first course.

Right: PICKLES AND RELISHES, CHANGDE

SWEET-AND-SOUR SPARE RIBS
tang cu pai gu

糖
醋
排
骨

Sweet tastes play little part in Hunanese home cooking, but dishes such as the following appear from time to time on restaurant menus. It's an irresistible appetizer, in which the ribs are clad in a rich, thick sweet-and-sour sauce, and was a well-known specialty of the Xiaoxiang Jiujia, a leading Changsha restaurant of the 1930s. In restaurants, the ribs are deep-fried before being bathed in the sauce, which gives them an appealing mouthfeel and a richer color, but at home you can simply boil them—they are still delicious. These ribs can be prepared some time in advance of your meal.

1 LB. MEATY SPARE RIBS, CUT
    INTO BITE-SIZE SECTIONS
TWO 1-OZ. PIECES FRESH GINGER,
    UNPEELED AND CRUSHED
4 SCALLIONS, WHITE PARTS
    ONLY, CRUSHED
1 TBSP. SHAOXING WINE
SALT
2 TSP. DARK SOY SAUCE
4 TBSP. WHITE SUGAR
1 TBSP. CHINKIANG VINEGAR
1 TSP. SESAME OIL
PEANUT OIL FOR COOKING

1. Place the ribs in a saucepan of water and bring to a boil over a high flame. Skim the water, then add one piece of ginger, 2 scallions, the Shaoxing wine, and salt to taste. Boil for 15 minutes, until the meat is cooked and tender; strain and set aside, reserving the cooking liquid.

2. *Optional deep-frying step*: Heat the oil for deep-frying in a wok over a high flame until it reaches 350–400°F. Add the ribs and fry for about 5 minutes, until golden; drain and set aside.

3. Pour off all but 3 tablespoons of the oil in the wok and reheat over a high flame. Add the remaining scallions and ginger and stir-fry until fragrant. Add the ribs and toss for a couple of minutes in the fragrant oil.

4. Add slightly less than 1 cup of the reserved cooking liquid, the dark soy sauce, and the sugar, with a little salt to taste (take care not to oversalt, because the liquid will eventually be reduced to a glaze). Simmer over a medium flame, spooning the liquid over the ribs, until the sauce has reduced to a heavy, syrupy consistency.

5. Add the vinegar and cook for another 1–2 minutes, until the flavors have fused. Off the heat, stir in the sesame oil and leave to cool before eating.

LOTUS ROOT "SANDWICH" FRITTERS
jiao zha ou jia

This rather delicious and texturally exciting snack was, I'm told, very popular in Changsha in the 1970s—the Hunanese equivalent of the shrimp cocktail. Crisp lotus root slices are stuffed with fragrant ground pork and deep-fried in a rich batter, so they are crunchy and juicy at the same time. They taste very good with a sprinkling of ground roasted Sichuan pepper. A similar method is used to make eggplant fritters in Sichuan province, but the use of lotus gives this dish a Hunanese stamp. I suspect these would also taste rather good with a sweet-and-sour dipping sauce, although I've not eaten them like this in China.

10½ OZ. FRESH LOTUS ROOT,
    WITH RELATIVELY SLENDER
    SECTIONS
½ TSP. SALT
PEANUT OIL FOR DEEP-FRYING
GROUND ROASTED SICHUAN
    PEPPER TO SERVE (SEE
    PAGE 28)

For the stuffing:
¼ LB. GROUND PORK
1 TSP. SHAOXING WINE
2 TSP. FINELY CHOPPED FRESH
    GINGER
1 SCALLION, GREEN PART ONLY,
    FINELY CHOPPED
1 EGG, BEATEN

For the batter:
⅔ CUP ALL-PURPOSE FLOUR
2 TBSP. POTATO FLOUR
2 EXTRA-LARGE EGGS, BEATEN

1. Peel the lotus root, discarding the junctions between the sections, then cut into fairly thin slices. Sprinkle with ½ teaspoon salt and set aside for 30 minutes.

2. To make the stuffing, combine the pork, wine, ginger, and scallion greens in a bowl, adding salt to taste. Add enough egg to make a soft but not runny paste; set aside.

3. To make the batter, combine the all-purpose and potato flours in a bowl, add the eggs and any leftovers from the egg used in the stuffing, and then just enough water to make a batter that is thick but still fluid.

4. Heat the oil for deep-frying in a wok over a high flame until it reaches 300°F.

5. Use chopsticks to sandwich small amounts of stuffing between pairs of lotus slices, then dip them in the batter. Deep-fry the sandwich fritters for about 5 minutes, until the pork stuffing changes color and is cooked through: the batter should remain pale in color. When they are cooked, set aside on paper towels to drain. (This step can be done some time in advance of your meal.)

6. When you are ready to eat, reheat the oil to 350°F. Add the fritters and fry for just a few minutes until crisp and golden. Serve hot with a sprinkling of Sichuan pepper.

FIRE-BAKED FISH STIR-FRIED WITH BELL PEPPER
hong jiao huo bei yu

In the Chinese traditional village, women were married out into distant families, and brides brought in to marry local men and continue the family name. For this reason, the men and children of many villages almost all share a single surname, and Chairman Mao's home village is no exception. The people who ran the guesthouse where I stayed were called Mao, as was the motorbike driver who gave me a ride. You can also see in the given names of local people the revolutionary fervor that gripped the region when Mao Zedong became a star. The twenty-eight-year-old motorbike driver, born during the Cultural Revolution, was called "Red Soldier Mao" (*mao hong bing*). And the wife of the local communist party secretary was called "New Army" (*xin jun*). Such names are mildly embarrassing in these days of rampant Chinese capitalism, especially when most girls are named after pretty things like flowers and sunsets.

One of Mao Zedong's favorite foods was fire-baked fish (*huo bei yu*), small fry that are gently baked dry in a wok over a fire, and then lightly smoked. These tasty little fish are usually fried or steamed with black fermented beans or chiles, which is how I ate them at the table of New Army Liu in Shaoshan Village. Since fire-baked fish are not available here, I've used whitebait in the following recipe.

SALT

1 TBSP. SHAOXING WINE

1 LB. FROZEN WHITEBAIT, THAWED

½ RED BELL PEPPER

1 FRESH RED CHILI

1¼ IN. PIECE FRESH GINGER

3 SCALLIONS, GREEN PARTS ONLY

½ CUP ALL-PURPOSE FLOUR

DRIED CHILLI FLAKES

1 TSP. SESAME OIL

PEANUT OIL FOR DEEP-FRYING

1. Add ½ teaspoon salt and the Shaoxing wine to the fish and mix well; set aside.

2. Remove the stem and seeds from the pepper, then cut it and the fresh chili into fine slivers. Peel the ginger and cut into fine slivers. Cut the scallion greens into sections or slivers to match the pepper and ginger; set all aside.

3. Heat the oil for deep-frying in a wok over a high flame until it reaches 375°F. Shake the fish dry in a colander, and then toss in the flour, making sure they are evenly coated. Deep-fry the fish for a few minutes until crisp and golden; set aside on paper towels to drain.

4. Pour off all but 3 tablespoons of the oil and reheat over a high flame. Add the bell pepper, chili, and ginger and stir-fry until sizzly and fragrant. Add plenty of chili flakes to taste, stir a couple of times, and then return the fish to the wok. Stir vigorously to coat the fish in the fragrant oil, adding salt to taste. Add the scallion greens and stir a few more times. Off the heat, stir in the sesame oil and serve.

SPRING ROLLS WITH THREE SILKEN THREADS
san si chun juan

If you are lucky in your wanderings in the markets of southern China, you might, in the right season, come across a street vendor making and selling spring roll wrappers. She will be seated on a stool beside a small coal-fueled stove topped by a modest griddle, with a bowl filled with a runny white dough. Every once in a while she will scoop up a handful of this dough, so fluid and mobile it will run between her fingers if she doesn't keep them moving, and touch it gently onto the griddle in a swift circular motion. A thin round of batter will adhere to the hot iron surface, where it quickly cooks and pops up around the edge, so she can lift it off, flip it over for a few seconds, and then add it to the pile. These delicate pancakes can be stuffed with shredded vegetables and eaten just like that, or wrapped around a stuffing and deep-fried like the spring rolls familiar in the West. The most memorable spring rolls I've eaten in Hunan were of the latter variety, and stuffed with a delicious mixture of bamboo shoots, smoked bacon, and Chinese chives. They were served as part of a selection of "small eats" (*xiao chi*) in the famous Changsha snack restaurant, Huogongdian. The recipe below is my attempt to re-create them.

Spring roll wrappers can be bought frozen in many Asian supermarkets, but they don't have the delicate crispness of the homemade variety. I've therefore included instructions below for making your own wrappers. Be warned this is a tricky business, and the first time you attempt it you might end up with something resembling Frankenstein in your kitchen. So try it when you have time to mess around and have fun, and make a double quantity of the dough so you can put some of it down to experience, and with a bit of luck end up with a number of usable wrappers by the end of the session.

12 SPRING ROLL WRAPPERS,
    BOUGHT OR HOMEMADE (SEE
    PAGE 53)
PEANUT OIL FOR DEEP-FRYING

For the filling:
5 OZ. BAMBOO SHOOTS (BRINED
    OR CANNED)
SALT

1. To make the filling, cut the bamboo shoots into thin slices and then into very fine slivers. Blanch them in lightly salted boiling water, and then shake dry; set aside.

2. Cut the rinds off the bacon and set them aside. Cut the bacon into thin slivers. Trim the chives, discarding the thicker stalky bits, and cut into 1½-inch pieces.

3. Dry-fry the bamboo shoots in the wok over a medium heat so they lose some of their water content; set aside. Over a high flame, dry-fry the bacon rinds until they yield up their oil, then discard them, leaving the oil in the wok. Add the bacon and stir-fry until the strands have separated and smell delicious.

ingredients and method continue on the next page

SPRING ROLLS WITH THREE SILKEN THREADS *continued*

¼ LB. SMOKED BACON SLICES WITH RINDS
2½ OZ. CHINESE CHIVES
LIGHT SOY SAUCE
1 TSP. SESAME OIL

4. Tip in the bamboo shoots and continue to stir-fry until they are sizzly and fragrant, seasoning with a little soy sauce to taste. Off the heat, stir in the sesame oil and chives.
5. Lay a spring roll wrapper on a clean plate with the stickier side facing upward. Use chopsticks to place 2–3 tablespoons filling in a line on the wrapper. (If you are using bought, square wrappers, you should lay them out with one corner facing you.) Fold the near edge (or corner) away from you and start to roll up the wrapper, turning in the sides as you go. Moisten the far edge of the wrapper with a dab of water just before you seal it against the roll. Repeat to fill all the wrappers.
6. Heat the peanut oil for deep-frying in the wok over a high flame until it reaches 350°F. Add the spring rolls in batches and deep-fry for a few minutes, until pale golden; remove and set aside on paper towels to drain.
7. Return the oil to 350°F and fry the rolls again until crisp and deeply golden. Serve immediately. (The first frying can be done early, and the spring rolls can also be frozen at that stage.)

MAKES 12 SPRING ROLLS

VEGETARIAN VERSION

Vegetarians might substitute slivers of soaked dried shiitake mushrooms for the bacon, and add them to the bamboo shoots with a little peanut oil. One other version I've encountered on the streets of Changsha was a stuffing of Chinese chives that had been very briefly stir-fried with some ground chiles and salt—simple but rather good.

¾ CUP COLD WATER

½ TSP. SALT

1⅓ CUPS ALL-PURPOSE OR BREAD
FLOUR, SIFTED

TO MAKE YOUR OWN SPRING ROLL WRAPPERS:

1. Put the water into a large bowl, add the salt, and stir to dissolve. Tip in the flour and mix with your hand or a wooden spoon until a thick, smooth, wet dough forms. Gently smooth the surface of the dough, cover with a thin layer of water (perhaps a little less than ½ cup) and leave to rest at room temperature for 2 hours.

2. Heat a dry, heavy-bottomed skillet over a gentle flame. Rub it with a little oil—you do not want the surface to be actually oily, so rub hard with a cloth or paper towels to remove all but the merest smear.

3. Tip away the surface water from the bowl, and use your hand to stir the dough: it should be very soft, moist, and almost runny, so it slowly runs off your hand.

4. Take a handful of dough, keeping your hand mobile to contain it. Sweep the dough across the hot pan surface—allowing a thin, circular layer to stick. The rest of the dough should cling to the dough in your hand when you move it away. Keep moving your hand to stop the dough slipping away, and use your other hand gently to pick up the edge of the wrapper, which should be just cooked, but still entirely pale—you don't want to brown it. Turn it over and cook the other side for a few seconds, before transfering it to a plate.

5. Repeat with the rest of the dough. If it starts to stick, scrape off any fragments so the surface of the pan is completely clean again, and rub with a very slightly oiled bit of cloth or paper towels. If the dough becomes a little too stiff, simply mix in a few drops of cold water.

6. Persevere—the wrappers will get better, and it's very satisfying work when you get the hang of it!

AROMATIC BROTH
lu shui

In the markets of Hunan, as in other parts of China, you will always find stalls selling meat, poultry, bean curd, and other titbits that have been simmered in a rich and aromatic stock, *lu shui*. The food will be glossy and caramel-colored, and can be eaten directly as a snack, perhaps dipped in chili flakes or tossed with piquant seasonings, or "returned to the wok" with peppers or garlic leaves for an enticing stir-fry. Many stalls have a potful of *lu shui* simmering away on a charcoal stove, so you can have whatever takes your fancy bathed again in the broth and seasoned while you wait.

You can buy packages of spices for *lu shui* in Chinese spice stores and sometimes in Chinese supermarkets in the West. They vary in their complexity—some specialists claim to use a secret blend of up to forty spices. I once bought an extravagant collection in a market in Yueyang, and enlisted the help of a crowd of about twenty people in identifying them. We found fennel seeds, cassia bark, bay leaves, *cao guo* or Chinese cardamom, gingko, star anise, "sand ginger," tangerine peel, male and female cloves (the latter have the same four-pointed top as the familiar male cloves, but a plump pod the size of an olive pit instead of the nail-like bud), licorice root, Sichuan pepper, Chinese gromwell, and at least ten other spices whose English names I have been unable to find.

The master broth is traditionally kept indefinitely, boiled up and strained every day, and replenished with spices and salt as necessary, and its flavor deepens over time: chefs tell me of *lu shui* that has been sustained for sixty years. At home, you can strain it and keep it in the freezer, to be thawed and boiled up for occasional use. The following is a basic recipe for *lu shui*.

2 QT. EVERYDAY STOCK (PAGE 287)

1½-IN. PIECE FRESH GINGER, PEEL LEFT ON, SLICED

2 SCALLIONS

A SELECTION OF SPICES TIED IN CHEESECLOTH (PERHAPS A SMALL HANDFUL OF DRIED CHILES, 1 TBSP. WHOLE SICHUAN PEPPER, 1 TBSP.

1. Place all the ingredients, including enough caramel color to stain the liquid a rich brown, into a big saucepan over a high flame and bring to a boil, skimming if necessary. Reduce the heat and simmer for an hour or so to let the flavor develop.

VARIATION

Dark soy sauce can be used as an easy substitute for the caramel, but it won't give such an appetizing and lustrous color to the food.

continued

AROMATIC BROTH
continued

FENNEL SEEDS, 3 SLIGHTLY
CRUSHED *CAO GUO*, A FEW
PIECES CASSIA BARK, 6 BAY
LEAVES, 4 STAR ANISE, 6
CLOVES, AND 6 CARDAMOM
PODS)
4 TBSP. SHAOXING WINE
1 TBSP. LIGHT SOY SAUCE
SALT (PERHAPS 1½–2 TSP.)
CARAMEL COLOR (PAGE 289)

COOKING FOOD IN *LU SHUI*

You can simmer all kinds of foods in this aromatic broth. Small pieces like chicken wings can be cooked directly, but for larger portions of poultry or cuts of meat the flavor will be best if you salt-cure them first, as in the following duck recipe. Meat and poultry is ready when it is so tender you can poke a chopstick into it with little resistance. All fresh meats and poultry will benefit from blanching first. Beef cooked in this manner makes a wonderful cold cut, but most chefs suggest you cook it in a separate broth from less-strongly flavored ingredients such as poultry. Firm bean curd is a hugely popular ingredient, but, again, it is best to cook it separately, and to discard the broth used to cook it afterward. Hard-boiled eggs, rolled in cold water to crack their shells, acquire a delicious flavor and a pretty crackled appearance (they are a lovely addition to a European meal of cold meats and salads). Many kinds of variety meat are also cooked in this way.

AROMATIC DUCK SALAD
re lu ya zi

This is a fabulous way to eat duck, either warm from the pot or after it has cooled. The aromatic broth gives it a moistness and superb depth of flavor, which is complemented by the spices, fragrant oils, and fresh scallion. You can also try tossing it into a salad of some crisp green leaves—not a Chinese way of eating, but most delicious.

2 DUCK LEGS (12 OZ. IN TOTAL)
SPICED SALT (SEE BELOW RIGHT)
¾-IN. PIECE FRESH GINGER,
    UNPEELED
1 SCALLION
1 TBSP. SHAOXING WINE
AROMATIC BROTH TO COVER
    (SEE PAGES 54–5)
2 SLENDER SCALLIONS TO SERVE

For the dressing:

1 TSP. FINELY CHOPPED FRESH
    GINGER
1 TSP. FINELY CHOPPED GARLIC
½ TSP. DRIED CHILI FLAKES
2 TSP. CHILI OIL
½ TSP. SESAME OIL
2 TBSP. AROMATIC BROTH

1. Prick the duck legs all over with a skewer. Sprinkle generously with spiced salt. Crush the ginger and scallion and add them with the Shaoxing wine, rubbing the seasonings into the duck. Refrigerate for 2–3 hours, covered, to allow the flavors to penetrate. Before cooking, wipe off as much of the salt and juices as possible, and discard them.

2. Bring the aromatic broth to a boil in a pan over a high flame. Reduce the heat, add the duck legs and simmer for 30–40 minutes, skimming occasionally, until so tender you can poke a chopstick into the flesh; drain and set aside.

3. Cut the meat from the duck legs, preferably while still warm. Cut the scallions at a steep angle into thin slices. Toss the duck and scallions with all the dressing ingredients. Serve warm or at room temperature.

VARIATIONS

★ BACK-IN-THE-POT AROMATIC DUCK
hui guo lu ya

Slice the aromatic duck and stir-fry it with dried chiles, cumin seeds, and finely chopped fresh ginger and garlic, adding sections of green scallion toward the end of the cooking, and a small dash of sesame oil when you have removed the pan from the heat.

★ CRISPY AROMATIC DUCK, HUNAN-STYLE
you zha lu ya

Salt and then cook a whole duck or duck portions as in the recipe above. Drain and dry the duck thoroughly, and then deep-fry it in very hot oil until crisp. It can be eaten directly, perhaps with a dip of ground roasted Sichuan pepper and salt or chili flakes, dressed with seasonings as in the recipe above, or even, if you like, eaten London-style with pancakes, cucumber and scallion, and sweet bean sauce.

★ AROMATIC PIG'S EAR SALAD
re lu zhu er

Pig's ears are fantastic cooked in this way, thinly sliced, so each slice is a kind of "sandwich" of tender skin with a wisp of crisp cartilage in the middle, and then tossed with the same seasonings. You should prepare the ears by singeing them in a gas flame to remove any hairs, and then scrubbing them clean. They don't need salting but can be directly cooked.

★ AROMATIC BEEF WITH CORIANDER
xiang cai ban niu rou

Salt chunks of beef and then simmer them until tender in the aromatic broth. Slice the cooked meat (warm or cool) and make into a salad with fresh coriander and similar seasonings to the recipe above, to taste.

★ AROMATIC BEAN CURD WITH A SPICY DRESSING
liang ban xiang gan

Cook fairly firm bean curd in aromatic broth until flavorful and nicely colored. Season as in the duck recipe above.

★ SPICED SALT
yan liao

To make spiced salt, stir-fry the following ingredients in a dry wok over a medium flame: 4 tablespoons salt, 4 tablespoons whole Sichuan pepper, a couple of pieces of cassia bark, 2 crushed *cao guo*, 5 bay leaves, 2 star anise, and 8 cloves. Stir them over the heat for about 10 minutes, until the salt is brownish and the spices have filled your kitchen with their deep, wonderful, overwhelming aromas. Store in an airtight jar.

FRAGRANT-AND-HOT SPARE RIBS
xiang la pai gu

We drove across the river, and wound our way up the Yuelu Mountain on the west side of town. From the summit we looked out over the Xiang river and the long strip of Tangerine Island, as bats circled overhead. A few lanterns hung here and there, but there was not much light save the moon, and pairs of young lovers sat on benches under the trees. Later, after an al fresco dinner on the side of the mountain, we left the car in a clearing and walked along a dark path, all around us dense undergrowth and towering tree trunks. We passed the Aiwan Pavilion, where the young Mao Zedong used to gather with his friends, and eventually reached a teahouse. We sat there for hours in the near darkness, sipping tea, the air humid and heavy with the scent of pine, shimmering with the hum of cicadas.

One of the dishes we ate that night was a concoction of spare ribs with ginger and lashings of chili. The following recipe, from Ren Jianjun, is equally delicious. You can simplify it by omitting the deep-frying: the ribs will still taste good, but won't have quite the same fragrance and mouthfeel.

2½ LB. MEATY SPARE RIBS, ¾-IN. SECTIONS

2 QT. AROMATIC BROTH (PAGES 54–5)

2 TSP. FINELY CHOPPED GARLIC

2 TSP. FINELY CHOPPED FRESH GINGER

1 TSP. CHILI BEAN PASTE

1 TSP. CHOPPED SALTED CHILES

¼ TSP. GROUND CUMIN

1 TSP. DRIED CHILI FLAKES

2 TSP. SESAME SEEDS

2 TBSP. FINELY CHOPPED RED BELL PEPPER

3 SCALLIONS, GREEN PARTS ONLY, FINELY SLICED

2 TSP. SESAME OIL

PEANUT OIL FOR DEEP-FRYING

1. Bring a large saucepan of water to a boil over a high flame. Add the ribs and blanch; drain.

2. Bring the aromatic broth to a boil. Reduce the heat, add the ribs, and simmer for about 40 minutes, until tender; drain and set aside. (This step can be done in advance.)

3. Heat the oil for deep-frying over a high flame until it reaches 350°F. Add the ribs and deep-fry until golden; set aside on paper towels to drain.

4. Pour off all but 3 tablespoons of the oil and heat over a medium flame. Add the garlic, ginger, chili bean paste, and chopped salted chilies and stir-fry until fragrant. Add the cumin, chili flakes, and sesame seeds and stir a couple of times.

5. Add 3 tablespoons water and the ribs, and toss them in the sauce. Finally, add the bell pepper and scallions, stir a few times until you can smell the scallions, and then, off the heat, stir in the sesame oil, and serve.

SPICY CORIANDER SALAD
liang ban xiang cai

凉拌香菜

This is one of the dishes Liu Wei's older brother made for a lunch party during the New Year holiday—a piquant and refreshing salad. We lit strings of firecrackers on the roof of his apartment block, and then settled down for a lazy afternoon of eating, drinking tea, playing mah jong, laughing, snoozing, watching television, and eating sweets and nuts—a typical Spring Festival day, they said. We also had a brief performance of Hunan opera from Liu Wei's brother, who used to be a professional opera singer.

1 BUNCH FRESH CORIANDER
(CILANTRO), ABOUT 3½ OZ.

2 TSP. CLEAR RICE VINEGAR

¼ TSP. SUGAR

SALT

1–2 GARLIC CLOVES, VERY FINELY
CHOPPED OR CRUSHED

2 TSP. CHOPPED SALTED CHILES

1 TBSP. CHILI OIL

1 TSP. SESAME OIL

1. Trim the root ends of the coriander and tear the stems and leaves into chopstickable lengths, perhaps 2½ to 2¾ inches. Wash well and shake and squeeze to remove as much water as possible.

2. Combine the vinegar, sugar, and salt to taste in a bowl and stir to dissolve. Add to the coriander with all the other ingredients, and use chopsticks to mix very well. Serve.

VARIATION

A similar salad combines coriander with thin ribbons of "hundred leaves," which is bean curd that has been pressed into leatherlike sheets, and sometimes then stewed in an aromatic broth (pages 54–5).

ROASTED PEPPERS WITH PRESERVED DUCK EGGS
shao la jiao pi dan

Sometimes you can find, in a Hunan vegetable market, someone crouched over a charcoal burner, roasting bell peppers over a makeshift grill, the dark aromas of the peppers' scorched flesh drifting out among the shoppers. The peppers will be bought to make the following dish, a Hunanese version of that Italian antipasto made with charred peppers, capers, and anchovies. In Hunan the peppers are paired with dark preserved duck eggs, and drizzled with a garlicky sauce of soy and vinegar. The eggs have a rich, savory taste (one food-writer friend of mine compares it to the taste of brown crabmeat), which goes well with the sleek, smoky peppers. Make this dish with red or green peppers, or a mixture, as you please. And if you find the preserved duck eggs too outlandish, the dressed peppers alone make a delicious appetizer.

3 RED BELL PEPPERS (ABOUT 1 LB. 2 OZ.)

4 PRESERVED DUCK EGGS ("1,000-YEAR-OLD EGGS")

2 TSP. VERY FINELY CHOPPED GARLIC

1½ TBSP. LIGHT SOY SAUCE

2 TSP. CHINKIANG VINEGAR

SALT

½ TSP. SESAME OIL

1. Char the bell peppers until they are soft and their skins are blackened. I do this by leaving them on a metal grill set over a small gas ring, turned down to the lowest flame, and turning them from time to time. It's a slow business, taking a good hour or so, but the scorched flavor is wonderful. You can also blacken them more quickly under the broiler, turning so as much as possible of the skin is charred.

2. When the peppers are charred, put them in a bowl and cover closely with a plate or lid. Leave until cool enough to handle, then peel one pepper at a time, reserving any juices in the bowl. Rinse it under cold water as you detach and discard the skin (it should come away easily). Open the pepper and discard seeds and stem, and then cut into ½-inch strips. Pile these up on a serving plate; repeat with the remaining peppers.

3. Peel the preserved duck eggs, rinse well, and then cut each into 6 segments. Arrange these around the peppers like the petals of a flower.

4. Combine the garlic with any juices from the peppers, and then stir in the soy sauce, vinegar, and salt to taste. Add the sesame oil and then pour over the peppers and eggs. Use chopsticks to mix the sauce into the peppers before eating.

SMACKED CUCUMBERS
pai huang gua

Zhangguying village is an extraordinary place. A vast sprawl of interlocking courtyard houses, threaded by long corridors and a meandering stream, it was built by a wealthy clan named Zhang during the Ming dynasty. There are traces of its past grandeur in the elaborate wood carvings and lofty halls, but these days the courtyards are filled with ramshackle farming implements. Amazingly, the village is still inhabited by the impoverished scions of the Zhang family. They prepare and eat their meals in the yards, as the weekend tourists wander through, unsure of the division between public museum and private home.

One evening, I sat in a lovely old courtyard after the day-trippers had gone. Sunlight spilt through an opening in the gray-tiled roof, birds twittered in the eaves, and a couple of men were playing Chinese chess nearby. As night fell the sound of sizzling came from woks in several directions, and some Zhangs I had been talking to invited me to share their dinner. We dipped into small dishes of homemade fermented bean curd laced with chili, and ate cucumber salad, home-smoked bacon, and a soup of fish and bean curd. After dark I took my leave, and stumbled back to my guesthouse to a chorus of frogs (nearly falling into the stream on the way—I was rescued by another Zhang, with a flashlight).

Smacked cucumbers is a common Hunan appetizer, named because of the way you whack the cucumbers with the flat of a cleaver blade to encourage them to absorb the flavors of the dressing.

1 CUCUMBER (ABOUT 13 OZ.)

SALT

Version 1:

2 TSP. CHOPPED SALTED CHILES

2 TSP. VERY FINELY CHOPPED
    GARLIC

3 TBSP. CLEAR RICE VINEGAR

A COUPLE PINCHES SUGAR

1 TSP. SESAME OIL

CHILI OIL

Version 2:

2 TSP. VERY FINELY CHOPPED
    GARLIC

2 TBSP. CLEAR RICE VINEGAR

2 TBSP. PEANUT OIL

1 TSP. DRIED CHILI FLAKES

1. Place the cucumber on a chopping board and whack hard, several times, with the flat of a cleaver blade, so the vegetable splinters and opens up with jagged cracks, then chop it into bite-size pieces. Place in a bowl, sprinkle with ½ teaspoon salt, and leave for about 30 minutes. After this time, drain off the water in the bowl.

2. To make Version 1, add the chopped salted chiles, garlic, vinegar, sugar, and salt to taste, mix well and leave for a few minutes to let the flavors blend. Just before serving, add the sesame oil and chili oil to taste, toss, and serve.

   To make Version 2, add the garlic and vinegar to the cucumber with more salt to taste, mix well, and set aside for a few minutes to allow the flavors to penetrate. Heat the oil in a wok over a high flame until smoking. Scatter the chili flakes over the cucumber, then sprinkle the hot oil over, which will sizzle. Mix well before serving.

THE SISTERS' DUMPLINGS
zi mei tuan zi

姊
妹
團
子

These sweet or savory dumplings, which are served in little bamboo steamers, are named in honor of two pretty sisters who sold them around the Fire Temple, Huogongdian (see pages 68–9), in the early 1920s. The basic *tuan zi* dumplings were a traditional snack, but these girls so delighted customers with their cooking skills and their demeanor that the dumplings have borne their name ever since.

For the dough:

2 CUPS GLUTINOUS RICE FLOUR

2 TBSP. RICE FLOUR

WATER

For the savory dumplings:

1 DRIED SHIITAKE MUSHROOM

1 SMALL PIECE FRESH GINGER,
  UNPEELED

2 OZ. GROUND PORK

2 TSP. SHAOXING WINE

½ TSP. SESAME OIL

LIGHT SOY SAUCE

SALT AND PEPPER

For the sweet dumplings:

1 TBSP. SESAME SEEDS

1 TBSP. ROASTED UNSALTED
  PEANUTS

4 TBSP. GRANULATED SUGAR

2 TSP. ALL-PURPOSE FLOUR

A FEW GRAINS RED YEAST RICE
  (A NATURAL FOOD COLORING
  MADE BY CULTURING THE
  FUNGUS *MONASCUS
  PURPUREUS* ON RICE) OR
  DROPS COCHINEAL (OPTIONAL)

1. To make the savory stuffing, soak the shiitake in hot water from the kettle for at least 30 minutes. Crush the ginger with the side of a cleaver blade and put into a small cup with a little cold water to cover. Chop the drained and squeezed shiitake finely and mix with the pork. Stir in the Shaoxing wine and sesame oil, and season to taste with soy, salt, and pepper. Add just enough of the ginger-fragrant water to make a paste.

2. To make the sweet stuffing, toast the sesame seeds in a dry skillet over a low heat until fragrant, taking care not to burn them. Place in a mortar with the peanuts and crush finely. Moisten the sugar with ½–1 teaspoon cold water, then add the nuts and the flour. You should end up with a stiff paste.

3. Line a steamer with a piece of clean cheesecloth.

4. To make the dough, combine both rice flours with enough cold water to make a stiff, putty-like paste.

5. Roll the dough into sausages and break off walnut-size pieces. Take a piece in your hand, roll into a sphere, then flatten gently and make an indentation in the middle. Place a little of one of the stuffings in the indentation, and draw up the edges of the dough to enclose it. Roll the sweet-filled dumplings into globes and place a dot of cochineal or a few red rice grains on top, if desired. Roll the meat-filled dumplings into globes, and then draw up the top of the dough into a pointy tip.

6. Place the finished dumplings in the steamer and steam over a high flame for 8–10 minutes. Serve immediately.

MAKES ABOUT 20 DUMPLINGS

DEEP-FRIED PEANUTS
you su hua ren

油酥花仁

Fried peanuts were served, alongside spicy fermented bean curd, pickled *jiao tou* garlic, and a cucumber salad, at the start of a lunch I shared with Mao Zedong's nephew in his home village, Shaoshan. Peanuts are generally thought to have originated in Peru, and only spread to China in the sixteenth century, although the discovery of peanut remains at ancient archaeological sites in eastern China has led some scholars to believe they were a native crop. In Hunanese cooking, they are mainly stewed with mixed spices, made into soups with pork and soybeans, or deep-fried on their own as in the following recipe. The deep-fried peanuts can be served on their own as an appetizer, or used as a crunchy garnish for cold noodles and other snacks.

1⅓ CUPS SHELLED PEANUTS, IN
   THEIR SKINS

SALT

PEANUT OIL FOR DEEP-FRYING

1. For best results, soak the peanuts overnight in cold water, then drain and allow to dry thoroughly before cooking.

2. Heat the oil in a wok over a low flame until it reaches 200–250°F. Add the peanuts and deep-fry for about 20 minutes, stirring often, until they are crisp and fragrant. You can test them by lifting a few up into a perforated spoon and shaking them around—they are ready when they make a light pinging sound against the metal surface.

3. Drain the peanuts and allow them to cool. Serve with a sprinkling of salt to taste.

SCRAPED JELLY RIBBONS IN HOT SESAME SAUCE
gua liang fen

刮凉粉

The Chinese make many interesting jellies, pastas, and "curds" from starchy vegetables. There are sweet potato noodles (*hong shu fen*), transparent, with a bouncy mouthfeel; mung bean vermicelli (*fen si*); custardlike "bean curd" made from rice (*mi dou fu*); a pale brown tonic jelly made from konnyaku yam (*mo yu*); and a wonderful mung bean jelly (*liang fen*). The latter is made by grinding the soaked beans with plenty of cold water, and then bringing the liquid to a boil. It is stirred until it becomes translucent, and turned out into a bowl, where it sets to a pearlescent jelly. Market traders turn the bowl-shaped jelly out onto a board and use a *gua zi*—a special tool with sharpened holes like a cheese-grater—to scrape off long, thick strands. It has a fabulous mouthfeel, cool, slippery, smooth, and refreshing, and is often served with robustly spicy seasonings like those in the following recipe, which I learned on the backstreets of Changsha.

I have never seen fresh *liang fen* on sale in my local Chinese shops, but "Tianjin green bean starch sheets" make a pretty good substitute. They are large, thin sheets of dried mung bean starch, glassy and transparent. Soak them in hot water for a while and they have a similarly cool and slippery texture, a good foil for the boisterous flavors of the sauce. (Pictured with Spring rolls on page 51.)

4 SHEETS OF TIANJIN GREEN
    BEAN STARCH (ABOUT
    1½ LB. AFTER SOAKING)

For the sauce:
2 TBSP. SESAME PASTE
2 TBSP. COLD WATER
1 TBSP. FERMENTED BEAN CURD,
    MIXED WITH ITS JUICES
2 GARLIC CLOVES, CRUSHED
1 TBSP. LIGHT SOY SAUCE
1 TBSP. CHINKIANG VINEGAR
1 TSP. SESAME OIL

To finish:
2–4 TBSP. CHILI OIL WITH
    SEDIMENT

5 TBSP. PRESERVED MUSTARD
    TUBER (ABOUT 1¾ OZ.),
    RINSED AND FINELY CHOPPED
⅓ CUP LIGHTLY CRUSHED FRIED
    OR ROASTED PEANUTS
2 SCALLIONS, GREEN PARTS
    ONLY, FINELY SLICED

1. Soak the green bean starch sheets in hot water from the kettle for about 30 minutes, until supple and slippery. Break them up with your hands, into pieces that can be picked up with chopsticks. Drain well and divide between 4 serving bowls.

2. Combine the sauce ingredients in a bowl, and then divide the sauce between the serving bowls. Drizzle the chili oil over to taste, and then scatter with the preserved mustard tuber, peanuts, and scallions. Serve, and invite your guests to mix everything together before they eat.

CHANGSHA COLD-TOSSED NOODLES
chang sha liang mian

The following recipe comes from Mr. Yao, a gruff-voiced street vendor who had set up a stall near Tianxinge, the pavilion that stands on the last remaining section of the old Changsha city walls. He used plain flour-and-water noodles, but egg noodles taste delicious with the same seasonings.

7 OZ. DRIED OR 1 LB. 6 OZ. FRESH
  CHINESE NOODLES

1½ TBSP. CLEAR RICE VINEGAR

2 TSP. LIGHT SOY SAUCE

1½ TBSP. FERMENTED BEAN CURD,
  MIXED WITH ITS OWN JUICES

1½ TBSP. SESAME PASTE

1½ TBSP. CHILI OIL WITH
  SEDIMENT

2 TSP. SESAME OIL

2 TBSP. PRESERVED MUSTARD
  TUBERS IN SLIVERS

HEAPING 2 TBSP. DEEP-FRIED
  PEANUTS (PAGE 64)

A SMALL HANDFUL CHOPPED
  FRESH CORIANDER
  (CILANTRO) LEAVES

A LITTLE PEANUT OIL

1. Cook the noodles in boiling water until soft and supple, and drain well. Lay them out on a tray so they dry as quickly as possible, mixing in a little peanut oil to prevent sticking.

2. When you wish to eat, transfer the noodles to a bowl, add the vinegar, soy sauce, fermented bean curd, sesame paste, and chili and sesame oils to the noodles, and mix well.

3. Divide the noodles between 2 serving bowls, scatter with the mustard tuber, peanuts, and coriander, and serve.

MAKES 2 SERVINGS

YUEYANG HOT-DRY NOODLES
yue yang re gan mian

On New Year's Eve the markets of Yueyang were thronged with people stocking up on fireworks, fruits and sweets, and decorations that included traditional Spring Festival couplets as well as gaudy pictures of Chairman Mao. Fireworks were piled casually on market stalls, and a few children set them off in the side alleys. Itinerant street vendors were hawking chopsticks, pepper, and homemade rice wine. And of course there were the snack sellers. The following is a well-known Yueyang snack, named because the cooked noodles are reheated to order, but served with a slathering of seasonings, rather than in a bowl of soup.

7 OZ. DRIED OR 1 LB. 6 OZ. FRESH
   CHINESE NOODLES

1 TBSP. CHOPPED SALTED CHILES

4 TSP. SESAME PASTE

1 TSP. CRUSHED GARLIC

2 TSP. LIGHT SOY SAUCE

1 TBSP. CHILI OIL WITH
   SEDIMENT

2 TBSP. PRESERVED MUSTARD
   TUBER IN SLIVERS

4 TSP. FINELY SLICED SCALLION
   GREENS

4 TSP. TOASTED SESAME SEEDS

1. Cook the noodles in boiling water until soft and supple, and drain well.

2. Put the noodles in a large bowl. Add the chopped salted chiles, sesame paste, garlic, soy sauce, and chili oil and mix well.

3. Divide the mixture into 2 serving bowls and scatter with the mustard tuber, scallions, and sesame seeds. Stir with chopsticks before eating.

MAKES 2 SERVINGS

★ The Fire Temple—Huogongdian

In the courtyard, a team of chefs are making traditional New Year rice cakes, pummeling glutinous rice to a paste in a billowing cloud of steam, and pressing it into molds decorated with auspicious symbols. Inside, the main dining room is packed with holiday visitors, and the dark wooden tables are laden with steamers of dumplings, plates of cold meats, and bowls of soup. A fortune-teller wanders around, shaking a potful of the bamboo sticks used in divination. Steam drifts up from mugs of tea, and the air is noisy with chatter.

Huogongdian, which lies in the heart of Changsha, is a restaurant and a Hunan institution. It was founded in 1747 as a temple, at which local people made offerings to the God of Fire, in an attempt to protect their closely built wooden homes and workshops from conflagration. As time went by, more and more people came to make their sacrifices at the temple, and the city's snack vendors, opera singers, and storytellers began to gather there, too. By the late nineteenth and early twentieth centuries, Huogongdian had become a center of Hunanese street food and folk culture, and had acquired the atmosphere of a temple fair. The lanes around it were filled with small snack stores, and an open-air stage was the scene of lively performances of Hunan opera and traditional songs. Famous personages came to visit and sampled the snacks, including the great military commander Zeng Guofan and, so they say, General Tso of General Tso's chicken fame (see pages 117–22).

It was in this area that some of Changsha's most famous street snacks came to prominence. Stinking bean curd is said to have been invented by the ancestor of a lady called Grandmother Jiang, whose family ran a bean-curd store in the lanes, and who worked in the restaurant herself within living memory. According to legend, this ancestor used to take home the leftover bean curd that the family had been unable to sell that day, and on one occasion disposed of some in a jar of brine. She left it there for some time, and when she finally took a peek in the jar, discovered that it had turned black and had a terrible smell. Strangely, she thought it was worth trying to fry it—and found it delicious. Stinking bean curd soon became the family specialty.

Changsha was devastated in the Great Fire of 1938, when most of this ancient and venerable city burned to the ground. The Great Fire was started deliberately, as a result of chaos and rumor amid

Above: THE GOD OF FIRE, HUOGONGDIAN

the Japanese invasion of China. The Nationalist leader Chiang Kai-shek had implemented a "scorched earth" policy of resistance to the Japanese, and issued orders that Changsha was to be torched rather than let the enemy take the city. But some accidental fires led to a tragic misunderstanding, and on the night of November 12, 1938, the city was burned, although there was no immediate threat from the Japanese. The inferno raged for three days and three nights, and hundreds of thousands of people were made homeless. One of the few structures to survive was the memorial archway (*pai fang*) of Huogongdian.

The temple was rebuilt on a smaller scale a few years later, with three lanes of modest wooden stores that were soon colonized by the snack-seller concerns, including Mrs. Jiang's stinking bean curd, Zhang Guisheng's deep-fried dough strands, Deng Chunxiang's red-braised pigs' feet, and the Jiang sisters' steamed glutinous rice dumplings. In 1956, the place was nationalized as part of the general socialization of Chinese industry, the old lanes were demolished, and two new buildings offered departments specializing in main meals, noodles, cakes and pastries, cool drinks, sweetmeats, and, of course, the traditional snacks.

Prominent communist leaders stopped by to sample the famous Huogongdian snacks, including Mao Zedong, who was profuse in his praise of the stinking bean curd. He visited in April 1958, and the armchair in which he sat is still preserved, cultishly, in a private dining room named after his home village, Shaoshan.

During the Cultural Revolution the Fire Temple was ravaged by Red Guards during the campaign against the Four Olds, and the local neighborhood committee removed its most important wooden tablet to use as a tabletop. In 2001, the temple was restored once again as part of a grand reconstruction that brought to Huogongdian a new teahouse with a stage for musical performances, and a new restaurant building. And above the entrance, in pride of place, stands again that old survivor of fire and revolution, the Huogongdian memorial arch.

During the New Year holiday, craftsmen and peddlers gather outside Huogongdian as they did in the old days. There are sugar-blowers from Henan province, inserting straws into balls of soft toffee and blowing them, before your astonished eyes, into the forms of horses, pigs, and goats. Sichuanese vendors proffer potent bowlfuls of sour-and-hot noodles; while Uighur Muslims barbecue their kabobs in a drifting cloud of lamb-fat and cumin. And still, after all these years, there are Hunanese peddlers stirring glutinous rice dumplings in their cauldrons of molten toffee, and deep-frying squares of stinking bean curd.

GLUTINOUS RICE CONES WITH CURED SAUSAGE
la wei zong zi

腊
味
粽
子

On the balcony of her flat, Deng Zhiyuan's mother twists the long bamboo leaves (*ruo ye*) into cones, and stuffs them with a mixture of glutinous rice, mung beans, and peanuts, and then some richly marinated pieces of pork. She folds the leaves over, tying them tightly with string, and then starts to make another cone. The finished cones (*zong zi*), tied together like a string of firecrackers, are boiled or steamed, and sold in the courtyard of her apartment building.

Zong zi are traditionally eaten at the Dragon Boat Festival on the fifth day of the fifth lunar month, in commemoration of the great poet and official of the State of Chu, Qu Yuan, who lived from the fourth to the third century BC. Qu Yuan is regarded as a patriotic hero who offered sage advice to the Duke of Chu, but fell victim to some nasty court intrigue. The Duke failed to heed his advice, with disastrous consequences, and some years later the shattered Qu Yuan drowned himself in the Miluo River in northern Hunan. Grieving local people are said to have thrown parcels of rice into the river in the hope that the fish would leave his body intact. Despite the popularity of this myth, the true origins of *zong zi* are uncertain. They are eaten all over China, but have a particular resonance in northern Hunan, where Qu Yuan lived and is buried.

There are many different kinds of *zong zi*. They can be stuffed with sausage, salted duck egg yolk, or sweet Chinese jujube dates; and can be wrapped not only in giant bamboo leaves, but also lotus leaves, sections of fresh bamboo, reeds, or corn husks, all of which lend them a particular fragrance. The following version is easy to make and particularly delicious, as the rice is infused with the fragrance of the leaves and the rich taste of the sausage. (A moist salami makes a fine substitute for the traditional wind-dried Chinese sausage.) You can find the indocalamus leaves—they are usually 16 to 20 inches long, and narrow and pointed—in good Chinese supermarkets; if not, I suggest you use lotus leaves instead.

1⅓ CUPS GLUTINOUS RICE

2½ TBSP. DRIED MUNG BEANS

20 INDOCALAMUS (GIANT
    BAMBOO) LEAVES

3½ OZ. CHINESE WIND-DRIED
    SAUSAGE OR SALAMI

SALT

1 BALL NATURAL-FIBER STRING

1. Rinse the rice and mung beans under cold running water, then cover generously in cold water and leave to soak overnight. Cover the giant bamboo leaves in hot water from the kettle and leave to soak overnight.

2. Drain the giant bamboo leaves. Use scissors to cut a couple of inches off the stiff stem ends, so the remaining leaf is floppy.

3. Cut the wind-dried sausage or salami into slices and then very small (¼-inch) cubes. Drain the rice and bean mixture,

and then add the sausage cubes and a little salt to taste; mix well.

4. To stuff, take 2 leaves, shiny-sides up with the leaf bases facing away from you, and lay one on top of the other so they half-overlap. Take the narrower ends of the leaves, which are facing toward you, and twist them up so they make a cone at the bottom of the leaves. Use a spoon to stuff 4–5 tablespoons (about 2 ounces) of the rice mixture into the leaf cone, pressing it down. Fold the rest of the leaves down over the rice to close the cone, and wrap tightly around it. You should end up with a tight, triangular cone. Bind the cone with string, looping it around all the corners of the cone and tying it tightly. Repeat with the rest of the leaves.

5. Lay the cones in a bamboo or metal steamer, and steam over a high heat for about 40 minutes, taking care to top up the steamer with boiling water from the kettle when necessary.

6. To eat, untie and unwrap the cones. Hold them in your hands and eat the rice directly from the leaf, or serve them on plates and use chopsticks to eat the rice. The *zong zi* can be eaten fresh from the steamer, but they seem to be most delicious when allowed to cool for about 10 minutes first.

MAKES 10

VARIATION

If you wish to use lotus leaves instead of bamboo leaves, soak 4 dried lotus leaves in hot water from the kettle for 30 minutes. Then cut them into quarters, and cut off and discard the parts near the middle with stiff leaf-veins running through them, so the 4 sections are floppy. To stuff the lotus leaves, place 4–5 tablespoons stuffing in the middle of each leaf section. Fold the end that was nearest the middle of the leaf across the stuffing, fold in the sides, and flip over so the rice is completely enclosed in the leaf. The lotus cones should hold their shape without string-binding, if you handle them gently.

SPICY STEAMED PORK BUNS
duo jiao xiao bao

剁椒小包

In the south of Changsha, a small park surrounds Tianxinge, the tower on the last remaining section of the Ming dynasty city walls, which somehow survived the devastating fire of 1938. Early in the morning, people go there to dance or to practice *tai qi*, and the snack sellers congregate around the entrance. We walked up to an old-fashioned teahouse perched at the top of the hill, where a crowd of retired men and women were playing games over breakfast. There we drank mugs of green tea, and ate steamed buns stuffed with pork and salted chiles, and glutinous rice dumplings studded with cured meat and shrimp.

Most of the old teahouses of Changsha have been demolished with the modernization of the city, including the Deyuan, which was famous for the generous size and delicious flavor of its steamed *bao zi* buns. Founded in 1875 as a snack store, it later evolved into an elegant establishment that served not only stuffed buns and steamed breads, but also all kinds of banquet delicacies cooked in the grand mandarin style. It was best known, however, for its *bao zi*, stuffed with a variety of fillings, including pork and shiitake, candied rose petal, yellow lump sugar and salted greens, sesame paste, and *char siu* barbecued pork. Sadly, having survived revolutions, civil war, burning, and a communist makeover in the 1950s, the Deyuan was finally bulldozed in the early 2000s. The following recipe is based on the buns that we ate in the Tianxinge park on that cool spring morning.

For the stuffing:

¾-IN. PIECE FRESH GINGER,
    UNPEELED AND SMASHED

7 OZ. GROUND PORK

2 TBSP. CHOPPED SALTED
    CHILES

¼ TSP. SESAME OIL

For the dough:

1¾ CUPS ALL-PURPOSE FLOUR,
    WITH A LITTLE EXTRA FOR
    DUSTING

¾ TSP. ACTIVE-DRY YEAST

2 TSP. SUGAR

4 TBSP. LUKEWARM WATER

A LITTLE PEANUT OIL

1. To make the stuffing, smash the ginger with the flat of a cleaver blade, cover with about 5 tablespoons cold water, and leave to infuse for a minute or two. Place the pork in a bowl. Add the ginger-infused water (straining out the ginger). Use your hand to mix the water into the pork, picking it up and slapping it against the bottom of the bowl to encourage the meat to absorb the water. Add the chiles and sesame oil and mix well. Place in the freezer for about 20 minutes.

2. Meanwhile, to make the dough, place the flour in a bowl. Mix the yeast and sugar with the water and stir to dissolve. Add the yeast mixture to the flour with enough lukewarm water to make a stiff but moist dough. Turn the dough out onto a lightly floured countertop and knead for about 10 minutes until it is smooth and glossy. Cover with a wet cloth and set aside at room temperature for about 10 minutes.

3. Roll the dough into 2 long sausages, each about 1¼ inches thick. Break or cut this dough into about twenty 1¼-inch pieces and dust very lightly with flour.

4. Smear the bottom of a steamer with a little oil to prevent sticking.

5. To fill and shape the *bao zi*, take a piece of dough and flatten it slightly with the palm of your hand, so you have a plump disc. Then use a rolling pin to roll it out into a 2¾-inch circle. It is best to make small rolling movements toward the middle of the circle, turning it as you go, so you end up with a disk that is slightly fatter in the middle (this will help the wrapper to keep its shape when you add the filling). Cradle the disk of rolled dough in one hand, and add 1 tablespoon filling in the middle, smoothing it down with a knife blade. Then use your other hand to make small pinching movements around the edge of the filling, turning the dumpling as you go. You should end up with a ball-shaped dumpling with a whorl-like pattern on the top. (Ask a Chinese friend to demonstrate this process if you can!)

6. Place the finished dumpling onto the oiled steamer. Repeat with the rest of the dough and filling. When the dumplings are ready, set aside for 20 minutes at room temperature until the dough has risen.

7. Finally, steam the dumplings over a high heat for 15 minutes, by which time they should be cooked through—break one in half to make sure. Serve immediately.

MAKES ABOUT 20 DUMPLINGS

2

MEAT DISHES 畜肉類

★ MEAT DISHES

Pork is the primary meat for the Hunanese, and has pride of place at the festive table. Almost every rural household rears their own pig in preparation for the Chinese New Year, feeding it on homegrown plants that have been chopped and stewed. The flavor of the meat from these home-reared animals is so famously good it provokes sighs of longing in city-dwellers who don't have rural relatives to keep them supplied. After the ritual slaughter of the household pig some days before New Year's Eve, the extended family gathers for a feast of offal, and the rest of the meat is salted and smoked.

Fresh pork is the mainstay of the traditional rural feast. At weddings and funerals, you will see pork knuckles, "tiger-skin" belly pork, and pearly meatballs, all cooked in deep bowls in stacked bamboo steamers. Red-braised pork, cooked slowly with spices into melting submission, is one of the best known of all Hunanese dishes, largely because it was a favorite of Chairman Mao's. Small amounts of pork find their way into many otherwise vegetarian dishes, lending their rich, savory flavor to fresh beans, bamboo shoots, and pickled vegetables. Lard is the traditional cooking fat of the countryside, and is still used widely in the cities to enhance the tastes of stir-fries and soups.

But if fresh pork is common in Hunan as in many parts of China, it is smoked pork for which the region is most renowned. Hunanese bacon is salted and then cured in the lingering smoke of the farmhouse kitchen fire, until, as local historian Li Peitian so memorably describes, it has "skin as richly red as amber, fat as luminous as crystal, lean meat like a rose, and coral-like bones." The meat is traditionally cured in the twelfth lunar month, known as *la yue*, the month of winter sacrifices: the Chinese name for bacon and other cured meats is still *la rou*, "winter-sacrifice meat." In the countryside, smoking meats remains part of the fabric of life, and even in the cities, sides of bacon are hung out to wind-dry, and ad hoc smokeries are constructed in the courtyards of apartment blocks.

The rugged west of Hunan (*xiang xi*), with its spectacular scenery and mixed population of Miao, Tujia, and Han Chinese peoples, produces the best smoked meats in the province: not only pork, but also beef, chicken, fish, and wild creatures that might include wild boar, goat, pheasant, muntjac, and rabbit. These delicious meats are used in all kinds of colorful stir-fries and steamed dishes, most famously in combination with smoked fish and chicken in the traditional dish "Smoky flavors steamed together" (*la wei he zheng*).

Another notable specialty of the west of Hunan is "sour pork" (*suan rou*), a traditional preserve of the Miao minority. They marinate pork in salt and spices for a few hours, then add cornmeal and more salt and pack it into pickle jars where it is left for a couple of weeks. The preserved pork, cooked with chili and other ingredients, is an essential feature of the Miao festive board.

Beef plays a minor role in Hunanese cookery. It has been consumed in the region since ancient times:

ox bones were retrieved from the Han dynasty tombs at Mawangdui, and "ribs of the fatted ox" were one of the foods designed to lure back the soul of the deceased in the great poet Qu Yuan's "Summons of the Soul." Oxen were also used in ritual sacrifices, but were considered so vital to the rural economy that periodical decrees from the emperor forbade their slaughter for food. Interestingly, in Mao Zedong's report on the burgeoning revolutionary movement in 1920s Hunan, he says one of the first actions taken by peasants in some areas when they seized power from their landlords was to ban the killing of oxen. "Oxen are a treasured possession of the peasants. 'Slaughter an ox in this life and you will be an ox in the next,' has become an almost religious tenet," wrote Mao.

Above: SMOKING MEATS, ZHANGGUYING

Water buffalo can still be seen pulling the plow in some parts of Hunan, but there seems to be no vestige of taboo when it comes to eating beef. It is, however, particularly associated with Muslim cookery. A few beef dishes feature in the roll call of classic Hunanese banquet dishes, especially "hairlike tripe slivers," in which crisp ox tripe is cut into the finest possible strands and stir-fried swiftly at a very high temperature. This dish is said to have been perfected by an old Muslim restaurant in Changsha. In the city of Liuyang, black goat (*hei shan yang*) is a local delicacy. Both beef and goat or mutton are considered in Chinese gastronomy to have an off-putting "muttony" odor, so spices, ginger, scallion, and wine are liberally applied when cooking them.

In the cold and damp of midwinter, every Hunanese person knows that it's best to eat heating foods to restore the equilibrium of the body. One of the most effective heating foods is a kind of meat I don't dare even to mention in the polite company of European and American readers, let alone suggest a recipe (let's just say it goes "woof"!). Prized for the richness of its fragrance, it is made into nourishing soups and stews. It is, however, usually only eaten until the Chinese New Year, when sheep or goat, cooked in the same manner, are regarded as more efficacious.

Being southerners, the Hunanese also lean toward their Cantonese neighbors in their occasional penchant for exotica: civet cat, snake, and donkey are just some of the more unusual meats I've been offered during my stays in the region.

CHAIRMAN MAO'S RED-BRAISED PORK
mao shi hong shao rou

毛氏紅燒肉

Red-braised pork is a dish that in Hunan is inseparably bound up with the memory of Chairman Mao: many restaurants call it "The Mao family's red-braised pork." Mao Zedong loved it, ate it frequently, and is said to have insisted his Hunanese chefs cook it for him in Beijing. It's a robust concoction, best eaten with plain steamed rice and simple stir-fried vegetables, but the sweet, aromatic chunks of meat are irresistible and it's always a favorite at my London dinner parties. In keeping with traditional Chinese gastronomy, which seeks to make a medical virtue out of every dietary predilection, the people of Mao's home village, Shaoshan, recommend red-braised pork as a health food: "Men eat it to build their brains," Chairman Mao's nephew Mao Anping assured me when I met him there a few years ago, "and ladies to make themselves more beautiful." His friend and neighbor, the Shaoshan communist party secretary, told me he ate two bowlfuls a day to keep his intellect in shape.

This is Mao Anping's recipe, but on the next page you will find some delicious variations, where the richness of the meat is offset by the addition of other, vegetarian, ingredients. The one that uses water chestnuts is a particular favorite of mine. In Shaoshan, cooks traditionally leave the skin intact for maximum succulence, and cut the meat into rather large chunks, perhaps 1½ inches long: I tend to make the pieces a little smaller. The recipe below takes its color from caramelized sugar, which gives it a lovely reddish gloss, but many people just use dark soy sauce at home.

1 LB. PORK BELLY (SKIN OPTIONAL)

2 TBSP. PEANUT OIL

2 TBSP. WHITE SUGAR

1 TBSP. SHAOXING WINE

¾-IN. PIECE FRESH GINGER, SKIN LEFT ON AND SLICED

1 STAR ANISE

2 DRIED RED CHILES

A SMALL PIECE CASSIA BARK OR CINNAMON STICK

LIGHT SOY SAUCE, SALT, AND SUGAR

A FEW PIECES SCALLION GREENS

1. Plunge the pork belly into a pan of boiling water and simmer for 3–4 minutes until partially cooked. Remove and, when cool enough to handle, cut into bite-size chunks.

2. Heat the oil and sugar in a wok over a gentle flame until the sugar melts, then raise the heat and stir until the melted sugar turns a rich caramel brown. Add the pork and splash in the Shaoxing wine.

3. Add enough water to just cover the pork, along with the ginger, star anise, chiles, and cassia. Bring to a boil, then turn down the heat and simmer for 40–50 minutes.

4. Toward the end of the cooking time, turn up the heat to reduce the sauce, and season with soy sauce, salt, and a little sugar to taste. Add the scallion greens just before serving.

continued on the next page

VARIATIONS

For all these variations, begin by making the original recipe (it can be prepared in advance, and freezes well). Local chefs have told me that women always prefer the water chestnut version, while men opt for pork with bean curd skin. Do feel free to improvise by adding other vegetable ingredients: one of the most wonderful versions of this dish I have ever tasted was pork braised with reconstituted dried cabbage. It is a peasant dish served in the Everyone Restaurant in Yueyang.

★ RED-BRAISED PORK WITH WATER CHESTNUTS *bi qi shao rou*

Peel the water chestnuts and deep-fry briefly until just taking color. Drain well, then return the chestnuts to the wok with some cooked red-braised pork, light soy sauce, sugar, ground white pepper to taste, and a little dark soy sauce to intensify the honey color. Turn up the heat to reduce the sauce and make everything sizzly and fragrant. Just before serving, adjust the seasoning, stir in some pieces of scallion greens and allow them barely to cook. The crisp chestnuts are a magnificent foil for the richness of the meat.

★ RED-BRAISED PORK WITH GARLIC CLOVES *suan zi shao rou*

Follow the water chestnut recipe above, but substitute whole garlic cloves for the chestnuts and make sure you fry them until they are tender and a little golden.

★ RED-BRAISED PORK WITH DEEP-FRIED BEAN CURD *you dou fu shao rou*

Add deep-fried bean curd puffs to some prepared red-braised pork, with extra everyday stock (page 287) or water, if necessary, and simmer until the bean curd has absorbed the flavors of the meat. Finish as in the water chestnut version above.

★ RED-BRAISED PORK WITH BEAN CURD SKIN *dou sun shao rou*

Soak the brittle yellow bean curd skin rolls in cold water overnight, or in hot water for about 30 minutes, then drain and cut on an angle into chunks. Cook with some prepared red-braised pork as in the bean curd puff recipe above.

★ RED-BRAISED PORK WITH "TEA-TREE" MUSHROOMS *cha shu gu shao rou*

Simmer some prepared red-braised pork with soaked and squeezed dry "tea-tree" mushrooms, stir-frying the mushrooms before adding the pork and then proceeding as in the recipes above. (You can stir-fry the mushrooms in some of the fat that rises to the top of the braised pork.)

★ STEAMED RED-BRAISED PORK WITH PRESERVED MUSTARD GREENS *suan cai zheng hong shao rou*

Put some prepared red-braised pork into a bowl, top with a good handful of thoroughly rinsed preserved mustard greens and then steam for 20–30 minutes to heat through. This is delicious.

★ RED-BRAISED SPARE RIBS *hong shao pai gu*

Cook spare ribs as in the pork recipe above.

QING QING'S BACK-IN-THE POT PORK
qing qing hui guo rou

The following recipe is based on a simple but delicious spare rib dish my friend Qing Qing made during a Hunanese cooking session at my house in London. I've adapted it to use sliced pork instead of ribs.

14 OZ. PORK BELLY, WITHOUT
    SKIN

3 SCALLIONS, GREEN PARTS
    ONLY

10 GARLIC CLOVES, PEELED

1¾-IN. PIECE FRESH GINGER

2 TBSP. BLACK FERMENTED
    BEANS, RINSED

1 TBSP. LIGHT SOY SAUCE

½ TSP. DARK SOY SAUCE

SALT

EVERYDAY STOCK (PAGE 287) OR
    WATER (OPTIONAL)

2 FRESH RED CHILES, SLICED

1 TSP. SESAME OIL

3 TBSP. PEANUT OIL FOR
    COOKING

1. Bring a saucepan of water to a boil. Add the pork belly and then simmer until it is cooked through and the juices run clear when you poke a skewer into it; drain and set aside to cool. (This step can be done some time in advance.)

2. Cut the pork belly into fairly thin slices. Cut the scallion greens into 1¼ to 1½-inch pieces. If the garlic cloves are large, cut them in half; otherwise, leave them whole. Thinly slice the ginger, with or without its peel (the peel adds extra flavor).

3. Heat the wok over a high flame until smoke rises, then add the oil and swirl around. Reduce the heat to medium, add the garlic and ginger and stir-fry until fragrant. Add the pork slices and continue to stir-fry until sizzly and tinged with gold.

4. Add the black beans, soy sauces, and salt to taste and continue stir-frying until the beans are fragrant. If at any point the food starts to stick a little on the base of the wok, simply pour in a tablespoon or two of stock or water and mix well.

5. Add the chiles and when you smell their aroma, the scallion greens. When the onion is barely cooked, remove the wok from the heat, stir in the sesame oil, and serve.

STEAMED SPARE RIBS WITH BLACK BEANS AND CHILES
dou chi la jiao zheng pai gu

This is a dish I ate with Sansan after a day spent exploring old houses in the countryside around Liuyang. As night fell, we went in search of somewhere to eat, and ended up at a farmhouse whose owners had started a restaurant serving "rustic food." It was a long, single-storied building with a series of interconnecting rooms that ran the whole length of the house, and it was so informal they actually set up our dinner table in somebody's bedroom. All the food that night was cooked over a wood fire, which the Hunanese swear makes everything taste ten times as delicious. After we had supped on ribs, bean curd, soup, and rice, the owners saw us off from an entrance bedecked in glowing red lanterns. We drove back along a bumpy track, the scattered lights of farmhouses shining on the opposite side of the river, against the dark, looming Liuyang hills.

This dish also works well as a noodle topping (see pages 260–1).

1 LB. SPARE RIBS, CUT INTO BITE-SIZED CHUNKS

2 TSP. LIGHT SOY SAUCE

1 TBSP. SHAOXING WINE

1 TSP. FINELY CHOPPED FRESH GINGER

1 TBSP. BLACK FERMENTED BEANS, RINSED

DRIED CHILI FLAKES TO TASTE

2 TSP. LARD (OPTIONAL)

1. Bring a large pan or wok of water to a boil over a high heat. Add the ribs and blanch.

2. Drain the ribs and place them in a heatproof bowl with the soy sauce, Shaoxing wine, and ginger, and mix well. Top with the black beans and generous amounts of chili flakes, and the lard if desired (actually the dish tastes lovely without it).

3. Steam the ribs over a high heat for about 30 minutes, until cooked through. Serve in the bowl, and stir well before eating.

TIGER-SKIN STEAMED PORK
hu pi kou rou

The following recipe is typical of the rich steamed dishes that are served at rural Hunanese feasts. The cooking method renders the pork delightfully moist and tender, and gives it a fatty, wrinkled skin, which explains its name. The time needed for steaming is imprecise, which is why it is so useful when catering for large numbers of people. After half an hour the dish is pretty good; after one hour it is delicious; after one-and-a-half hours it is yet more wonderful, and so on. I haven't yet discovered an upper limit. You can also prepare it in advance, and simply return it to the steamer to heat through before serving.

You will need a deep bowl that can hold around 3½ cups liquid to make this dish.

1 LB. 10 OZ. PORK BELLY, WITH SKIN, IN ONE PIECE

2 TBSP. SWEET FERMENTED GLUTINOUS RICE WINE (SEE PAGE 277) OR SHAOXING WINE

¼ TSP. SALT

2 TBSP. LIGHT SOY SAUCE

2 TSP. DARK SOY SAUCE

2½ TBSP. BLACK FERMENTED BEANS, RINSED

1¾ CUPS PEANUT OIL FOR FRYING

1. Place the pork in a pan, cover with cold water, and bring to a boil. Reduce the heat and simmer for 8–10 minutes until nearly cooked, but still a little pink in the thickest places. Remove the pork from the liquid and pat dry with a clean dish towel or paper towels; do not throw away the cooking water. Rub the pork with the wine.

2. Heat the oil for frying in the wok over a high flame until it reaches 350°F. Add the pork, skin-side down, and fry for about 3 minutes, until the skin is a rich, dark red-brown.

3. Remove the pork from the oil and return it to the original cooking water. Bring the water to a boil, then reduce the heat and simmer for about 5 minutes, until the skin is puckered all over (the "tiger-skin" effect). Drain and cool slightly, reserving the liquid for the stockpot, if you wish.

4. Place the pork, skin down, on a chopping board and cut as evenly as possible into ½-inch slices. Layer the slices over the bottom of a heatproof bowl, making sure each piece of skin is in contact with the bowl. Put any ragged bits of meat on top. Scatter the meat with the salt, soy sauces, and black beans, and place in a steamer.

5. Steam the meat for at least 30 minutes, preferably 1½ hours. To serve, cover the bowl with a deep serving dish and swiftly invert. Remove the bowl and place on the table.

FARMHOUSE STIR-FRIED PORK WITH GREEN PEPPERS
nong jia chao rou

This is one of the most popular of all Hunan dishes, and you'll find it in almost every restaurant and every home, yet it is rarely included in cooking books. I have recorded many versions of it; in the beautiful village of Zhangguying, where the scent and sizzle of its stir-frying drifted out into an ancient courtyard; in my friend Fan Qun's family home in the countryside, when we ate it for dinner on New Year's Eve; and in restaurants all over the province. The following recipe draws, I hope, on the best of each of them.

I've used the long, only mildly hot peppers known as Italian frying peppers, but ordinary bell peppers, cut into squares, can be used as a substitute. Use a mixture of red and green peppers if you like.

9 OZ. ITALIAN FRYING PEPPERS

1¾ OZ. PORK BELLY OR THICKLY
    SLICED BACON

7 OZ. LEAN BONELESS PORK

1 TSP. SHAOXING WINE

1 TSP. LIGHT SOY SAUCE

½ TSP. DARK SOY SAUCE

2 GARLIC CLOVES, SLICED

2 TSP. BLACK FERMENTED
    BEANS, RINSED

SALT

½ TSP. POTATO FLOUR MIXED
    WITH 2 TBSP EVERYDAY
    STOCK (PAGE 287) OR WATER
    (OPTIONAL)

ABOUT 3 TBSP. PEANUT OIL OR
    LARD FOR COOKING

1. Cut off and discard the stems of the peppers, and slice at a steep angle into 1¼-inch chunks. (Don't worry about the seeds—this is a peasant dish!) Cut the pork belly and the lean pork into fairly thin slices; set aside the pork belly. Add the Shaoxing wine and the soy sauces to the lean pork and mix well; set aside.

2. Smear the wok with a little oil or lard and heat over a medium flame. Add the peppers and stir-fry, pressing them against the side of the wok with your wok scoop or ladle, for about 5 minutes, until they are fragrant and tender and their skins a little golden and puckered. Remove the peppers from the wok and set aside.

3. Remove any pepper seeds from the wok, and reheat the wok over a hot flame until smoke rises, then add 2 tablespoons of the oil or lard and swirl around. Add the pork belly and stir-fry until the slices are tinged with gold.

4. Toss in the garlic and black beans and stir-fry briefly until fragrant, and then add the lean pork. When the pork has almost changed color and lost most of its water content, return the peppers to the wok and continue to stir-fry for another minute or so, adding salt to taste.

5. If using the potato-flour mixture to add a professional gloss, give the mixture a stir and tip it into the wok at the final stage, stirring just long enough for the sauce to cling to the meat.

STEAMED PORK KNUCKLE IN AROMATIC SAUCE
jiang zhi zhou zi

This is an old-fashioned Hunanese banquet dish, made with a cut of meat that is especially popular in China. (The front shoulder or picnic includes the hock.) The long, slow cooking makes the fat soft and succulent, so it is, as they say, "richly fat without being greasy" (*fei er bu ni*).

1 FRONT PORK KNUCKLE OR
   FRONT SHOULDER, BONED
   WITH SKIN LEFT ON (ABOUT
   2¼ LB. BONED WEIGHT)

1¾-IN. PIECE FRESH GINGER,
   UNPEELED AND IN ONE PIECE

2 SCALLIONS

3 TBSP. CRUSHED YELLOW ROCK
   SUGAR

2 TBSP. CARAMEL COLOR (SEE
   PAGE 289) OR DARK SOY
   SAUCE

3½ TBSP. SHAOXING WINE

1 TSP. SALT

3⅓ CUPS EVERYDAY STOCK (PAGE
   287)

Some or all of the following spices:

A COUPLE PIECES CASSIA BARK

3 STAR ANISE

A SMALL HANDFUL DRIED
   CHILES

½ TSP. WHOLE SICHUAN PEPPER

½ TSP. FENNEL SEEDS

2 CLOVES WITH THEIR POWDERY
   HEADS PINCHED OFF AND
   DISCARDED

1 *CAO GUO* (SEE PAGE 25)

1. Lay the pork, skin down, on a chopping board and make a crisscross of deep cuts into the meat, about ¾ inches apart, taking care not to cut through the fat and skin. Bring a saucepan of water to a boil, add the pork, and simmer for about 5 minutes until partially cooked; drain, discarding the water.

2. Tie the dry spices up in a piece of cheesecloth. (This is not essential, but more convenient than using them loose.)

3. Crush the ginger with the flat side of a cleaver or a heavy object (do not peel it), and lay in the bottom of a flameproof casserole with the scallions. Add the pork, skin down, with the sugar, caramel color or soy sauce, wine, and salt, then tuck in the bundle of spices. Pour the stock over.

4. Bring the casserole to a boil, then reduce the heat and simmer over a gentle flame for at least an hour, preferably two. The meat will already be delicious by this stage, but the dish is traditionally finished off by steaming, as follows.

5. Take the meat out of the cooking liquid and tuck it, skin down, into a deep heatproof bowl. The meat should ideally fit neatly into the bowl, with the skin covering most of the surface; set aside.

6. Heat the wok over a medium flame until hot, then add the peanut oil. Add the black beans and chili flakes to taste and stir-fry until fragrant, and then lay them on the meat. Pour over enough of the cooking liquid to nearly cover the pork, place the bowl in a steamer, and steam over a high heat for 20–30 minutes.

A COUPLE PIECES DRIED
LICORICE ROOT
A COUPLE PIECES DRIED "SAND
GINGER"

For the steaming:
2 TBSP. PEANUT OIL
2 TBSP. BLACK FERMENTED
BEANS, RINSED
DRIED CHILI FLAKES

7. To serve, drain the liquid from the bowl into another container. Lay a deep serving dish over the bowl and swiftly invert it. Remove the bowl, to leave the glossy, aromatic pork in the middle of the dish. Spoon some of the steaming juices over and serve.

NOTE

The dark, aromatic cooking liquid (*lu shui*) can be reused to cook many foods, such as chicken wings and drumsticks and hard-boiled eggs (see pages 54–5 for details).

STIR-FRIED PORK WITH SILVERFISH
yin yu chao rou si

銀
魚
炒
肉
絲

Tiny silverfish are one of the most treasured products of the Dongting Lake area. According to legend, the Monkey King once stole some peaches, the fruit of immortality in Daoist mythology, from the Queen Mother of the Western Heavens. Furious, she set out with her soldiers in hot pursuit of the thief, and in her disarray lost a pair of precious jade hairpins. They tumbled into the waters of the Dongting Lake, where they metamorphosed into a pair of silvery fish. The fish multiplied, and before long were as numerous and dazzling bright as the stars in the night sky.

You can find packets of dried silverfish in good Chinese supermarkets. They are tiny, paper-thin, and wispy, with small, dotlike black eyes, and take only a few minutes to soak back into softness. The following stir-fry is a delectable entwining of pale pork slivers, tiny wisplike fish, and a few strands of green scallion, their flavors enhanced by the fresh piquancy of ginger.

1 OZ. DRIED SILVERFISH

9 OZ. LEAN BONELESS PORK OR
    CHICKEN BREAST

2 SCALLIONS, GREEN PARTS
    ONLY

1 TBSP. FINELY CHOPPED FRESH
    GINGER

SALT

1 TSP. CLEAR RICE VINEGAR

SCANT 1 CUP PEANUT OIL FOR
    COOKING

For the marinade:

2 TSP. SHAOXING WINE

¼–½ TSP. SALT

2 TSP. POTATO FLOUR

2 TBSP. COLD WATER

1. Rinse the silverfish under cold water, then put them in a bowl, cover with cold water, and squeeze them a few times in your hand; set aside to soak for 5–10 minutes, by which time they should be soft and supple.

2. Cut the pork or chicken into very thin slices, and then, along the grain of the meat, into very fine slivers. Place in a bowl, add the marinade ingredients, and mix well; set aside.

3. Cut the scallion greens into 2- to 2½-inch pieces, and then into fine slivers to match the meat; set aside.

4. Heat the oil in a wok over a high flame until it reaches 275°F. Add the meat and use chopsticks to separate the slivers. When the slivers are turning white, but are not yet completely cooked, remove them with a slotted spoon, and set aside. Pour off all but 3 tablespoons of the oil.

5. Return the wok to the heat. Add the ginger and sizzle until fragrant. Add the fish and stir-fry for a minute, adding salt to taste, and splashing in the vinegar toward the end of this time.

6. Return the meat to the wok and stir-fry until fully cooked, seasoning with more salt, if necessary. Add the scallion greens toward the end of the cooking time. Serve.

PEARLY MEATBALLS
zhen zhu rou wan

珍珠肉丸

I was woken at five-thirty in the morning by the sound of firecrackers resounding up and down the valley. Outside, a pall of white smoke hung in the air, and crowds of villagers were milling around, some of them dressed in robes of funeral white. They had gathered to welcome back the body of an old lady, a native of the village, who had died at her home in Yueyang. When her coffin arrived with three busloads of relatives, the crowds assembled into a long procession, some bearing paper wreaths, others a gong, still others playing plaintive tunes on *suo na* horns. Then they walked along the stream that runs through the village, among the carefully terraced rice fields, and up into the hills to the old lady's grave. Later, the old lady's sons provided a funeral lunch in the dilapidated splendor of their ancestral home. Dozens of tables had been laid out in the main hall, and shafts of bright sunlight caught the cigarette smoke drifting up from the throng of guests. The menu consisted of the traditional steamed bowls, including many dishes that were white or pale in color, as was fitting for a funeral. There were bean curd skin with chili and scallion, steamed pork knuckle (front shoulder or picnic), chicken legs, pale bean curd with pigs' blood, a soup of eggs and white wood ear fungus, and pork meatballs studded with grains of rice.

The following recipe is a slightly more extravagant version of the meatballs we ate that day: the meat is mixed with dried shrimp and water chestnuts, the rice with morsels of pink ham and dark shiitake mushrooms. Use a short-grained rice, and the dumplings will be as pearly as their name suggests; use a long-grained rice as I have done in the photograph, and the grains will prick up like porcupine quills. A similar method can be used to cook spare ribs, which are marinated and then mixed with the glutinous rice before steaming.

Please note that the rice for this dish should be soaked for a few hours, or preferably overnight, in advance of the cooking.

continued on the next page

1 CUP GLUTINOUS RICE

6 DRIED SHIITAKE MUSHROOMS

1 SLICE COOKED HAM, DARK PINK
    IF POSSIBLE (ABOUT 1 OZ.)

A LITTLE PEANUT OIL

2 SCALLIONS, GREEN PARTS
    ONLY, FINELY SLICED

1–2 TSP. SESAME OIL

For the meatball mixture:

2 TBSP. DRIED SHRIMP

12 CANNED OR 10 FRESH WATER
    CHESTNUTS

14 OZ. GROUND PORK, A LITTLE
    FATTY IF POSSIBLE

2 TBSP. FINELY CHOPPED FRESH
    GINGER

2 TBSP. SHAOXING WINE

1 EGG

2 TBSP. POTATO FLOUR MIXED
    TO A PASTE WITH 2 TBSP.
    WATER

SALT AND PEPPER TO TASTE

1. Rinse the rice thoroughly in cold water, and then soak for 3 hours in hot water from the kettle, or in cold water overnight; drain and set aside.

2. Meanwhile, soak the dried shrimp, for the meatball mixture, and the shiitake mushrooms in separate bowls of hot water from the kettle for about 30 minutes to reconstitute. After soaking, drain, squeeze dry, and finely chop them separately. Finely chop the ham; set aside.

3. Peel the water chestnuts if you are using fresh ones, then chop them finely. (Do not do this in a food processor: they are used to bring a little crunch to the meatballs and should not be completely pulverized.)

4. Combine the meatball ingredients and mix well. On a plate, mix the ham and shiitake with the drained glutinous rice. Oil a heatproof plate that will fit into your steamer.

5. Shape the meat mixture into walnut-size balls and roll in the rice to coat generously. Lay the meatballs in one layer on the oiled plate: you might need to steam them in 2 batches, depending on the size of your steamer.

6. Steam over a high heat for 10 minutes, until cooked through: break one in half to check that it is cooked. Serve directly on the plate, with a scattering of scallion and sesame oil.

NOTE

In Hunan, the cooked meatballs are often piled into a bowl and then resteamed before serving.

STEAMED GROUND PORK WITH EGGS
rou bing zheng dan

肉餅蒸蛋

These days people in China are able to laugh at some of the idiocies of the Cultural Revolution. The father of one of my closest friends grins sheepishly as he recalls how he used to do a public "loyalty dance" to Chairman Mao, tracing the lines of the Chinese character for "loyalty" with his footsteps on the ground. Even the most mundane activities, such as shopping, could be a surreal experience, given the need for exaggerated political correctness. The following was recounted by one of my friends as a typical market conversation of the era:

Shopper (to market vendor): Comrade, good morning. Chairman Mao said "Serve the People." One pound of pork, please.

Market vendor: "Be resolute, don't be afraid of making sacrifices, overcome ten thousand difficulties and strive for victory." Here you are. That'll be X Chinese yuan, and may I please have your ration coupons?

The following is a simple supper recipe that requires a little less than a pound of pork. Liu Qing Qing showed me how to make the dish.

4 MEDIUM OR 10–12 SMALL
    DRIED SHIITAKE MUSHROOMS
A SMALL PIECE FRESH GINGER,
    UNPEELED
10 OZ. GROUND PORK
1 TSP. SESAME OIL
SALT AND PEPPER
1–1¼ CUPS EVERYDAY STOCK
    (PAGE 287), COOL
4 EGGS
2 SCALLIONS, GREEN PARTS
    ONLY, FINELY SLICED

1. Soak the mushrooms in boiling water for about 30 minutes. Crush the ginger with the flat of a cleaver blade and place in a cup with a little cold water to cover.

2. Place the pork in a mixing bowl. Drain and finely chop the reconstituted shiitake and add to the pork. Add 3 tablespoons of the ginger soaking water, the sesame oil, and salt and pepper to taste and mix well. Stir in the stock, a little at a time to let the meat absorb it, until you have a very loose paste.

3. Pour the pork paste into a shallow heatproof bowl. Break the eggs over the pork. Place the bowl in a steamer and steam over a high heat for 15 minutes until the pork is cooked through. Serve with a scattering of scallion greens.

STEAMED BACON AND SMOKED BEAN CURD WITH WINTER-SACRIFICE BEANS
la ba dou zheng la wei

In the markets of Hunan, you can come across clay jars of moist, yellowish soybeans, perhaps speckled with morsels of chili. These are *la ba dou*, which I have loosely translated as "winter-sacrifice beans." *La ba* actually refers to the eighth day of the twelfth lunar month, which was once a time for making sacrifices to the gods, and it remains a key date in the season for making winter preserves, including these intensely flavored beans (see page 29 for more information on their production).

If you can't find winter-sacrifice beans in your local Chinese grocery, substitute 2–3 tablespoons black fermented beans and a spoonful or two of chili oil with sediment (or dried chili flakes and plain cooking oil to taste). The black beans can be briefly stir-fried in a little oil first to enhance their fragrance. This dish demands proper smoked bacon, fairly thickly cut, and some people fry it a little before steaming.

Eat this with plenty of plain steamed rice to counterbalance its robust, wintry flavors. Vegetarians can omit the bacon and make a delicious version of the dish with only the bean curd, avid meat-eaters vice versa, but the two together are marvelous. For less intense flavors, try interleaving the bacon with slices of plain white bean curd, which will absorb its smoky flavors to delightful effect.

7 OZ. SMOKED BACON SLICES, THICKLY CUT, RINDS DISCARDED IF NECESSARY

7 OZ. SMOKED BEAN CURD

½ CUP WINTER-SACRIFICE BEANS

½ TSP. DRIED CHILI FLAKES

1 TBSP. PEANUT OIL OR LARD

FRESH CORIANDER (CILANTRO) OR PARSLEY TO GARNISH (OPTIONAL)

1. Place the bacon in a steamer and steam over a high heat for 5–10 minutes, until cooked. Cut each slice into about 3 pieces. Cut the bean curd into thickish slices to complement the bacon.

2. Lay alternate slices of bacon and bean curd into the bottom and up the side of an earthenware or china bowl. Place any remaining slices on top. Spoon the beans, the chili flakes, and the oil or lard over. (You can prepare up to this stage in advance.)

3. Place the bowl in a steamer and steam for at least 30 minutes, or up to an hour, until the flavors have blended.

4. You can simply serve the dish in the steaming bowl, and just give everything a good stir with chopsticks before digging in. For greater elegance, however, cover the bowl with a serving dish, swiftly invert, and then serve it unmolded with a garnish of fresh coriander (cilantro) or parsley.

STIR-FRIED SMOKY BACON WITH SMOKED BEAN CURD
xiang gan zi chao la rou

香干子炒腊肉

In the kitchen of the Jade Belt restaurant in Zhangguying, the preserved meats hang from a bamboo pole suspended in the slow, drowsy smoke of the fire. There is pork, obviously, the fat smoked to a honey-colored yellow, the lean meat a dark crimson on the outside, pink within. But there is also wild muntjac, chicken, wild boar, catfish, and rabbit, all of which are local specialties. The rich flavors of these meats go particularly well with pungent vegetables like green garlic and scallion, and a little chili. One spring day we ate the bacon stir-fried with smoked bean curd that was made in a workshop just over the way—a fabulous combination. Vegetarians can follow a similar recipe, doubling the quantity of bean curd and omitting the bacon; avid meat-eaters vice versa. And if you can't find smoked bean curd, five-spiced bean curd makes a delicious substitute.

7 OZ. SMOKED BACON SLICES,
THICKLY CUT, RINDS
DISCARDED IF NECESSARY

5 OZ. SMOKED BEAN CURD

10 DRIED CHILES OR 2 FRESH
RED CHILES

5 CHINESE LEEKS OR SCALLIONS,
GREEN PARTS ONLY

LIGHT SOY SAUCE

SALT

2 TBSP. PEANUT OIL OR LARD
FOR COOKING

1. Place the bacon in a steamer and steam over a high heat for 5–10 minutes, until cooked through. Cut each slice into about 3 pieces. Cut the bean curd into slices to complement the bacon: very firm bean curd can be cut very thinly, more crumbly types a little thicker. If you are using dried chillies, snip them into ½-inch pieces, discarding seeds as far as possible; fresh chiles should be cut on a steep angle into thin slices.

2. Heat the oil or lard in a wok over a high flame. Add the bacon and stir-fry for a few minutes until it has lost some of its water content and released its fat. Now add the bean curd and sizzle until both are tinged golden.

3. Push the bacon and bean curd up the side of the wok, letting the oil fall to the bottom, and tip the chiles into the oil. Stir-fry them briefly until fragrant in the space you have created, then mix everything together. Add the leek or scallion and soy sauce and salt to taste. When the greens are just cooked, tip the dish onto a plate and serve.

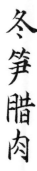

STIR-FRIED BACON WITH WINTER BAMBOO SHOOTS
dong sun la rou

When I stayed with the family of my friend Fan Qun over the Spring Festival holiday, her father and elder brother went foraging on the hillsides for winter bamboo shoots, the sweetest, crispest, and most highly prized bamboo. At midnight on New Year's Eve, we ran outside into the starry night and set off our firecrackers. All the way up the valley, the sky flashed and echoed as all the neighbors did the same. And then we went inside, where Fan Qun's mother had warmed up a potful of winter bamboo soup on the fire.

There's something incredibly beautiful about bamboo shoots. They push up from the forest undergrowth, their crisp flesh wrapped in a leafy cover that is silky with tiny hairs and mottled like a wildcat's coat. They must be eaten before they sprout leaves, because this is the moment when the velvet wrapper splits and the pale green bamboo bark begins to thrust upward, tall and strong. Winter bamboo shoots, the finest of them all, are gathered before they have even emerged from the earth, and their presence is only betrayed by slightly raised patches of ground. Their papery, purplish husks peel off to reveal pale, delicate flesh, which can be boiled, stewed, or stir-fried.

The following recipe is a typical Hunanese winter treat, using not only winter bamboo but also the bacon that is smoked in the last month of the lunar year, the month of winter sacrifices (*la yue*). If you can find fresh bamboo shoots in a Chinese shop, snap them up. Cut them open lengthwise, and then peel off the damp, furry outer layer and papery husk to reveal the ivory stem, crisp and secret as the heart of an artichoke. Discard any fibrous parts near the bottom of the shoot, and then slice. Many cooks recommend blanching of the shoots before cooking: either to remove their astringent taste, or to dispel toxins, depending on who is talking. Canned winter bamboo can be used as a substitute, but it is not nearly as good as the fresh shoot.

5 OZ. CHINESE BACON OR
   SMOKED BACON SLICES
3 OZ. FRESH WINTER BAMBOO
   SHOOTS
2 FRESH RED CHILES
A GOOD HANDFUL CHINESE
   CHIVES, CHINESE LEEKS, OR
   SPRING ONION GREENS
1 TSP. FINELY CHOPPED GARLIC
1 TSP. FINELY CHOPPED FRESH
   GINGER
1 TSP. DRIED CHILI FLAKES
   (OPTIONAL)
LIGHT SOY SAUCE
1 TSP. SESAME OIL
3 TBSP. PEANUT OIL OR LARD
   FOR COOKING

1. If using Chinese bacon, wash it and then steam it for 20 minutes. Allow it to cool until you can handle it, then slice thinly. If using Western smoked bacon, simply cut into 1½-inch strips.

2. If using fresh bamboo shoots, remove the husk from the shoots and cut into thin slices to match the bacon. If using canned winter bamboo, simply slice. Cut the chiles on an angle into thin slices, discarding the seeds and stems. Cut the chives into 1½-inch pieces.

3. Blanch the fresh or canned bamboo shoot in boiling water, and then drain.

4. Heat the wok over a high flame until smoke rises, then add the oil or lard and swirl around. Add bamboo slices and allow to sizzle. Add the bacon, garlic, ginger, chili flakes, and fresh chiles and stir-fry until fragrant, seasoning with light soy sauce.

5. When everything is sizzly and delicious, add the Chinese chives and stir-fry briefly until hot and fragrant. Remove the wok from the heat, stir in the sesame oil, and serve.

VARIATIONS

The Hunanese use smoked meats, not only bacon but also smoked beef, muntjac, wild boar, and many kinds of variety meat, in a huge variety of stir-fries. The meats are usually washed and boiled before being sliced. Aside from bamboo shoots, Chinese leeks (otherwise known as green garlic leaves) are a fantastic accompaniment, as are garlic stems. You can also use red and green bell peppers, semidried Asian radish (*daikon*), yard-long green beans, carrot, or cloud ear fungus. More exotic local ingredients that are stir-fried with bacon include fiddlehead ferns and a kind of artemisia (*lou hao* or *ni hao* in Hunan dialect). If you are using vegetables that require a longer cooking time, like carrots, stir-fry them first until almost cooked, and return them to the wok later, when the bacon is nice and sizzly.

SMOKY FLAVORS STEAMED TOGETHER
la wei he zheng

腊味合蒸

One winter's day I was exploring the old streets of the port district of Yueyang, when suddenly I came across a desolate brick pagoda, towering up above a cluster of old houses, weed-grown, and abandoned. According to legend, Cishi Pagoda dates back more than 1,000 years, to a period when water demons were wreaking havoc on the lives of local people. The locals decided to build a pagoda to vanquish these evil spirits, but a powerful official started extorting money from people to fund it. They were saved by the intervention of a widow whose family had been fishermen for generations, and who turned over her life savings. Sadly, she died before it was completed, but it was named in her honor, and over time people began to make offerings to her as a spirit.

The present construction is thought to date back to the thirteenth-century Song dynasty, although some sources claim it was built in the eighth century, during the Tang. The temple that once stood nearby has long since been demolished, and the tower narrowly escaped destruction in the Cultural Revolution, but it still has a ravaged majesty, especially when glimpsed from a boat on the waters of the lake.

When I visited, just before the Chinese New Year, people were smoking their bacon and fish over smouldering fires at the foot of the pagoda. The following recipe traditionally uses cold-smoked chicken, pork, and fish, which are steamed together so their flavors intermingle. I've used smoked bacon, first broiled or baked to give it a tinge of color, which brings it closer to the richness of Chinese smoked bacon, with smoked trout, which was the tastiest of the smoked fish I tried in my experiments. The dish is usually turned out onto a serving platter, but it actually looks lovely served in the bowl.

9 OZ. SMOKED BACON SLICES, THICKLY CUT WITH RINDS

10 OZ. SMOKED TROUT

3 TBSP. SHAOXING WINE

2 TBSP. BLACK FERMENTED BEANS, RINSED

1 TBSP. DRIED CHILI FLAKES

2 TSP. SESAME OIL

1. Trim the rinds from the bacon, and broil or roast the rashers until cooked and very slightly colored. Take the smoked trout flesh from the bone and cut into thick strips, discarding the head, tail, and skin. Lay the bacon and the trout separately, and neatly, into a heatproof bowl, so half the bowl is filled with bacon and half with trout. Top with the Shaoxing wine, black beans, and chili flakes.

2. Place the bowl in a steamer and steam over a high heat for 40 minutes. Serve in the steaming bowl, with a drizzling of sesame oil. Or (to be more traditional), cover the steaming bowl with a deep serving dish and swiftly invert, so you have a dome-shaped pile of meat and fish on the serving dish. Sprinkle the sesame oil over.

STIR-FRIED NEW YEAR RICE CAKE WITH SMOKED BACON
la rou chao ci ba

腊肉炒糍粑

Every year, in the last lunar month, many Hunanese households make their own New Year rice cakes. A mixture of rice and glutinous rice is soaked for two or three days, steamed, and then pounded to a paste in a heavy mortar made of gray stone, with a pestle as tall as a broomstick. (You can still see these mortars in the yards of most farmhouses.) The paste is then pressed into wooden molds, which are usually carved with auspicious designs, and left out to dry. The finished rice cakes, immersed in cold water to prevent them from cracking, keep for some time and are eaten in various different ways.

In the farmhouse belonging to my friend Fan Qun, I have sat around a bowl of glowing wood embers in midwinter, toasting slabs of *ci ba* on a long pair of iron tongs until they are crisp and golden, and then hollowing them out with chopsticks and stuffing them with white sugar that partially melts inside. But my favorite recipe is the one below, which another friend, Xiao Hong, showed me how to make with *ci ba* and intensely flavored bacon she had brought back to Changsha from her village. It's a typical New Year's holiday dish, drawing as it does on two of the traditional preserved products of the last lunar month.

You can buy *ci ba* in good Chinese supermarkets, vacuum-packed and ready to cook.

14 OZ. NEW YEAR RICE CAKE
(BOUGHT READY TO COOK)
7 OZ. SMOKED BACON SLICES,
THICKLY CUT WITH RINDS
5 SCALLIONS
2 FRESH RED CHILES
SALT
2 TSP. SESAME OIL
2 TBSP. PEANUT OIL FOR
COOKING

1. Cut the rice cake into slices about ¼ inch thick; set aside. Remove the rinds from the bacon and cut the bacon into slices to match the rice cake. Cut the scallions on a steep angle into long slices, separating the white and green parts. Thinly slice the chiles, discarding stems and seeds as far as possible.

2. Heat the wok over a high flame until smoke rises, then add the oil and swirl around. Add the bacon rinds and stir-fry until they have released their flavor, rendered their fat, and are golden; remove from the wok and discard.

3. Add the bacon to the wok and stir-fry until opaque, separating the slices. Add the rice cake and scallion whites and stir-fry until the rice cake and bacon are both fragrant and the rice cake is tinged with gold. Toward the end of the cooking time, add the chili slices and salt to taste.

4. Add the scallion greens and stir a few times so they are barely cooked, then, off the heat, stir in the sesame oil and serve.

★ CELEBRATING THE CHINESE NEW YEAR

We arrived a few days too late to see the slaughter of the New Year pig. Like every other family in the village, Fan Qun's had reared one especially, and they had celebrated its slaughter with a feast of fresh variety meat and a blitz of firecrackers. By the time we arrived the meat had been salted, and was hanging on the smoking rack above the kitchen fire, with a number of fish.

The Chinese New Year, or Spring Festival, marking the start of the new lunar year, is the most important feast in the Chinese calendar, and that New Year was the first time the immediate family had been together for several years. Their family home lies amid a rugged, romantic landscape, where a small stream flows alongside terraced fields and the hills are forested with pine and bamboo.

After a welcoming lunch, we were sent out to catch the ducks, which were roaming around in the fields outside. They were determined to evade capture, and quacked, flapped, and waddled their way down the terraced valley, swimming swiftly across the ponds. Fan Qun's father and eldest brother pursued them with long bamboo rods, while the rest of us tried to block the sides of the fields. It took about half an hour before they were cornered, and dispatched with the sharp blade of a cleaver.

Later that afternoon, Fan Qun's husband finished painting his Spring Festival inscriptions on strips of scarlet paper, and pasted them up around the house, as the rest of us sat around braziers of glowing embers, warming our feet and chatting.

We woke on New Year's Eve to the sound of the three nieces singing. It was freezing cold and frost lay on the wintry fields. We breakfasted on great steaming bowls of noodles with pickled radish and chili, pumpkin, bean curd, and pork-bone and soybean soup. In the kitchen, Fan Qun's sister-in-law Zhong Lachu had already started to cook. She was washing great chunks of smoky meat from the New Year pig, scaling and soaking smoked fish, chopping vegetables, and setting a great potful of dried radishes (their skins a beautiful rainbow of pinks, purples, and creams) to cook over the fire.

In the main hall of the house, a table was set with offerings to the ancestors: two red candles and a bundle of incense; half the pig's head; a huge pomelo; a whole smoked carp; a slab of fresh

Left: FAN QUN'S NIECES WITH THE NEW YEAR'S EVE FEAST

bean curd; a mug of tea, and a mug of wine. Before lunch, the same table was taken outside the house to make sacrifices to Heaven and Earth. The men of the family burned sheaves of paper money and made their kowtows, before lighting a huge string of firecrackers that sent out small, violent puffs of smoke.

Above: THE TABLE OF NEW YEAR OFFERINGS

The main New Year's Eve feast included sweet glutinous rice puffs, cold chicken's feet in chili sauce, home-reared pork with green bell peppers, a Cantonese roast duck brought home by one of the brothers, smoked carp, a sumptuous chicken soup with medicinal herbs, dried squid with jujube dates, a stew of smoked pig's intestines, dried radish soup, stir-fried cucumber, stir-fried eggplant and green bell peppers, stir-fried cabbage, golden needle mushrooms, bean curd, and rice with sweet potatoes. The drink used for celebratory toasts was Coca-Cola.

After lunch, we took some of the leftover foods up the fields to the hillside grave of a great uncle who had recently died. Small dishes of food and drink were laid out by his tomb, and there was more kowtowing, and burning of paper money and cigarettes and incense, and the rapid rattle of another string of firecrackers.

We spent the rest of the day playing mah jong, nibbling, and chatting. At midnight, we went outside and set off fireworks, bangers that echoed for miles around, and rockets that sent streams of sparks into the dark sky. And then there was a sudden silence, just the freezing night and a moonless sky scattered with bright glinting stars. Afterwards we piled inside for another meal that included a marvelous soup of winter bamboo shoot that had been simmering in the embers of the fire, and stayed up into the early hours playing games.

New Year's Day itself began with steaming cups of glutinous rice wine and a hearty breakfast of rice with about nine dishes, and then we all walked along the winding track up the valley, visiting every neighboring house to offer New Year's greetings and share some tea and sweetmeats. Later, we went to visit other relatives in a nearby village. There, in an old farmhouse, the men of the household were cooking over a wood-fired range, as about two dozen people milled around, eating and drinking and warming themselves at the open hearth in the kitchen. After a lively, noisy lunch, the sun was already setting, so we set off on the long walk home. Soon it was completely dark and silent, the road lit only by the windows of farmhouses in the distance, and flickering candles set before shrines to the gods of the earth.

BEEF WITH CUMIN
zi ran niu rou

狄
然
牛
肉

The powerful aroma of cumin is always associated with Xinjiang, the great northwestern Muslim region where it is grown. On city streets all over China, you will find it drifting up from portable grills where Xinjiang Uyghur street vendors cook their trademark lamb kabobs, scattering the sizzling meat with chili and cumin. In Hunan, the spice finds its way into "strange-flavor" combinations, Uyghur-influenced barbecues and a limited number of restaurant dishes. This one is irresistible. Tender slices of beef luxuriate in a densely spiced sauce, speckled with the gold and ivory of ginger and garlic, scarlet chili, and green scallions, and suffused with the scent of cumin. You can use prime steak if you wish, but I usually make do with a braising steak such as chuck or round: the method of cutting it across the grain makes it seem almost as tender.

This particular recipe is one from the Guchengge restaurant in Changsha, and it's one I fell in love with immediately. I'm sure you will too.

12 OZ. TRIMMED BEEF STEAK, SUCH AS SIRLOIN (SEE INTRODUCTION ABOVE)

2 TSP. FINELY CHOPPED FRESH GINGER

1 TBSP. FINELY CHOPPED GARLIC

2 FRESH RED CHILES, SEEDS AND STEMS DISCARDED AND FINELY CHOPPED

2–4 TSP. DRIED CHILI FLAKES

2 TSP. GROUND CUMIN

SALT

2 SCALLIONS, GREEN PARTS ONLY, FINELY SLICED

1 TSP. SESAME OIL

1¼ CUPS PEANUT OIL FOR FRYING

For the marinade:

1 TBSP. SHAOXING WINE

½ TSP. SALT

1 TSP. LIGHT SOY SAUCE

1 TSP. DARK SOY SAUCE

1 TBSP. POTATO FLOUR

1 TBSP. WATER

1. Cut the beef across the grain into thin slices, ideally 1½ by 1¼ inches. Add the marinade ingredients and mix well.

2. Heat the peanut oil to about 275°F. Add the beef and stir gently. As soon as the pieces have separated, remove them from the oil and drain well; set aside.

3. Pour off all but 3 tablespoons of the oil. Over a high flame, add the ginger, garlic, fresh chiles, chili flakes, and cumin and stir-fry briefly until fragrant. Return the beef to the wok and stir well, seasoning with salt to taste.

4. When all the ingredients are sizzlingly fragrant and delicious, add the scallion greens and toss briefly. Remove from the heat, stir in the sesame oil and serve.

BEEF SLIVERS WITH CORIANDER (CILANTRO)
xiang cai niu rou si

香菜牛肉絲

In many parts of China coriander (cilantro) is used as a garnish, especially for dishes using beef and mutton, which are thought to benefit from its refreshing fragrance. The herb can, however, also be used as a vegetable, as in the following dish, where it accompanies slender strands of beef in a light, bright stir-fry.

9 OZ. LEAN BEEF (FLANK STEAK
    IS GOOD)

2 FRESH RED CHILES

1 BUNCH FRESH CORIANDER
    (CILANTRO), ABOUT 5 OZ.

1 TBSP. FINELY CHOPPED GARLIC

1 TSP. LIGHT SOY SAUCE

SALT

1 TSP. SESAME OIL

1¾ CUPS PEANUT OIL FOR FRYING

For the marinade:

1 TSP. SHAOXING WINE

¼ TSP. SALT

½ TSP. LIGHT SOY SAUCE

1 TSP. DARK SOY SAUCE

2 TSP. POTATO FLOUR MIXED
    WITH 1½ TBSP. COLD WATER

1. Cut the beefsteak into thin slivers about 2½ inches long and less than ¼ inch thick. Add the marinade ingredients, mix well and set aside while you prepare the other ingredients.

2. Discard the stems and seeds of the chiles and cut into thin slivers to match the beef; set aside. Rinse the coriander and shake or spin dry. Discard any coarser stems, and cut the rest, leaves and all, into sections to match the beef.

3. Heat the oil in a wok over a high heat to about 275°F. Add the beef and stir-fry for 30–60 seconds until the slivers have separated (use chopsticks to ease them apart as they fry); remove with a slotted spoon and set aside.

4. Drain off all but 3 tablespoons of the oil and return the wok to a high flame. Add the garlic and chili and stir-fry until fragrant. Return the beef to the wok, add the coriander and stir-fry vigorously for a couple of minutes, adding the soy sauce and salt to taste, if necessary. When the coriander is barely cooked, switch off the heat, stir in the sesame oil, and serve.

BEEF SLIVERS WITH "WATER BAMBOO"
jiao bai niu rou si

Water bamboo (*jiao bai* or *jiao gua*), also known as wild rice stem, is a weird and wonderful Chinese vegetable with a delicate taste and a pleasingly crisp texture, and one which seems to be increasingly available in Western Chinatowns. It is an aquatic plant whose lower stems swell up when attacked by a specific fungus: it is then that they are harvested and eaten. The Chinese have grown water bamboo since ancient times, and are thought to have deliberately made use of its fungus-swollen stems for at least 2,000 years. The edible part of the stem is enclosed in a papery husk reminiscent of bamboo, but it is normally peeled before sale. The peeled shoots are a pale ivory yellow, with greenish tips, and roughly the size of carrots.

9 OZ. LEAN BEEF (FLANK STEAK
    IS GOOD)

9 OZ. WATER BAMBOO

2 FRESH RED CHILES

2 SCALLIONS, GREEN PARTS
    ONLY

¾ TSP. DARK SOY SAUCE

½ CUP EVERYDAY STOCK (PAGE
    287)

LIGHT SOY SAUCE AND SALT

½ TSP. POTATO FLOUR MIXED
    WITH 1 TBSP. COLD WATER

1 TSP. SESAME OIL

1 CUP PEANUT OIL FOR FRYING

For the marinade:

1 TBSP. SHAOXING WINE

¼ TSP. SALT

2 TSP. LIGHT SOY SAUCE

1 TBSP. POTATO FLOUR

1 TBSP. COLD WATER

1. Cut the beef into thin slices, and then, against the grain, into fine slivers about 2 inches long. Place in a bowl, add the marinade ingredients, mix, and set aside.

2. Cut the water bamboo into pieces, then into thin slices and then fine slivers to match the beef; set aside. Discard the stem and seeds of the chiles and cut them into fine slivers; set aside. Cut the scallion greens into pieces if they are slender, or, if not, into fine slivers; set aside.

3. Heat the oil in a wok over a high flame to about 275°F. Add the beef and fry very briefly, stirring to separate the slivers, until nearly cooked, then remove with a slotted spoon and set aside.

4. Drain off all but about 3 tablespoons of the oil and return the wok to the heat. Add the water bamboo and chili slivers and stir-fry until barely cooked. Add the beef, the dark soy sauce, and the stock with light soy sauce and salt to taste. Bring to a boil and simmer briefly to allow the flavors to mingle.

5. Finally, add the flour mixture and scallions, stirring well as the sauce thickens. Off the heat, add the sesame oil and serve.

VARIATION
For beef slivers with "wild mountain chiles" (*ye shan jiao niu rou si*), use Turkish pickled green chiles as a substitute for the water bamboo.

SLOW-BRAISED BEEF WITH POTATOES
tu dou wei niu rou

Most Hunanese think nostalgically of the flavors of farmhouse cooking, when stews would be cooked in a blackened pot, set into the embers of a wood fire and heated slowly for hours on end. You can still find people cooking this way in the countryside, but in the cities they make their stews in clay pots, lined with a bamboo mat to prevent sticking, and set on the very smallest gas flame. With the current fashion for rustic dining, many restaurants now display waist-high clay jars by their entrances. Inside, the embers of a wood fire smoulder on the ground, and many small clay pots are arranged on circular shelves on the walls of the jar. These stews and soups can be cooked for as long as eight hours, so any meat and poultry within them ends up meltingly tender and marvelously fragrant.

The following recipe is based on one I enjoyed at the Tanzhou Wagang restaurant in Changsha, which was made with beef ribs and potatoes, although I've adapted it to the Western oven.

1¾ LB. RICH STEWING BEEF

1½-IN. PIECE FRESH GINGER

2 TBSP. CHILI BEAN PASTE

1 SMALL PIECE CASSIA

½ STAR ANISE

8–10 DRIED RED CHILES

2½ CUPS WATER

1 TBSP. DARK SOY SAUCE

2 TBSP. LIGHT SOY SAUCE

1 TSP. CLEAR RICE VINEGAR

SALT

1 LB. POTATOES

PEANUT OIL FOR COOKING

1. Preheat the oven to 300°F. Cut the beef into bite-size chunks and blanch in boiling water; drain and set aside.

2. Slice the ginger (you can leave the peel on for extra flavor, or peel it, as you please); set aside.

3. Heat 3 tablespoons peanut oil in a wok over a medium flame. Add the chili bean paste and stir-fry until the oil is red and richly fragrant. Add the ginger, cassia, and star anise and continue to stir-fry until they, too, are fragrant. Add the chiles and stir a few times more.

4. Tip the beef into the wok and stir-fry for a couple of minutes in the fragrant oil, then add the water. Bring to a boil, then add the soy sauces, vinegar, and salt to taste, remembering that the liquid will reduce greatly by the end, so don't oversalt. Pour into an ovenproof casserole or Chinese sand-pot (*sha guo*).

5. Place the casserole in the oven and cook for 1½–2 hours. When the time has nearly been reached, peel the potatoes, cut them into chunks, and fry in hot oil until golden. Add them to the stew, stir well and then cook for an hour or so longer, by which time the potatoes should be cooked, the meat meltingly tender, and the liquid greatly reduced.

QUICK-FRIED LAMB
xiao chao yang rou

小炒羊肉

The city of Liuyang lies on the banks of the Liuyang River, amid gentle, wooded hills to the east of the Hunanese capital. There, "the mountains are beautiful, the water is beautiful, and the people are even more beautiful" (*shan mei, shui mei, ren geng mei*), so they say. Although the two cities are no more than about fifty miles apart, Liuyang has its own distinctive character, and its people speak a dialect that is incomprehensible to the inhabitants of Changsha. Liuyang is a world center of firework production, and is known poetically in Chinese as "the home of smoke-flowers" (*yan hua zhi xiang*).

A meal in Liuyang, like its most famous product, is an explosion of glittering colors: the lovely green of fresh soybeans, the brilliant red of fresh or pickled chiles, the warm sunset of a pumpkin soup. I remember one day, when gray mist had reclaimed the hills, sitting around a table laden with dishes as torrential rain rattled on the rooftops outside and thunder cracked the sky. This is one of the dishes we ate, a colorful stir-fry traditionally made with one of Liuyang's famous products, the black goat (*hei shan yang*), but which works equally well with lamb.

10 OZ. LEAN BONELESS LAMB

1 TBSP. SHAOXING WINE

1 TSP. LIGHT SOY SAUCE

½ TSP. DARK SOY SAUCE

¼ TSP. SALT, PLUS EXTRA TO TASTE

2 FRESH RED CHILES OR ½ RED
    BELL PEPPER

2½ OZ. FRESH CORIANDER
    (CILANTRO) OR CHINESE
    CELERY

2 TSP. FINELY CHOPPED FRESH
    GINGER

2 TSP. FINELY CHOPPED GARLIC

1 TSP. DRIED CHILI FLAKES
    (OPTIONAL)

1 TBSP. FINELY CHOPPED CHINESE
    ANGELICA ROOT (OPTIONAL)

1 TSP. SESAME OIL

3 TBSP. PEANUT OIL FOR COOKING

1. Cut the lamb across the grain into thin slices. Place the slices in a bowl, add the Shaoxing wine, soy sauces, and salt and mix well; set aside.

2. Cut the red chiles into thin slices; if using bell pepper, cut into small squares. Cut the coriander stems or celery into 2-inch pieces, reserve some leaves for a garnish and set aside the other leaves for other uses.

3. Heat the wok over a high flame until smoke rises, then add the peanut oil and swirl around. Add the ginger, garlic, fresh chili or bell pepper, chili flakes, and angelica root, if using, and stir-fry briefly until fragrant.

4. Add the lamb and continue stir-frying, adding salt to taste, if necessary. When the lamb is almost cooked, add the coriander or celery, and stir a few times until barely cooked. Turn off the heat, stir in the sesame oil and serve, with coriander leaf garnish, if desired.

VARIATION

The same method can be used to cook beef.

YUEYANG BARBECUED LAMB CHOPS
yue yang shao kao yang pai

岳陽燒烤羊排

Late at night in Yueyang, after dinner and an evening in a teahouse, Mr. Tang and his friends like to meet at a barbecue restaurant in a tucked-away corner in the middle of town. Outside, there's a man tending the charcoal, basting fish and meats with sticky sauce and scattering them with spices. When I went there one evening, we ate lamb or goat ribs, encrusted with chili and cumin and served with plenty of coriander (cilantro) on a metal dish that sizzled over a burner on our table. In trying to reproduce it at home, I prefer to use the Yueyang seasonings to cook lamb chops, rather than ribs, and to eat them seared and fragrant while still pink and juicy inside. This method would be anathema in China, where rare meat is generally regarded with revulsion, but I find it produces an extremely delicious result. If you would like to eat the ribs as they are cooked in Yueyang, I have added a variation below.

2 TBSP. LIGHT SOY SAUCE

2 TSP. SWEET BEAN SAUCE

2 TBSP. SHAOXING WINE

¼ TSP. FIVE-SPICE POWDER

12 RIB LAMB CHOPS

SALT

6 SCALLIONS, GREEN PARTS ONLY

1 BUNCH FRESH CORIANDER
   (CILANTRO), ABOUT 5 OZ.

4 TBSP. PEANUT OIL

GROUND CUMIN

DRIED CHILI FLAKES

SESAME OIL

1. Combine the soy sauce, sweet bean sauce, Shaoxing wine, and spice powder in a nonmetallic bowl, and then apply to the lamb chops, with a little salt to taste, if you wish. Mix well and leave to marinate for at least 30 minutes.

2. Meanwhile, finely slice the scallion greens. Tear the coriander leaves for the garnish; set aside.

3. Heat a grill pan over a high flame until very hot. Brush the lamb chops with the oil and cook for 2–3 minutes, then flip over and scatter generously with cumin and chili flakes. Continue cooking for 2–3 minutes longer (2 minutes on each side if you like your meat pink and juicy), scattering with scallions when nearly done.

4. Place the chops on a serving dish, sprinkle with a little sesame oil (a couple of teaspoons), and scatter with coriander leaves.

VARIATION

★ **YUEYANG BARBECUED LAMB RIBS** *shao kao yang pai*

To eat the ribs as I did in Yueyang, generously cover 12 ribs (about 1¾ pounds) with cold water. Bring to a boil, skimming, then reduce the heat, add 2 tablespoons Shaoxing wine, a couple pieces cassia bark, a few slices fresh ginger, 1 star anise, and a few dried chiles. Simmer for about 5 minutes; drain and set aside. Then proceed as in the recipe for lamb chops above, but omit the five-spice powder from the flavoring mix. Serve on a bed of coriander, on a sizzling pan set onto a tabletop burner.

3

POULTRY
AND EGGS

禽蛋類

★ POULTRY AND EGGS

Some of Hunan's most famous dishes are made with chicken, although in the past it was more of a luxury for special occasions than an everyday meat. In the countryside, most people keep a few chickens, which peck around the fields, eating odds and ends of grain and insects, and providing eggs until they end up in the cooking pot. The flavor of these free-range birds (known literally as "earth chickens," *tu ji*) is vastly superior to that of their factory-farmed cousins, and they are much in demand in city restaurants.

Chickens are generally used whole, and on the bone, in traditional Hunanese cooking, partly because the bones add flavor, and partly because the Chinese tend to find pleasure in teasing the flesh away from them with tongue and teeth. Sometimes a farmyard chicken, chopped up for the cooking pot, will reveal a whole string of embryonic eggs. These are cooked with the rest of the bird, and have a curious texture, a little firmer than egg yolk but less flavorful. Chicken is also smoked, and hangs above the farmhouse fire alongside sides of bacon and fish.

Chicken eggs are widely used in everyday Hunanese cookery, and those of a special local breed that lays yolkless eggs are an essential component of one celebrated banquet delicacy (see the last recipe in this chapter). They also have their ritual functions: in my friend Fan Qun's village, boiled eggs dyed red are given to children to mark the birth of a baby, and on the third day of the third lunar month, everyone in Hunan seems to make a kind of soup of chicken eggs boiled with shepherd's purse (*ji cai*, or *di cai* in Hunan dialect), Chinese jujube dates and ginger—it is supposed to drive out the windiness of the season and relieve internal heat.

The Dongting Lake area is particularly known for its wild ducks, which migrate down from Mongolia and Siberia to pass the winter. Local people traditionally hunt them, and make them into rich stews or smoke them alongside the winter bacon. The lakes and ponds that are part of the Hunanese landscape are also ideal duck-rearing terrain, so many farmers

Above: BOILED EGGS WITH SHEPHERD'S PURSE

keep a bird or two. The markets of Yueyang sell pressed ducks (*jiang ban ya*), dark, sweet, and aromatic preserved birds that have been splayed open with bamboo sticks and flattened—they are delicious on their own or stir-fried with green bell peppers. And one of the most intriguing duck dishes I've come across was "blood-pudding duck" (*xue ba ya*), a spicy stew of duck with a kind of black pudding made from duck blood and glutinous rice. It was fabulous, and somehow reminiscent of Scottish haggis. The dish was served in a riverside restaurant in the picturesque town of Fenghuang, in the far west of Hunan.

Fresh duck eggs are mixed with pungent vegetables or tree shoots and made into omelets, but they are most important as a preserve. Salted duck eggs (see page 286), preserved in brine or in a paste of salt mixed with mud or ashes, are tasty when simply hard-boiled, but their yolks really come into their own as an intensely flavored cooking ingredient (see page 213).

Above: BUYING A DUCK, ZHANGGUYING

Preserved duck eggs, otherwise known as "century eggs" or "thousand-year-old eggs," are caked in a paste made from soda, quicklime, salt, and ash, often with the addition of tea leaves or rice husks, and then left to mature for a rather prosaic three months. When the paste is scraped off and the shells broken, the eggs have creamy grey yolks, and dark brown, translucent albumens that are threaded with beautiful flowerlike patterns which seem to be etched beneath the surface. These eggs can be eaten straight from the shell or used in cooking (see page 60).

The excavations of the Han dynasty tombs at Mawangdui showed that the noble elite of this region were accustomed to eating not only chickens and ducks, but also wild geese, pheasants, cranes, turtledoves, owls, pigeons, magpies, and sparrows. You don't see such exotic fowl in the marketplace these days, although pigeons and quail pop up from time to time, and one classic Hunanese cookbook does list a recipe for deep-fried turtledoves.

DONG'AN CHICKEN
dong an zi ji

This is one of Hunan's most famous dishes, a delicate concoction of chicken flavored with chili and clear rice vinegar that is said to have originated in Dong'an county. Its precise history is lost in the mists of legend, although most sources claim it is based on a dish called "vinegar chicken" (*cu ji*) that was eaten in Dong'an county as far back as the eighth century, during the Tang dynasty. Some embellish the tale to say it was invented by three old ladies who ran a modest restaurant. One evening, so the story goes, some merchants called and demanded dinner at a time when the women had sold out of almost everything, so they had to slaughter a couple of chickens and rustle up a new dish on the spot. The resulting recipe was so extraordinarily delicious that the merchants spread the word far and wide, and the dish entered the canon of classic Hunan delicacies.

There are two different versions of the tale of how "vinegar chicken" eventually became known as "Dong'an chicken." Some say a Qing dynasty military commander named Xi Baotian loved the dish, and often served it to his guests at banquets; because Xi was from Dong'an, people started calling it "Dong'an chicken." Others claim that after the success of the Northern Expedition in 1927, a Nationalist army commander, Tang Shangzhi, served "vinegar chicken" at a banquet in Nanjing. His dinner guests were profuse in their praise, and asked what the dish was called. Tang felt that the original name was a bit blunt and inelegant, so he told them it was called Dong'an chicken, and the name stuck.

I have based the recipe below on one told to me by one of the great Hunanese chefs, Shi Yinxiang, a delightful man now in his eighties, who used to cook for Chairman Mao whenever he returned to his home province.

ABOUT 4 QT. WATER OR—
BETTER STILL—EVERYDAY
STOCK (PAGE 287)
1 FREE-RANGE OR CORN-FED
CHICKEN, ABOUT 2¾ LB.
1¾-IN. PIECE FRESH GINGER,
UNPEELED
3 SCALLIONS
1 FRESH RED CHILI

1. Bring the water or stock to the boil in a large saucepan over a high flame. Add the chicken and return the liquid to the boil, skimming the surface, as necessary. Crush half the ginger and one scallion with the flat side of a cleaver or a heavy object, then add to the pan with the chicken. Reduce the heat and poach the chicken for 10 minutes. Remove the chicken from the cooking liquid and allow it to cool; reserve the cooking liquid. The chicken should be about three-quarters cooked.

ingredients and method continue on the next page

3 DRIED CHILES (OPTIONAL)

2 TSP. SHAOXING WINE

2 TBSP. CLEAR RICE VINEGAR

½ TSP. SICHUAN PEPPER OIL OR

    ½ TSP. WHOLE SICHUAN

    PEPPER

SALT TO TASTE

¾ TSP. POTATO FLOUR MIXED

    WITH 2 TSP. COLD WATER

1 TSP. SESAME OIL

4 TBSP. LARD OR PEANUT OIL

    FOR COOKING

2. When the chicken is cool enough to handle, remove the flesh from the carcass and cut as far as possible into bite-size strips, along the grain of the meat. I never discard the skin. (The bones and scrappy pieces of meat can be returned to the cooking liquid and made into stock.)

3. Cut the fresh chili in half lengthwise and discard the seeds and pithy part, then cut into very fine slivers about 1½ inches long. Peel the remaining ginger and cut it into slices and then slivers similar to the chili. Cut the green parts of the remaining 2 scallions into slivers of a similar length; set aside.

4. Heat the wok over a high flame until smoke rises, then add the lard or peanut oil and swirl around. When the oil is warming up but before it is smoking hot, add the fresh chiles and ginger, along with the dried chiles and Sichuan pepper, if using, and stir-fry until fragrant, taking care that the seasonings do not take color or burn.

5. Add the chicken and continue to stir-fry. Splash the Shaoxing wine around the edges of the chicken. Add the vinegar, Sichuan pepper oil, if using, and salt to taste. Add up to ½ cup of the chicken poaching liquid (if the chicken is very juicy no additional liquid will be necessary), bring to a boil and then turn the heat down a little and simmer briefly to allow the flavors to penetrate the chicken, spooning the liquid over.

6. Add the potato flour mixture to the liquid and stir as the sauce thickens. Throw in the scallion greens and stir a few times. Remove from the heat and stir in the sesame oil. Serve.

★ THE STRANGE TALE OF GENERAL TSO'S CHICKEN

General Tso's (or Zuo's) chicken is the most famous Hunanese dish in the world. A delectable concoction of lightly battered chicken in a chili-laced, sweet-sour sauce, it appears on restaurant menus across the world, but especially in the eastern United States, where it seems to have become the epitome of Hunanese cuisine. Despite its international reputation, however, the dish is virtually unknown in Hunan itself. When I went to live there in 2003, I scoured restaurant menus in vain for it, and no one I met had ever heard of it. And as I deepened my understanding of Hunanese food, I began to realize General Tso's chicken was somewhat alien to the local palate, because Hunanese people have little interest in dishes that combine sweet and savory tastes. So how on Earth did this strange, foreign concoction come to be recognized abroad as *the* culinary classic of Hunan Province?

Above: GENERAL TSO

General Tso's chicken is named after Tso Tsung-t'ang (now usually transliterated as Zuo Zongtang), a formidable nineteenth-century general who is said to have enjoyed eating it. He was born in 1812 in Xiangyin county, Hunan province, and died in 1885 after a glittering career in the Qing dynasty civil and military administration. He led successful military campaigns against various rebel groups, but is best known for recapturing the great western desert region of Xinjiang from rebellious Uyghur Muslims. The Hunanese have a strong military tradition, and General Tso is one of their best-known historical figures. But although many Chinese dishes are named after famous personages (like, for example, the Sichuanese Gong Bao chicken), there is no record of any dish named after General Tso in the classic texts on Hunanese food and cooking.

The real roots of the dish lie in the chaotic aftermath of the Chinese civil war, when the leadership of the defeated Nationalist party fled to the island of Taiwan. They took with them many talented people from the mainland, including a number of notable chefs, and foremost among them was a young Hunanese man named Peng Chang-kuei. Peng was born in 1919 into a poverty-stricken household in the Hunanese capital Changsha. As a teenager, he served as apprentice to Cao Jingchen, a famous chef who had just opened his own restaurant. Cao had previously served as private chef to the Nationalist official and great Hunanese gourmet Tan Yankai, and was one of the most outstanding cooks of his generation. He worked in a period generally known as the golden age of Hunanese cooking, when the capital Changsha was the center of a flourishing culinary scene.

After his hard years of apprenticeship, Peng Chang-kuei won acclaim as a chef in his own right. By the end of World War II he was in charge of Nationalist government banquets, and when the

Nationalists met their final, humiliating defeat at the hands of Mao Zedong's Communists in 1949, he fled with them to Taiwan. There, he continued to cater for official functions, devising menus for presidential feasts and visiting VIPs, and inventing many new dishes.

When I met Peng Chang-kuei, a tall, dignified man in his eighties, during a visit to Taipei in 2004, he could no longer remember exactly when he first cooked General Tso's chicken, although he says it was sometime in the 1950s. "General Tso's chicken did not preexist in Hunanese cuisine," he said, "but originally the flavors of the dish were typically Hunanese—heavy, sour, hot, and salty."

In 1973, Peng went to New York, where he opened his first restaurant on 44th Street. At that time, Hunanese food was unknown in the United States, and it wasn't until his cooking attracted the attention of officials at the nearby United Nations HQ, and especially of the American Secretary of State Henry Kissinger, that he began to make his reputation. "Kissinger visited us every time he was in New York," says Peng Chang-kuei, "and we became great friends. It was he who brought Hunanese food to public notice." In his office in Taipei, Peng still displays a large, framed black-and-white photograph of Kissinger and himself raising wine glasses on their first meeting at his restaurant, Peng's.

Above: PENG CHANG-KUEI AND HENRY KISSINGER

Peng Chang-kuei was no hidebound traditionalist, and, faced with new circumstances and new customers, he worked creatively, inventing new dishes and adapting old ones. "The original General Tso's chicken was Hunanese in taste, and made without sugar," he says, "but when I began cooking for non-Hunanese people in the United States, I altered the recipe." In the late 1980s, having made his fortune, he sold up and returned to Taipei. His New York venture was to have an enormous impact on the cooking of the Chinese diaspora. Not only General Tso's chicken, but other dishes that he invented, have been widely imitated, and his own apprentices have helped to disseminate his style of cooking.

The final twist in the tale is that General Tso's chicken is now being adopted as a "traditional" dish by some influential chefs and food writers in Hunan itself. In 1990, Peng returned to his hometown, Changsha, where he opened a high-class restaurant that included General Tso's chicken on its menu. The restaurant itself did not last long, and the dish was never popular ("too sweet," one local chef told me), but some leading figures in the culinary establishment did learn how to make it. And when they began to travel abroad to give cooking demonstrations in the 1990s, it seems likely that their overseas audiences would have expected them to produce that famous "Hunanese" dish, General Tso's chicken. Perhaps it would have seemed senseless to refuse to acknowledge a dish upon which the international reputation of Hunanese cuisine was largely based—especially when very little, if anything, else was known about Hunanese cuisine. Maybe, also, it would have been embarrassing to admit that the most famous "Hunanese" dish in the world was the product of the exiled Nationalist society of Taiwan and not of Hunan itself, with all the implications of the relative success of Taiwan's development over the course of the twentieth century. Whatever their motivations, they began to include the dish in publications about Hunanese cooking, especially those aimed at a Taiwan readership.

The vast majority of Hunanese people have still never heard of General Tso's chicken, and I have never seen it on a Hunanese restaurant menu, but some of the cosmopolitan culinary elite now claim it as a historical dish. Only the older generation, including Peng Chang-kuei and the senior chefs he met during his time in Changsha, remember the details of how the dish was created, and acknowledge with a smile that it is an invented tradition.

But even if General Tso's chicken is not an "authentic" Hunanese dish, it has to be seen as part of the story of Hunanese cuisine. It doesn't tell the same story as the dishes eaten in remote Hunanese villages, where some cooking methods haven't changed for millennia, but it is a key part of recent culinary history. After all, it embodies a narrative of the old Chinese apprentice system and the Golden Age of Hunanese cookery; the tragedy of civil war and exile; the struggle of the Chinese diaspora to adapt to American society; and in the end the opening up of China and the reestablishment of links between Taiwan and the Mainland.

And since the dish has, through the vagaries of history, become known as *the* Hunanese dish par excellence, how could I even think of omitting it from this book? So please cook it, and savor it, and dream as you do so of the Hunanese past, and the invention of new mythologies in the cultural melting pots of the modern world.

GENERAL TSO'S CHICKEN (TAIWAN VERSION)
zuo zong tang ji

左宗堂鶏

This version of the dish is based on one I learned in the kitchen of the Peng Yuan restaurant in Taipei. It was invented by veteran chef Peng Chang-kuei, who still runs the restaurant with his son, Peng T'ieh-cheng. The dish is hot and sour, and lacks the sweetness of the Americanized version, which follows. (See pages 117–19 for the full story of this dish.) You can use chicken breast instead of thigh meat if you prefer.

4 BONED CHICKEN THIGHS WITH
    SKIN (ABOUT 12 OZ. TOTAL)
6–10 DRIED RED CHILES
2 TSP. FINELY CHOPPED FRESH
    GINGER
2 TSP. FINELY CHOPPED GARLIC
2 TSP. SESAME OIL
PEANUT OIL FOR DEEP-FRYING
For the marinade:
2 TSP. LIGHT SOY SAUCE
½ TSP. DARK SOY SAUCE
1 EGG YOLK
2 TBSP. POTATO FLOUR
2 TSP. PEANUT OIL
For the sauce:
1 TBSP. DOUBLE-CONCENTRATE
    TOMATO PASTE MIXED WITH
    1 TBSP. WATER
½ TSP. POTATO FLOUR
½ TSP. DARK SOY SAUCE
1½ TSP. LIGHT SOY SAUCE
1 TBSP. CLEAR RICE VINEGAR
3 TBSP. EVERYDAY STOCK (PAGE
    287) OR WATER
THINLY SLICED SCALLION
    GREENS TO GARNISH

1. Unfold the chicken thighs and lay them, skin side down, on a chopping board. (If some parts are very thick, lay your knife flat and slice them in half, parallel to the board.) Use a sharp knife to make a few shallow crisscross cuts into the meat—this will help the flavors to penetrate. Then cut each thigh into bite-size slices, an uneven ¼ inch or so in thickness. Place the chicken slices in a bowl.

2. To make the marinade, add the soy sauces and egg yolk to the chicken and mix well, then stir in the potato flour and lastly the oil; set aside while you prepare the other ingredients.

3. Combine the sauce ingredients in a small bowl; set aside. Use a pair of scissors to snip the dried chiles into ¾-inch pieces, discarding seeds as far as possible.

4. Heat enough oil for deep-frying to 350–400°F. Add the chicken and deep-fry until it is crisp and golden. (If you are deep-frying in a wok with a relatively small volume of oil, fry the chicken in batches.) Remove the chicken with a slotted spoon and set aside. Pour the oil into a heatproof container, and clean the wok if necessary.

5. Return the wok to a high flame with 2–3 tablespoons of the oil. Add the dried chiles and stir-fry briefly until they are fragrant and just changing color (do not burn them). Toss in the ginger and garlic and stir-fry for a few seconds longer, until fragrant. Then add the sauce and stir as it thickens.

6. Return the chicken to the wok and stir vigorously to coat the pieces in sauce. Remove from the heat, stir in the sesame oil and then serve, sprinkled with scallion greens.

GENERAL TSO'S CHICKEN (CHANGSHA VERSION)
zuo zong tang ji

左宗堂鷄

This version of General Tso's chicken is one I learned in the kitchens of the Yuloudong restaurant in the Hunanese capital, Changsha. It is not on the menu of the restaurant, but one of the chefs there had learned the recipe from someone connected indirectly with Peng Chang-kuei, and he very kindly showed me how to make it. Its sweetness makes it closer to the Americanized version of the dish than the previous Taiwan recipe. (See page 117–19 for the full story of the dish.)

The dish is usually made with boned chicken leg meat, although you can use breast if you prefer. I've suggested using boned thighs, which are widely available.

4 BONED CHICKEN THIGHS WITH
    SKIN (ABOUT 12 OZ. TOTAL)
6–10 SMALL DRIED RED CHILES
¾-IN. PIECE FRESH GINGER,
    PEELED AND SLICED
1 TBSP. DOUBLE-CONCENTRATE
    TOMATO PASTE MIXED WITH
    1 TBSP. WATER
3 SCALLIONS, GREEN PARTS
    ONLY, SLICED
1 TSP. SESAME OIL
PEANUT OIL FOR COOKING

For the marinade:
2 TSP. LIGHT SOY SAUCE
½ TSP. DARK SOY SAUCE
1 EGG YOLK
4 TBSP. POTATO FLOUR

For the sauce:
½ TSP. POTATO FLOUR
2 TSP. WHITE SUGAR
2 TSP. CHINKIANG VINEGAR
¼ TSP. DARK SOY SAUCE

2 TSP. LIGHT SOY SAUCE
3 TBSP. EVERYDAY STOCK (PAGE
    287) OR WATER

1. Prepare the chicken and add the marinade ingredients as in Steps 1 and 2 of the recipe on page 120: the main difference being that the chicken slices will be caked in potato flour.

2. Combine the sauce ingredients in a small bowl; set aside. Use a pair of scissors to snip the dried chiles into ¾-inch pieces, discarding the seeds as far as possible.

3. Deep-fry the chicken as in Step 4 in the previous recipe. Remove with a slotted spoon and set aside. Pour the oil into a heatproof container, and clean the wok if necessary.

4. Return the wok to a high flame with 2–3 tablespoons of the oil. Add the dried chiles and stir-fry briefly until they are fragrant and just changing color (do not burn them). Toss in the ginger and stir-fry for a few seconds more, then add the tomato paste and stir-fry until the oil is stained a deep orange.

5. Add the mixed ingredients for the sauce, stirring as it thickens. Tip in the chicken and stir vigorously to coat it in sauce. Add the scallions and stir a few times, then, off the heat, stir in the sesame oil and serve.

STEAMED CHICKEN WITH CHOPPED SALTED CHILES
duo la jiao zheng ji

刹辣椒蒸鷄

This is a marvelous dish, utterly simple to make but most seductive with its gentle heat and subtle flavors. I first tasted it at the Gan Chang Shun noodle bar in Changsha, where it was served in a small clay steaming bowl as a topping for noodles. If you would like to eat it as a noodle topping, see the chapter on noodles; otherwise, serve it in the steaming bowl and eat it with rice, spooning the delicious cooking juices over.

The famous Gan Chang Shun was founded in 1883 by a man named Gan Changlin who had started his career as a noodle-bar apprentice at the age of twelve ("Chang Shun" can be roughly translated as "long success"). It soon became known for the quality of its noodles and its warmly welcoming atmosphere, and in 1884, on the occasion of the fiftieth birthday of the Dowager Empress Cixi, the Hunan provincial governor is said to have ordered 2,000 bowls of noodles at Gan Chang Shun as part of the celebrations. Gan Changlin himself died in 1904, but the restaurant remained in his family until it was nationalized in the 1950s, serving fresh noodles made on the premises with a great variety of different toppings. Like many old Hunan restaurants, however, Gan Chang Shun was badly affected by the Cultural Revolution: the quality and variety of its noodles declined, and it was actually renamed as The East Noodle Restaurant until 1986, when it reverted to its original name.

1 BONELESS, SKINLESS CHICKEN
   BREAST HALF (ABOUT
   10 OZ.)

1 TSP. FINELY CHOPPED FRESH
   GINGER

1 TBSP. SHAOXING WINE

1½ TBSP. CHOPPED SALTED
   CHILES

SALT

1 SCALLION, GREEN PARTS ONLY
   (OPTIONAL)

1. Cut the chicken into bite-size chunks. Add the chunks to a saucepan of boiling water and blanch just until the water returns to the boil, then drain.

2. Place the chicken in a heatproof bowl with the ginger, Shaoxing wine, chiles, and salt to taste and mix well. Place the bowl in a steamer and steam over high heat for 20–30 minutes, until the chicken is cooked through. Serve in the bowl, with a garnish of finely sliced scallion greens, if desired.

LIUYANG BLACK BEAN CHICKEN
liu yang dou chi ji

While I was living in Hunan, I spent some time with a group of great friends, all women aged from their thirties to their sixties, who shared a great love of food. They seemed to spend much of their time driving out of town on excursions to buy special delicacies, hosting lavish banquets that their husbands rarely attended, and staying up all night to play mah jong. Their banquets were always held in private rooms at restaurants, and were uproarious with laughter and witty repartee. The male guests, who often included high-ranking officials, tended to sit around quietly, seemingly overwhelmed by the sheer outrageousness of the ladies. As they say, Hunanese women are a little spicy, like their food.

Whenever we drove out to Liuyang, we would go on an urgent gastronomic tour, swooping down on the central market to pick up armfuls of freshly picked vegetables and spicy stewed meats. One of the gang would buy a bagful of golden, doughnutlike puffs of glutinous rice dough, dusted liberally with sugar, for her husband. We would stop in a side street known for its pickle vendors. Their stalls were stacked with glass jars in the manner of an old English candy store, filled with a rainbow of exotic titbits that glowed like Venetian glass in the sun. There was pink salted ginger, black papaya, sweet-sour jujube fruits, and ivory radish strips with a splattering of scarlet chili. Sometimes we would also visit a street lined with small food stores selling local delicacies. One honey specialist had an amazing business card with a photograph of a man with his bare head and face almost entirely covered in swarming bees. Inside, the shelves were stacked with jars of royal jelly and pollen and, among others, loquat blossom honey, wild chrysanthemum honey, and kiwi fruit blossom honey. Other shops sold boxes of sweetmeats and bagfuls of dried goods: salted ginger, long-stalked mushrooms, tangled purslane, tiny baked fish, and sour Chinese plums encrusted in chiles.

Chief among Liuyang's prized local food products are black fermented beans, whose fame is said to have been spread by monks who tasted them while visiting a local Buddhist temple as far back as the Tang dynasty. The following recipe makes generous use of these richly savory black beans, and it is scrumptious. A similar dish is made using Laoganma, a sauce made from black fermented beans and chilies that is produced in neighboring Guizhou province and immensely popular in Hunan (simply use it instead of the black beans and chili).

continued

LIUYANG BLACK BEAN CHICKEN

1 LB. BONED CHICKEN THIGHS
    WITH SKIN

SALT

1 TBSP. LIGHT SOY SAUCE

1 HEAD GARLIC

2½-IN. PIECE FRESH GINGER

4 SCALLIONS, GREEN PARTS
    ONLY

4 TBSP. BLACK FERMENTED
    BEANS, RINSED

1 TBSP. CLEAR RICE WINE OR
    SHAOXING WINE

2–3 TSP. DRIED CHILI FLAKES

2 TSP. CLEAR RICE VINEGAR

1 TSP. SESAME OIL

2 CUPS PEANUT OIL FOR DEEP-
    FRYING

1. Cut the chicken into bite-size chunks. Put the chunks in a bowl, add ¼ teaspoon salt and the soy sauce and mix well; set aside while you prepare the other ingredients.

2. Peel the garlic cloves, cutting any very large ones in half. Peel and slice the ginger. Cut the scallion greens into 1½-inch pieces.

3. Heat the oil for deep-frying over a high flame until it reaches 350–400°F. Add the chicken and stir-fry until it has changed colour, then remove from the wok with a slotted spoon and allow the oil to return to 350–400°F. Return the chicken to the hot oil and deep-fry again until tinged golden; remove and set aside.

4. Drain off all but 3 tablespoons oil from the wok, then return it to a medium flame. Add the ginger and garlic and stir-fry for a few minutes until they are fragrant and the garlic cloves are tender. Add the black beans and stir-fry until fragrant, splashing in the rice wine as you do so. Add the chili flakes and stir-fry for a few moments until they have lent their heat and red color to the oil.

5. Return the chicken to the wok and toss it in the fragrant oil, splashing in the vinegar and adding salt to taste. When everything is sizzly and delicious, throw in the scallions, and stir a few times until barely cooked. Then, off the heat, stir in the sesame oil and serve.

STIR-FRIED CHICKEN SLIVERS WITH YELLOW CHIVES
jiu huang ji si

韭
黃
雞
絲

Yellow, or hothouse, chives are grown in darkness, so they don't develop the deep green color of everyday Chinese chives, but remain a shy, pearly yellow. This method of blanching dates back to the Han dynasty, some 2,000 years ago. My friend Sansan remembers yellow chives as a rare and expensive luxury in her childhood, and says then they were only eaten on special occasions like the family New Year's Eve dinner. They are more common nowadays, but there is still something special about their pale fragility, and the strong, seductive aroma that will fill your kitchen. They don't keep well, and are usually cradled in protective paper when you buy them in a Western Chinese supermarket.

The following recipe can easily be made with pork, but I prefer to use chicken because its pale flesh complements the delicate leaves so pleasingly. In restaurants, chefs would add a little starch-and-water to make a glossy sauce at the end, but there's no real need to do this at home.

2 SMALL BONELESS CHICKEN
    BREAST HALVES WITH SKIN
    (ABOUT 10 OZ. TOTAL)
9 OZ. YELLOW CHIVES
SALT AND WHITE PEPPER
1 TSP. POTATO FLOUR MIXED
    WITH 1 TBSP. COLD WATER
    (OPTIONAL)
1 CUP PEANUT OIL OR LARD FOR
    COOKING

For the marinade:
¼ TSP. SALT
2 TSP. Shaoxing WINE
2 TSP. POTATO FLOUR

1. Cut the chicken into very thin slices, and then, along the grain, into fine slivers. Place in a bowl, add the marinade ingredients and mix well; set aside.

2. Discard the base ends of the chives and cut the stems into 1½-inch pieces.

3. Heat the oil or lard in a wok until it reaches 275°F. Add the chicken and fry briefly, using chopsticks to separate the slivers. When the chicken has changed colour but is not quite cooked, remove the slivers with a slotted spoon and set aside. Drain off all but 3 tablespoons oil from the wok.

4. Return the wok to a high flame, and when the oil is hot add the chives and stir-fry a few times, adding a little salt to taste. Then add the chicken and stir-fry until it and the chives are just cooked, adding a little pepper and more salt to taste, if necessary. If you are using the potato-flour mixture, add it just before the end of the cooking time and stir briskly as it thickens and clings glossily to the chicken slivers. Serve immediately.

NUMBING-AND-HOT CHICKEN
ma la zi ji

麻辣子鷄

The Hunanese love to point out that the most important culinary difference between themselves and their Sichuanese neighbors is that while in Hunan they eat chili-hot food, those in Sichuan like their chiles to be mixed with Sichuan pepper in "numbing-and-hot" (*ma la*) combinations that ruin every other flavor. Most Hunanese people find the lip-tingling taste of Sichuan pepper strange and unpalatable—so it's surprising that one of the most famous Hunanese dishes is this "numbing-and-hot" chicken. Admittedly, the Hunanese are fairly lily-livered in the amount of Sichuan pepper they use, but it's still an interesting deviation from culinary norms.

Numbing-and-hot chicken is an old-fashioned dish most sources date back to the reign of the Tongzhi Emperor of the Qing dynasty (the 1860s–70s), when it was already being served in Changsha restaurants. During the early twentieth century, a period of intense competition in the catering trade, big-name restaurants in Changsha vied with one another to create the ultimate version of the dish, but it is most strongly associated with the Yuloudong, largely because one notable guest in the 1920s was so moved by its deliciousness that he wrote a calligraphic inscription about it.

The dish is normally made with an entire baby chicken, boned and cut into cubes, but to simplify things I suggest you use boneless meat, and dark meat for maximum flavor.

continued on the next page

12 OZ. BONED CHICKEN THIGHS
OR BREAST HALF, IF YOU
PREFER, WITH SKIN

1 SMALL RED BELL PEPPER,
THIN-SKINNED IF POSSIBLE

1 FRESH RED CHILI, OR 1 TSP.
DRIED CHILI FLAKES

3 SCALLIONS, WHITE PARTS
ONLY

1 TSP. WHOLE SICHUAN PEPPER

1 TSP. SESAME OIL

1¼ CUPS PEANUT OIL FOR DEEP-
FRYING

For the marinade:

1 TBSP. SHAOXING WINE

1 TBSP. LIGHT SOY SAUCE

¼ TSP. DARK SOY SAUCE

1 TBSP. POTATO FLOUR MIXED
WITH 1 TBSP. COLD WATER

For the sauce:

1 TBSP. LIGHT SOY SAUCE

1 TBSP. CLEAR RICE VINEGAR

½ TSP. POTATO FLOUR

3 TBSP. EVERYDAY STOCK (PAGE
287) OR WATER

1. Cut the chicken as evenly as possible into bite-size cubes. Place the chicken cubes in a bowl, add the marinade ingredients and mix well; set aside while you prepare the other ingredients.

2. Discard the stem and seeds of the pepper, and cut into small squares to complement the chicken. If using a fresh chili, slice it thinly, discarding the stem and seeds as far as possible. If the scallions are slender, cut them into 1¼- to 1½-inch pieces, otherwise slice them on a steep angle. Crush the Sichuan pepper using a mortar and pestle. Combine the sauce ingredients in a small bowl; set aside.

3. Heat the oil for deep-frying in the wok over a high flame to 350–400°F. Add the chicken and stir briskly for about 30 seconds, until the pieces have separated and have become pale; remove from the oil with a slotted spoon. Allow the oil to return to 350–400°F, then fry the chicken again until golden; remove and set aside. Drain off all but 3 tablespoons of the oil.

4. Return the wok to the heat and, working quickly over a high flame, tip in the red bell pepper, fresh or dried chiles, scallions, and Sichuan pepper and stir-fry briefly until they are wonderfully fragrant.

5. Stir in the chicken. Give the sauce a stir and tip it in to the wok. Stir briskly as the sauce thickens. Finally, off the heat, stir in the sesame oil and serve.

CHICKEN WITH GINGER
lao jiang men ji

The burning packages of paper money and sheaves of incense sticks blazed yellow in the darkness, sending jagged shadows dancing up the walls of the lane, and releasing clouds of aromatic smoke into the air. One by one, every member of Sansan's family made their offerings, setting light to bags of ritual banknotes, some for her deceased grandparents, some for the local land god. They burned a cardboard trunk containing paper replicas of things the grandparents might need on their return to the world of the dead, clothing, gloves, combs, and cleavers. And then they scattered rice and water into the flames, to appease the appetites of any Hungry Ghosts who might have been roaming the city on that inauspicious night, looking for mischief.

Earlier, we had fed the ancestors. Black-and-white photographs of Sansan's grandparents presided over a makeshift altar, a table piled with offerings of fruit, cake, and wine, before which incense sticks glowed and paper money smouldered. Sansan's uncle, Qiu Yongan, cooked, and the food was ritually offered on the altar, after which we could eat it ourselves.

The seventh lunar month, or Ghost Month, is traditionally the time when the gates of the underworld open, and the spirits of the dead are free to roam the earth. It's a dark month, an unlucky time to move house or marry. Ancestors are welcomed back into the family and provided with all they need to sustain them for the coming year, but the menacing Hungry Ghosts, the spirits of those who died violent deaths or left no descendants to honor them, must also be mollified with offerings.

CHICKEN WITH
GINGER
continued

The following recipe is based on one that Qiu Yongan made for his deceased parents (and us) on that spooky night in the high summer of 2004. He used a whole chicken, but I've adapted the recipe to use boned chicken thighs. The chicken is fried and then simmered (*men*) for a while in liquid, which leads to a gentle, succulent dish. You can also make it entirely by frying for a more sizzly finish (see note below). Add some dried chili flakes to either version if you please.

1 LB. BONED CHICKEN THIGHS
    WITH SKIN

¼ TSP. SALT

2 TSP. LIGHT SOY SAUCE, PLUS
    EXTRA FOR SEASONING

3-IN. PIECE FRESH GINGER,
    UNPEELED AND SLICED

1 TBSP. CLEAR RICE WINE OR
    SHAOXING WINE

A FEW DRIED CHILI FLAKES
    (OPTIONAL)

⅔ CUP EVERYDAY STOCK (PAGE
    287) OR WATER

SALT

3 SCALLIONS, GREEN PARTS
    ONLY, FINELY SLICED

1 TSP. SESAME OIL

3 TBSP. PEANUT OIL FOR
    COOKING

1. Cut the chicken into bite-size chunks, add the salt and 2 teaspoons light soy sauce, and mix well.

2. Heat the peanut oil in a wok over a medium flame. Add the ginger and stir-fry until richly fragrant. Add the chicken and continue to fry until it is tinged golden. Splash the wine into the side of the wok, add some chili flakes, if you like, and let their spicy fragrance infuse the oil.

3. Pour in the stock or water and bring to a boil, then reduce the heat and simmer, seasoning with salt and soy sauce to taste. When the liquid is much reduced, add the scallions and stir a few times. Off the heat, stir in the sesame oil and serve.

VARIATION

For a drier dish, do not add the stock but simply continue to stir-fry until everything is sizzly and aromatic and the chicken is cooked through, adding small amounts of water or stock, if necessary, to prevent sticking. If you use this method, you might also wish to add ½ teaspoon or so dark soy sauce to give it a richer color. Finish as in the recipe above with scallions and sesame oil.

STEAMED CHICKEN IN LOTUS LEAVES
he ye fen zheng ji

In the summer, lotus leaves cover the entire surface of the ponds in the Hunanese countryside. In the following recipe, they are used to wrap chicken pieces that have been marinated and coated in rice meal. After cooking, the rice meal has a pleasantly moist and cakelike texture, and the chicken is infused with the bewitching fragrance of the leaves. A more common version of this dish uses sliced pork belly or spare ribs, but since I included a Sichuanese lotus leaf-steamed pork recipe in my last book, I thought you could have the more elegant chicken variation in this one. Local recipe books suggest wrapping a single chicken slice in each leaf, but I tend to make the packages a little larger at home. If you can't be bothered to make so many, just lay a whole lotus leaf in a heatproof bowl, pile in the chicken, fold the edges of the leaf over and tuck in, trimming off any excess. After steaming, turn out the package onto a plate and cut a hole in the top with scissors. Obviously this is easier, and it looks splendid on the table, but the package will take longer to heat through and the lotus fragrance won't penetrate as deeply.

Dried lotus leaves are available in better Chinese supermarkets, and need a quick soaking in hot water from the kettle to make them pliable. If you are by any chance using fresh lotus leaves, blanch them in boiling water before use.

¼ CUP LONG-GRAIN RICE

¼ CUP GLUTINOUS RICE

1 STAR ANISE

1 LB. BONED CHICKEN THIGHS, BREASTS, OR WHAT-EVER CUT SUITS YOU, WITH SKIN

3 OZ. PORK BELLY OR WELL-MARBLED UNSMOKED BACON

2–4 DRIED LOTUS LEAVES, SOAKED IN HOT WATER

PEANUT OIL

1. Toast the long-grain rice, glutinous rice, and star anise in a dry wok over a medium flame, stirring constantly, until the rice is brittle and yellowish; set aside. When cool, remove the star anise and grind the rice in a food processor. Do not grind to a fine powder—the mixture should be of a similar coarseness to couscous. (This step can be done some time in advance.)

2. Cut the chicken into slices about ¼-inch thick and place in a bowl. (If you are using breasts, cut on a steep angle into large slices.) Cut the pork or bacon into fine slivers and add to the chicken. Add the marinade ingredients, mix well, and leave for 15 minutes or so to let the flavours penetrate.

3. Remove the lotus leaves from the water and pat dry. Cut each lotus leaf into about 8 segments, discarding any raggedy pieces. Trim off the coarse, spiny bottom of each segment, and lay on a plate or cutting board with the shiny side of the leaf underneath. Brush the leaves with a little oil to prevent

STEAMED CHICKEN
IN LOTUS LEAVES

continued

For the marinade:

1 TBSP. SHAOXING WINE

2 TSP. LIGHT SOY SAUCE

¼ TSP. SALT

1 TBSP. FINELY CHOPPED FRESH
GINGER

2 SCALLIONS, WHITES ONLY,
FINELY CHOPPED

sticking.

4. Stir the rice meal and a scant ½ cup cold water into the chicken and pork mixture and mix well.

5. Use chopsticks to place a few slices of chicken in each leaf segment, then turn the sides of the leaf in and roll up to make a rectangular package. (I would aim to make about 12 packages in all.) Lay the packages prettily in a heatproof bowl, in a single layer if possible. (The recipe can be prepared in advance to this stage.)

6. Shortly before you eat, set the bowl in a steamer and steam over a high heat for 30–40 minutes, until the chicken is cooked through and infused with the fragrance of the leaves. Let your guests open the lotus-leaf packages themselves.

NOTE

If you would rather not add pork to the filling, add 4 tablespoons peanut oil at the start of Step 4, when you add the rice meal to compensate for its absence.

CHANGDE CLAY-BOWL CHICKEN
chang de bo zi ji

In winter, one of the really striking features of the Hunanese dinner table is the presence of potfuls of food murmuring away on tabletop burners. They might be small metal woks, casserole dishes, pottery bowls, or large metal pans filled with soup. This manner of eating is currently fashionable all over Hunan, but is particularly associated with the city of Changde in the north of the province. There, I once came across a tableful of men tucking into an ox penis hotpot, a dish that is seen as a reliable boost for virility. Had they all been feeling hen-pecked that morning, I wondered, or were they just preparing for an evening's debauchery?

In northern Hunan, the winters are cold and windy, and farming families, mostly idle in this slackest of seasons, still huddle around open fires in their kitchens, or warm their feet at metal pans stocked with glowing embers. The tabletop hotpots are another way to fend off the rigors of the season. Originally, they were partially glazed clay pots or bowls, and the burners were made of terracotta and fueled by embers from the kitchen fire. They kept the food hot in the drafty old farmhouses, and created a convivial atmosphere around the dinner table. You can still find these small clay stoves in the countryside, but in the cities they have been replaced by gas burners or gel-fueled stoves.

The following recipe is based on one I learned in Changde. There it is made with chicken on the bone, but you can use about 1¾ pounds of boned chicken pieces, preferably a mixture of white and brown meat, instead.

continued on the next page

1 ORGANIC OR FREE-RANGE
   CHICKEN (ABOUT 2¾ LB.)
A SMALL HANDFUL DRIED
   CHILES
10 GARLIC CLOVES, PEELED
1-IN. PIECE FRESH GINGER,
   PEELED AND SLICED
A COUPLE PIECES CASSIA BARK
   OR 1½-IN. CINNAMON STICK
1 TBSP. CHILI BEAN PASTE
2 CUPS CHICKEN STOCK
2 TBSP. SHAOXING WINE
¼ TSP. DARK SOY SAUCE
1 TBSP. LIGHT SOY SAUCE
SALT
3 SCALLIONS, GREEN PARTS
   ONLY, CUT INTO 1½-IN.
   PIECES
A COUPLE STRIPS RED OR GREEN
   BELL PEPPER—OR BOTH
1–2 TSP. SESAME OIL
1 CUP PEANUT OIL FOR COOKING

1. Cut the chicken into bite-size chunks with a heavy cleaver: start by severing the legs and wings, then cut apart the breast and back sides of the chicken; discard the parson's nose (tail). Cut both back and breast sides in half lengthwise, and then chop into chunks. Separate each thigh and drumstick, and the 2 joints of wing, and chop these into chunks, too. (In China, the wingtips and ends of the legs would also be cooked.)

2. If you wish to end up with a very hot dish, cut the chiles into pieces, otherwise, leave them whole; set aside.

3. Heat the wok over a high flame until smoke rises, then add the peanut oil and heat until it reaches about 350°F. Add the chicken and deep-fry until it becomes pale and loses some of its water content, then remove the chicken with a slotted spoon. Allow the oil to return to 350°F and fry the chicken again until it is cooked through and golden; set aside. It's best to do this in a couple of batches.

4. Add the garlic cloves to the hot oil and fry until fragrant and tinged with gold; set aside.

5. Pour off the oil. Clean the wok and return to the stovetop over a high heat until smoke rises, then add 3 tablespoons oil and swirl around. Tip in the ginger and cassia and fry until fragrant. Add the chili bean paste and continue to stir-fry until the oil is red. Add the dried chiles and stir-fry briefly until just changing color.

6. Quickly add the chicken and garlic, along with the stock, Shaoxing wine, soy sauces, and a little salt to taste. Bring to a boil, then reduce the heat and simmer, uncovered, over a medium flame for 10–15 minutes, stirring from time to time, to allow the flavors to penetrate the chicken. By this stage, the liquid will have reduced, leaving a rich, flavorful sauce.

7. If you are serving the chicken in traditional style, over a tabletop burner, simply turn it into a heated clay pot, top with the scallions and bell pepper strips, drizzle with the sesame oil, and serve. Otherwise, add the pepper strips, and then the scallions toward the end of the cooking time, so they are barely cooked, and drizzle the sesame oil over just before serving.

JUNSHAN CHICKEN WITH SILVER-NEEDLE TEA
jun shan ji pian

君山鷄片

The isle of Junshan lies amid the reeds of the Dongting Lake, and its beauty has been praised by Chinese poets since the Tang dynasty. We went there by boat on a misty day, and followed a path that twisted and turned through a forest of bamboo and bracken, the foliage yielding from time to time to plunging views of the rocks below. Birds cackled and twittered in the trees, and in the small clearings were neat terraced rows of tea bushes. The silver-needle tea (*yin zhen cha*) produced on the island is one of China's most famous, and was sent in tribute to the Qing dynasty emperors. It is a "yellow tea," made by a long and delicate process that involves firing, heating over charcoal, and gentle, enclosed oxidation. The dried leaves are pale and narrow, and covered in tiny white hairs. When infused in a glass, they hang vertically in the pale golden liquid, and sometimes gently rise and fall.

The following dish is a local banquet delicacy made with Junshan silver-needle tea, although any good Chinese green tea can be used as a substitute. The key to success is not to overheat the oil, so the chicken slices remain very tender and slippery, and you can appreciate the delicate fragrance of the tea.

2 BONELESS CHICKEN BREAST
    HALVES WITH SKIN (ABOUT
    12 OZ. TOTAL)
1 TBSP. CHINESE YELLOW OR
    GREEN TEA LEAVES
SALT
½ TSP. POTATO FLOUR MIXED
    WITH 2 TSP. COLD WATER
1 TSP. SESAME OIL
1¼ CUPS PEANUT OIL FOR
    COOKING

For the marinade:
¼ TSP. SALT
2 TSP. SHAOXING WINE
1 TBSP. POTATO FLOUR
1 LARGE EGG WHITE

1. Holding your knife at an angle to the board, cut the chicken into thin slices. Put the slices in a bowl, add the marinade ingredients, and mix well. If there is any excess egg white that does not cling to the chicken, discard it.

2. Bring a kettle of water to a boil, and then let the water cool to 176°F before pouring ½ cup over the tea leaves. Strain off the water immediately, then add 5 tablespoons fresh water at the same temperature to the leaves, and leave to infuse.

3. Heat the oil over a medium flame until it reaches 275°F. Add the chicken and swiftly separate the slices with a pair of chopsticks. When the chicken slices are pale but not completely cooked, remove them with a slotted spoon and set aside.

4. Drain off all but 3 tablespoons oil and return the wok to a high flame. Add the chicken and salt to taste and stir-fry. When the chicken is just cooked, pour in the tea infusion, leaves and all, and when the liquid boils, add the potato-flour mixture and stir as it thickens the juices. Immediately remove from the heat, stir in the sesame oil, and serve.

"DRY-WOK" SPICY DUCK
gan guo ya zi

A "dry wok" (*gan guo*) is a small wok that sits on a tabletop burner among other dishes, and is usually filled with cooked food in a light gravy. It is less soupy than a hotpot, but is eaten in a similar way, with guests using chopsticks to pluck pieces out of the simmering sauce. The "dry wok" itself is a modern innovation, but its roots lie in the clay-pot chafing dishes that are particularly popular in the north of Hunan. If you have a tabletop burner and a small wok (of the kind sold in Chinese or Indian supermarkets), you can serve the following dish in the Hunanese manner, sizzling away as your guests help themselves with chopsticks. Otherwise, simply enjoy it as a stew.

In Hunan, the ducks tend to be smaller and less fatty than the ones available in the West, and are chopped on the bone into bite-size pieces. In making this recipe at home, I bought a whole duck, cooking the breasts and legs, and popping the excess fat and the carcass in the oven to render down into delicious duck fat (good for roasting potatoes among other things). If you'd rather, buy four portions of jointed duck.

continued on the next page

1 DUCK (ABOUT 5½ LB.), OR 4
DUCK PORTIONS WITH SKIN
(LEG, BREAST, OR A MIXTURE)

1-IN. PIECE FRESH GINGER,
UNPEELED AND SLICED

2 PIECES CASSIA BARK

½ STAR ANISE

2 TBSP. CHILI BEAN PASTE

2 TBSP. SHAOXING WINE

1 BAY LEAF, FRESH OR DRY

1 *CAO GUO* (SEE PAGE 25)

1 TSP. DARK SOY SAUCE

LIGHT SOY SAUCE

SALT

PEANUT OIL FOR FRYING

To finish:

2 GARLIC CLOVES, SLICED

AN EQUIVALENT AMOUNT FRESH
GINGER, PEELED AND SLICED

A SMALL HANDFUL DRIED
CHILES

½ RED BELL PEPPER, SEEDED AND
CUT INTO BROAD SLICES

3 SLENDER SCALLIONS, TRIMMED
AND CUT INTO BITE-SIZE
PIECES

FRESH CORIANDER (CILANTRO)
TO GARNISH

1. If you are using a whole duck, cut away the whole leg joint close to the carcass, then divide the thigh and lower leg and use a heavy cleaver to chop each piece into 2 or 3 chunks. Cut the breasts from the breastbone and cut into bite-size chunks. The wings can also be cut away and chopped into chunks if you wish to add them to the dish, or they can just be saved for adding to the stockpot.

2. Heat 1 cup peanut oil in a wok over a high flame until it reaches 350°F. Add the duck and fry for a couple of minutes to allow it to lose some of its water content. Remove with a slotted spoon, allow the oil to return to 350°F, and then refry the duck pieces until lightly browned; set aside. It is best to fry the duck in a couple of batches.

3. Drain off all but 2 tablespoons of the oil and reheat over a high flame. Add the ginger, cassia, and star anise and stir-fry until fragrant. Add the chili bean paste and fry some more until the oil is red. Add the duck, and splash in the wine around the edge, stirring well.

4. Turn the duck and all its flavorings into a saucepan or flameproof casserole and barely cover with water. Bring to a boil, add the bay leaf, *cao guo*, and dark soy sauce, with light soy sauce and salt to taste. Turn the heat down and simmer gently, uncovered, for an hour or so, until the duck is tender and flavorful and the liquid reduced. (This step can be done in advance.) Discard the whole spices as far as possible.

5. When you are ready to eat, set a small wok to heat over a low flame or in the oven. Heat your normal wok over a high flame until smoke rises, then add 2 tablespoons oil and swirl around. Add the garlic, ginger, and dried chiles and sizzle briefly until fragrant. Add the prepared duck and the liquid left in the cooking pot, bring to a boil, and check seasoning.

6. Turn the stew into the small wok, top with the bell pepper and scallions, and a sprig of coriander, then take, sizzling, to the table. If you are serving the dish in a bowl, rather than over a burner, simply add the bell pepper and onion to the stew while still on the heat before serving with a garnish of coriander.

DONGTING STIR-FRIED DUCK BREAST
dong ting xiao chao zi ya

洞庭小炒子鷄

Many rural people in Hunan raise their own ducks, but there are also specialist duck-keepers. I remember one twilight in the village of Zhangguying, when the local duck-keeper drove his flock into the village, in a fluid chaos of undulating necks and beaks. When people came to buy, he rushed into the flock with a bamboo cane, snatched up a duck or two and then weighed them, live, on hand-held scales.

Ducks are most commonly chopped up on the bone and made into various kinds of stews, but the following recipe uses boneless breast meat. It's a simple but fantastically delicious dish with seductive undertones of chili and garlic, and is based on one that I enjoyed eating at Luo Leiguang's restaurant in Changsha. The red chiles add a vibrant spiciness, but you can use bell peppers instead if you prefer.

2 BONELESS DUCK BREAST
    HALVES WITH SKIN (ABOUT
    13 OZ. TOTAL)

4 SCALLIONS

4 LONG, POINTY FRESH RED
    CHILES OR ½ RED BELL
    PEPPER

2 GARLIC CLOVES, SLICED

AN EQUIVALENT AMOUNT FRESH
    GINGER, PEELED AND SLICED

SALT

1 TSP. SESAME OIL

2 TBSP. PEANUT OIL FOR
    COOKING

For the marinade:

1 TBSP. SHAOXING WINE

1 TBSP. LIGHT SOY SAUCE

½ TSP. DARK SOY SAUCE

1. Holding the knife at an angle to the chopping board, cut the duck breasts into even, fairly thin slices. Place in a bowl with the marinade ingredients, mix well, and set aside while you prepare the other ingredients.

2. Trim the scallions. Cut the white and pale green parts into ½-inch pieces, and the green parts into pieces about the same size and keep separate. Cut the red chiles crosswise into ¼-inch slices, or, if you are using the bell pepper, cut it into small squares; set aside.

3. Heat the wok over a high flame until smoke rises, then add the peanut oil and swirl around. Add the duck and stir-fry until the slices are nearly cooked. Add the garlic, ginger, scallion whites, and red bell pepper, if using, and stir-fry until fragrant. Add the red chili, if using, and continue to stir-fry, seasoning with salt to taste.

4. When the chiles have added their spicy notes to the duck, and everything smells delicious, stir in the scallion greens, and then, off the heat, the sesame oil.

SQUAB WITH FIVE SPHERES
wu yuan ru ge

This is a magical Chinese tonic dish, so named because it is made with five "spherical" ingredients. The dish has a marvelously sweet and fruity aroma. It is traditionally steamed, but I've also seen it cooked slowly in a tall clay jar heated by wood embers, so I've taken the liberty of adapting the recipe to be made in an oven, which produces much the same effect and is more convenient than steaming. Duck, chicken, and other fowl can be cooked with "five spheres," and the spheres can include apricots or quail eggs, so feel free to improvise.

4 SQUAB

14 OZ. PORK BELLY

1 TBSP. HONEY

SCANT ½ CUP SHAOXING WINE

⅔ CUP PEANUT OIL FOR COOKING

5 TBSP. YELLOW LUMP SUGAR OR
    4 TBSP. HONEY

1½-IN. PIECE FRESH GINGER,
    UNPEELED AND IN ONE PIECE

2 SCALLIONS, WHITE PARTS
    ONLY

SALT AND PEPPER

The "five spheres":

A GOOD HANDFUL RED CHINESE
    DATES (*HONG ZAO*), RINSED

A GOOD HANDFUL DRIED LONGAN
    FRUITS OR DRAGON-EYE
    FRUITS (*LONG YAN*), RINSED

A GOOD HANDFUL DRIED LOTUS
    SEEDS (*LIAN ZI*), RINSED

4 TBSP. DRIED CHINESE
    WOLFBERRIES (*GOU QI*),
    RINSED

12–15 FRESH LYCHEES

1. Preheat the oven to 300–325°F.

2. Heat a large saucepan of water over a high flame. Add the squab and pork belly and blanch just until the water returns to the boil, skimming the surface as necessary; drain and set aside. (This step can be omitted.)

3. Stir the honey into 2 tablespoons of the Shaoxing wine until it dissolves. Heat the wok over a high flame until smoke rises, then add the peanut oil and swirl around. Dry the squab and use a pastry brush to paint them with the honey mixture, then brown them in the hot oil.

4. Place the browned squab with the pork belly, yellow lump sugar or honey, and the rest of the wine in a flameproof casserole. Add the dates, longans, lotus seeds, and wolfberries to the pot. Peel the lychees and put them in, too. Crush the ginger slightly with the flat of a cleaver or a heavy object and place in the pot with the scallion whites. Add enough water to just cover, with salt and pepper.

5. Bring the liquid to a boil, cover the casserole, and place in the preheated oven for 45–60 minutes, until the birds are tender. Adjust the seasoning and serve with a sprinkling of pepper.

VARIATION

To steam the dish, just place everything in a deep heatproof earthenware bowl instead of a casserole, and steam over a medium heat for the same amount of time, until tender.

GOLDEN COINS
jin qian dan bing

金錢蛋餅

This most unusual egg dish is made from hard-boiled eggs that are sliced and fried to resemble "golden coins," before being stir-fried with a few seasonings. It looks beautiful on the plate: a radiant mix of yolk-yellow, scarlet, and green. The ginger and vinegar help to cut the richness of the eggs.

5 EXTRA-LARGE EGGS, HARD-
　BOILED AND COOLED
　COMPLETELY

4 TBSP. ALL-PURPOSE FLOUR

1½ TSP. CLEAR RICE VINEGAR

½ TSP. POTATO FLOUR

2 TBSP. EVERYDAY STOCK (PAGE
　287) OR WATER

½ TSP. SESAME OIL

1 TBSP. FINELY CHOPPED FRESH
　GINGER

1 TBSP. FINELY CHOPPED FRESH
　RED CHILI OR SWEET RED
　BELL PEPPER

SALT

3 SCALLIONS, GREEN PARTS
　ONLY, FINELY SLICED

PEANUT OIL OR LARD FOR
　COOKING

1. Peel the eggs and cut crosswise into thick slices. Coat the slices lightly in flour, shaking off any excess. Combine the vinegar, potato flour, stock or water, and sesame oil in a small bowl; set aside.

2. Heat ½ cup peanut oil or lard until it reaches 350°F. Add the egg slices in 2 or 3 batches and fry for just a few minutes until a little golden (the oil will froth up as they cook); remove with a slotted spoon and set aside.

3. Clean the wok and heat it over a high flame until smoke rises, then add 2 tablespoons oil or lard and swirl around. Add the ginger and chili or bell pepper and stir-fry briefly until fragrant.

4. Return the eggs to the wok and gently stir-fry to coat them in the seasonings, adding salt to taste. Don't worry if some fall apart. Add the prepared sauce and the scallions, and stir-fry for a few seconds more. Serve immediately.

STIR-FRIED EGGS WITH GREEN PEPPERS
qing jiao chao dan

青椒炒蛋

After the chaos of the early Cultural Revolution, a generation of city youths was sent down to the countryside for years to be "educated by the peasants." They were billeted in remote villages, and spent their days in exhausting agricultural labor. One friend of mine was rusticated at the age of seventeen and spent three years in a remote border region, living in the mountains with a few other female students. There were no roads, and neither electricity nor running water, so they had to fetch water from a valley several miles below, carrying it up to their village in wooden pails strapped to their backs in bamboo frames. Their home was a disused storehouse, and they slept on beds made from corn stalks and leaves. They grew corn and potatoes on the rugged, hilly land, with a few beans, pumpkins, cabbages, and radishes. The work was heavy, but it was supposed at the time to be morally uplifting: "Chairman Mao told us fighting the sky and the earth was an infinite joy," says my friend.

She and her companions lived on an inadequate diet, and were always hungry. They tried to supplement their daily meals of cornmeal, potatoes, and cabbages with a few eggs, but had to be careful about keeping poultry. "If you raised your own animals it counted as 'taking the capitalist road' and you could be punished," she says, "but we secretly kept a couple of chickens and let them loose in the middle of the night to peck around for grains and seeds."

The following is an utterly simple, home-cooked egg dish, but the lazy piquancy of the peppers is delightful with the soft scrambled egg. I've made the dish in England with various different types of bell pepper, and find it works best with the long Turkish ones that have fairly thin skins and a gentle hotness.

9 OZ. GREEN BELL PEPPERS

4 EXTRA-LARGE EGGS

SALT

3 TBSP. PEANUT OIL FOR
   COOKING

1. Discard the stems of the peppers and cut on an angle into bite-size chunks (don't worry about the seeds). Beat the eggs with salt to taste in a small bowl.

2. Smear the wok with a little oil and heat over a medium flame. Add the bell peppers and stir-fry for about 5 minutes, pressing them against the side of the wok with your wok scoop or ladle, until they are fragrant and tender, their skins a little golden and puckered.

3. Add the rest of the oil, and when it is hot pour in the eggs and mix well. Scramble the eggs and peppers, adding a little more salt to taste, if necessary. I prefer not to stir the eggs too constantly, so they set into folds. When the eggs are just cooked, turn onto a serving dish and eat.

STIR-FRIED EGGS WITH SILVERFISH
yin yu chao dan

Tiny, wispy silverfish used to flourish in the Dongting Lake; these days, they are mainly farmed, but they remain a celebrated local product. It was apparently once believed they grew out of leftover morsels of finely ground fish that were thrown into water, and one of their Chinese names can be roughly translated as "leftovers fish" (*kuai can yu*).

This recipe is based on one taught to me by Liu Xiaoming, a former fisherman who now works as a cook in a small restaurant on Junshan Island. The fish add a wonderful savory taste to the scrambled eggs.

1 OZ. DRIED SILVERFISH

2 SCALLIONS, GREEN PARTS
    ONLY

3 EXTRA-LARGE EGGS

SALT

1 TSP. FINELY CHOPPED FRESH
    GINGER

1 TBSP. CLEAR RICE VINEGAR

3 TBSP. PEANUT OIL FOR
    COOKING

1. Rinse the fish under cold running water, then put in a small bowl and cover with cold water. Squeeze them a few times in your hand, and then leave to soak for 5–10 minutes while you prepare the other ingredients, by which time they should be soft and supple.

2. Cut the scallion greens into 1½- to 2-inch pieces and then into slivers; set aside. Beat the eggs with salt to taste.

3. When the silverfish are tender, drain them, and pat dry with kitchen paper. Heat the wok over a high flame until smoke rises, then add the peanut oil and swirl around. When the oil is very hot, add the ginger and sizzle briefly until fragrant. Add the fish and stir-fry for a minute or so, adding salt to taste, and splashing in the vinegar toward the end of the cooking time.

4. Pour in the eggs and stir-fry until just cooked, adding the scallions toward the end of the cooking time.

DUCK EGG AND CHIVE OMELET
jiu cai jian ya dan

韭菜煎鴨蛋

We walked along the northern side of Junshan Island, looking out over the marshes to a silvery horizon. There we met a weatherworn but smiling woman, a bamboo slat over her shoulders, from which were suspended some weighing scales and a pair of baskets containing several dozen eggs. She and her husband lived in a flimsy tent on the edge of the marshes, with a charcoal-burning stove, a bed, and a few pots and pans. A wooden rowing boat was moored nearby, in the margins of the Dongting Lake. They tended a flock of white ducks that splashed in the green marshy shallows, and took their eggs to market. The following is her recipe for a duck egg and chive omelet.

In China, this omelet is usually made in a wok (many people don't even have flat skillets at home): you simply pour the beaten egg mixture into the bottom of the wok and use a ladle to scoop up the runny part and drizzle it around the edge to build up a wide and even circle of omelet. I find a skillet more practical, however, and I suggest you use it instead.

2½ OZ. CHINESE CHIVES OR 7
    SCALLIONS, GREEN PARTS
    ONLY
3 DUCK EGGS
SALT
3 TBSP. PEANUT OIL FOR
    COOKING

1. Trim the chives and chop finely, discarding any tough sections at the bottom of the leaves. (Or finely chop the scallion greens, if using.) Beat the eggs, adding salt to taste, and then add the chopped chives or scallions, mixing well.

2. Heat the peanut oil in a skillet over a high flame. When hot, remove briefly from the stovetop and pour in the egg mixture, swirling it around to cover the bottom of the pan evenly. Return to the stovetop and fry until golden. Gently push and slide the half-cooked omelet out onto a plate, invert the skillet over it, and tip swiftly upside-down. Fry the other side of the omelet until golden. Serve immediately.

VARIATIONS

★ CHINESE CHIVE OMELET
jiu cai jian dan

Follow the recipe above, but use 4 chicken eggs instead of 3 duck eggs.

★ TOON TREE SHOOT OMELET
xiang chun jian dan

This is made with the chopped, tender shoots of the Chinese toon tree (*Toona sinensis*). These maroon-tinged leaves are a delicacy in both Hunan and Sichuan provinces, although I have never seen them for sale in the West.

RADISH SLIVER OMELET
luo bu si jian dan

蘿蔔絲煎蛋

This dish has a peculiar resonance for me, because I ate it during a period of extraordinary intrigue. I had ventured out to a town known for certain specialty foods, and looked up some contacts at the local cooking school. I was warmly welcomed by a delightful member of the school's staff, and shared with him and his family an evening of passionate discussions about food. He introduced me to various food experts and chefs, all of whom were friendly and welcoming, and we arranged another meeting the following day. I went to keep the appointment, and was disconcerted by a sudden chill in the atmosphere. It turned out that a senior member of staff had returned to work, and was deeply suspicious about me. He greeted me with a frigid politeness, but told his colleagues I was trying to steal "commercial secrets," and put pressure on them to avoid me. It was a flashback to the days when all foreigners were suspected of espionage, and it put several lovely people in very awkward positions. This sudden freeze heralded, for me, a bizarre period of secret, late-night assignations in teahouses, furtive handovers of information on culinary history, and cunning plans involving friends in Sichuan and the National Library in Beijing.

This dish, then, was served at a lunch hosted by the suspicious boss, which was memorable for its fake camaraderie and generally stilted atmosphere. But the dish, a radish omelet, was so delicious, and so extremely simple to make, that I thought I'd include it in this book.

10 OZ. ASIAN RADISH (*DAIKON*)

SALT AND PEPPER

4 EGGS

5 SCALLIONS, GREEN PARTS
    ONLY, FINELY SLICED

3 TBSP. PEANUT OIL

1. Cut the radish into very thin slices, and then in very fine slivers. Sprinkle with ½ teaspoon salt, mix well, and leave for 30 minutes. Meanwhile, beat the eggs with salt to taste. Add the sliced scallions and set aside.

2. Squeeze as much water as possible out of the radish slivers.

3. Heat the peanut oil in a wok or skillet over a high flame. Add the radish slivers and stir-fry for a few minutes to dry out some of the remaining moisture. Turn the heat down a little, add the eggs and mix gently to incorporate. As the omelet cooks, gently push in from the edge so the egg forms soft, loose folds. When the underside is golden, turn the omelet over and fry the other side until also golden. Serve with a sprinkling of pepper to taste.

STEAMED EGGS
zheng ji dan

★

This extremely simple dish is a regular in households and restaurants across Hunan. Beaten eggs are combined with stock and steamed to make a delicate custard, as soft and smooth as crème caramel. The stock adds a satisfying savory taste, which is enhanced before serving with a drizzling of sesame oil. It's a kind, comforting supper dish: best eaten with plain steamed rice and a simple stir-fried green vegetable, at the end of a tiring day. In China, this is particularly recommended for infants and invalids. Most people would use a pork-bone stock for this recipe, but my friend Qing Qing makes a delicious version with a vegetarian black bean infusion (see page 287). The key to success in this dish is to cook the eggs very gently, and not for too long. So steam them over a medium heat: otherwise they can become a little stringy. If you are using a bamboo steamer, some steam will escape naturally; with a metal steamer, I find it's best to leave the lid ever-so-slightly ajar, to avoid an intense build up of pressure, which will overcook the eggs.

1¼ CUPS EVERYDAY STOCK (PAGE 287)

4 EXTRA-LARGE EGGS, BEATEN (ABOUT 7 OZ. TOTAL)

SALT

1 TSP. VEGETABLE OIL OR MELTED LARD

1 TSP. SESAME OIL

2 SCALLIONS, GREEN PARTS ONLY, THINLY SLICED

LIGHT SOY SAUCE

1. Bring two-thirds of the stock to a boil, and then combine with the rest of the stock so the liquid is fairly hot but not boiling. Stir the stock into the eggs with a little salt to taste. Add the vegetable oil or lard. Pour into a shallow heatproof bowl and place in a steamer. Bring the water in the steamer to the boil, then steam for about 10 minutes over a medium heat until the custard has just set.

2. Serve immediately, with a scattering of sesame oil and scallions, and soy sauce to taste.

YOLKLESS EGGS WITH SHIITAKE MUSHROOMS
hua gu wu huang dan

花菇無黃蛋

This dish is a perfect illustration of the wit and artistry of traditional Chinese haute cuisine. It consists of a number of what appear to be normal hard-boiled eggs, laid on a bed of leafy greens and bathed in a rich sauce made with fine shiitake mushrooms. Bite into one of the eggs, however, and you will find no yolk cradled within its unusually delicious and tender white. Changsha waiting staff like to tell unwary foreign guests of the existence of a local breed of chicken that lays yolkless eggs. In fact, the dish is the product of an absurdly complicated cooking process that was perfected in the 1930s by a chef named Cai Haiyun. It involves filling emptied eggshells with a mixture of egg white and fine chicken stock, and steaming them so gently the eggs end up smooth and entire in shape, and almost custard-tender.

Under extreme pressure over the deadline of this book, I tested this crazy recipe with my mother. It was a nightmare. We tried cooking egg after egg in different conditions in a vain attempt to produce one with a suitably delicate texture. We steamed them at various temperatures, cooked them in cool ovens, warmed them in bains-maries, and even tried heating them in a microwave at the lowest setting. But each egg, when we broke it, was a disappointment. Some remained liquid inside, others ended up with ragged, curdled flesh, and the ones in the microwave exploded like volcanoes. It became clear that all the Hunanese recipe books I had consulted were hopelessly inaccurate. In despair, I wanted to give up, but my mother insisted on persevering, and in the end we cracked it. We were delirious with pleasure and relief when our final experimental egg turned out perfect. Of course, such elaborate recipes were the product of an era when chefs could rely on teams of apprentices to help them, and when wealthy gourmets would compete with one another in the refinement of the food served at their dinner parties. When I mentioned to a Hunanese chef friend that I had attempted it, he was thunderstruck, and told me that it was regarded as so challenging that it was actually an examination dish for the highest grade of Hunanese chef. Anyway, here is the recipe, and I hope it works for you if you are mad enough to try it. It is, in the end, delicious, and delightful.

5 DRIED SHIITAKE MUSHROOMS, SOAKED IN HOT WATER FROM THE KETTLE FOR 30 MINUTES

8 LARGE EGGS

1–1¼ CUPS CHICKEN STOCK

SALT

2¾ CUPS COOKED RICE

4 TBSP. PEANUT OIL OR LARD

16 BABY BOK CHOY, TRIMMED WITH ANY WILTED AND DISCOLORED LEAVES DISCARDED

1 TSP. LIGHT SOY SAUCE

½ TSP. POTATO FLOUR MIXED WITH 1 TBSP. COLD WATER

2 TSP. SESAME OIL

WHITE PEPPER

1. Drain the shiitake, cut off and discard their stems and cut the caps into even slices; set aside.
2. Tap the pointy end of an egg with the heavy back corner of a cleaver to crack the shell, and then pull off a small circle of shell from the tip. Drain the egg white out of this small hole into a bowl. Next, puncture the yolk and drain it into a separate bowl. Rinse the shell carefully and shake dry. Repeat with the remaining eggs.
3. Bring the chicken stock to a boil, and then allow to cool to 140–149°F. Measure the combined volume of the egg whites, and add to them an equal quantity of hot chicken stock (we found ¾ cup to be about right) and season with salt to taste. Stir together, but do not introduce frothy air bubbles by beating or whipping. Push the mixture through a sieve to get rid of any stringy bits of egg white.
4. Lay the cooked rice in a thick layer on a heatproof dish that will fit into a bamboo steamer.
5. Place the empty eggshells in an egg carton, holes facing upward. Use a funnel to fill them with the egg-white and stock mixture. Cover the holes with small pieces of paper, made pliable by rinsing under the hot tap. Use a pin to prick a tiny hole in each piece of paper. Stand the filled eggs up in the layer of cooked rice in the dish.
6. Place the dish in a bamboo steamer in a wok with a layer of water for steaming. Place the lid on the steamer. Bring the water in the steamer to the boil slowly over a medium flame. When you see steam puffing out from the sides of the steamer, turn the heat right down and steam extremely gently for 30 minutes.
7. Place the cooked eggs, in their shells, into a bowl of iced water and leave for about 5 minutes. Meanwhile, reheat the remaining stock and pour it into a heatproof bowl.
8. Shell the eggs very gently, then immerse them in the hot stock. Place the bowl in a steamer and steam very gently to keep them warm.
9. Heat 1 tablespoon peanut oil or lard in a wok over a medium flame. Add the bok choy hearts and stir-fry for a few minutes until cooked but still a little crunchy, adding salt to taste. Lay them neatly around the edge of a serving dish.
10. Place the warmed eggs in the middle of the serving dish, so they are surrounded by bok choy leaves.
11. Return the wok to the heat with the rest of the oil or lard. Add the sliced shiitake and stir-fry until they are fragrant. Add the rest of the chicken stock and the soy sauce and bring to a boil. Stir in the potato flour mixture until the liquid thickens and reduces. When it is silky and glossy, pour the liquid with the mushrooms over the waiting eggs. Drizzle the sesame oil over and sprinkle with a little pepper. Breathe a sigh of relief, and serve.

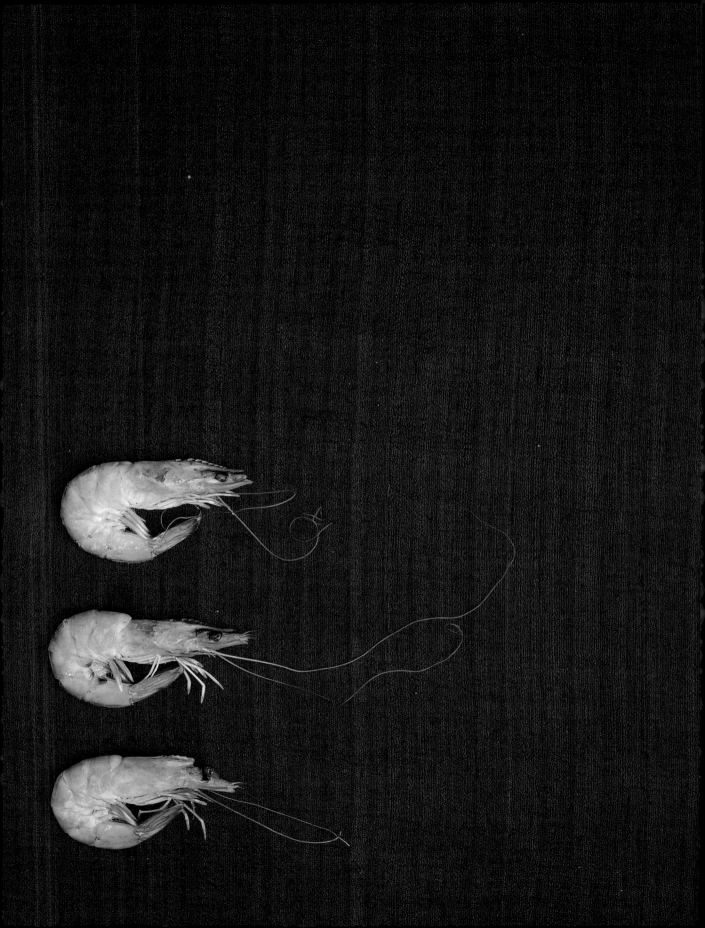

4

FISH DISHES

水産類

★ FISH DISHES

Hunan province has been known since ancient times as one of the richest agricultural regions of China, and a "land of fish and rice" (*yu mi zhi xiang*). The province is threaded by rivers, from the far west, where multicolored dragonflies flit over the Tuojiang River as it flows through the ancient town of Fenghuang, to the east, where the Xiang River passes through Changsha on its way to the Dongting Lake and then through the Yangtze to the eastern coast. You can still occasionally find fishermen plying a small-scale trade in Changsha, their sampans moored at the tip of Tangerine Island, where they offer "fire-baked small fry" (*huo bei yu*) or a few yellow catfish. In the villages, many people raise their own fish in ponds among the paddy fields, or catch them in small lakes and reservoirs.

This watery landscape means freshwater fish and other aquatic foods play a vital part in the Hunanese diet. As in other parts of China, a whole fish is an essential part of the New Year's Eve feast because its name is a pun on "plenty" (*nian nian you yu* can mean both "fish every year" and "every year a surplus"). It is served last, and must not be finished that night. In the past, those who could not afford a fish for their New Year's Eve dinner table would sometimes place a wooden replica on the table instead, like the pair of beautiful carved carp I once found in an antiques market in Changsha.

Above: SMOKED CARP AND BACON, ZHANGGUYING

In particular, the lakeside city of Yueyang is renowned for its fish. The Tang dynasty poet Li Shangyin famously wrote "Dongting fish can be gathered without even changing the fishing nets. They are as clamorous as ants before rain, as numerous as Autumn flies." A Song dynasty chronicle made mention of a local custom of offering a thick fish soup when entertaining guests. Legend has it the Qianlong Emperor visited Yueyang during a tour of southern China, and was so impressed by a feast of fish and river food he was served there that he gave it the name "The Baling Fish Banquet" (*ba ling quan yu xi*), using the ancient name for Yueyang, Baling.

In the 1970s, a local chef named Zhang Keliang brought together some twenty local fish dishes in a special feast to which he gave this legendary name. The feast was served in a well-known Yueyang restaurant, founded in 1936, the Weiyu Jiujia. Like many of the grand old restaurants, it had been badly damaged by the political vicissitudes of the Maoist era. According to unpublished sources, it was nationalized in 1956 and at some point renamed "Love the Masses" (*ai qun*), and the family who had founded it were persecuted as capitalists during the Cultural Revolution. But the grand fish feast seems to have won great local acclaim at the end of the revolutionary period, and the name lives on to this day. The full fish feast shows off up to eighteen different kinds of fish and other aquatic foods in a dazzling variety of forms, including dishes such as "Goldfish playing among the lotus," "Crystal fish jelly," "Fish slices with silver-needle tea," and "Shrimp with fresh green soybeans."

As in many parts of China, in Hunan fresh fish means live fish, so they are sold in great basins of water in the markets, and kept swimming around in the sinks in restaurant kitchens. There are also many local ways of preserving them. Sun-dried fish are sold at stalls on Junshan Island and in the markets of Yueyang. Small fry of a variety of species are fire-baked—the *huo bei yu* so beloved of Chairman Mao. And in the winter, almost every household seems to smoke their own fish. My friend Fan Qun salts her own carp, and hangs them to wind-dry on her balcony, where their patterned skin gleams with dark shades of pewter and iron, their bellies with pale aluminum and gold. In the far west of Hunan, the ethnic Miao and Tujia people pickle their fish in red wine lees, the boozy grains staining the pale fish a vibrant pink in the clay pickling jars. This pickled fish (*qu yu* or *zha yu*), usually steamed with black fermented beans and chiles, must be served at celebratory feasts.

Aside from fish, there are shrimp, soft-shelled turtles, tortoises, eels and loaches, and small

freshwater crabs. When I stayed with some friends in the northern Hunan plains, their young cousin went out in the middle of the night with a torch and a homemade eel-catching tool, and came back later with a bucketful of eels, loaches, and crabs, which we cooked and ate the following day.

In Changsha, crayfish are a local obsession. If you wander down at night to the South Gate (*nan men kou*), a tree-lined street in the middle of town, the place is abuzz with food stalls and small, noisy restaurants. Little armies of crayfish crawl around in great wooden tubs: they are cooked to order with ginger and garlic, and lashings of chili, and are juicily delicious. Many of these restaurants also offer spicy stews made with fish roe and swim bladders, another delicacy.

Left: MIAO WOMAN EATING, WESTERN HUNAN

RED-BRAISED BREAM
hong shao bian yu

紅燒鯿魚

In Zhangguying, thirty people had gathered to celebrate the birth of a child three days before. The beautiful baby lay asleep in his mother's arms, oblivious to the stream of visitors passing through their bedroom. In the main room of the house, a table was laden with dishes, including jujube fruits in a syrupy sauce, stir-fried cucumber and string beans, eels with red bell pepper, a chicken-and-scallion stir-fry, preserved duck eggs with chiles, stewed pig's foot, and a glorious red-braised fish.

This is a beautiful, irresistible recipe: a whole fish in a rich chestnut-red sauce, splashed with jagged morsels of chopped chiles and strands of bright red bell pepper and scallion green. I've used a bream, but you can use the same method to cook sea bass or red snapper. Some cooks deep-fry (*zha*) the fish as a short cut, but the flavor is better if you shallow-fry (*jian*) as I've suggested.

1 GILTHEADED BREAM OR SEA
    BASS (ABOUT 1 LB. 5 OZ.),
    DRESSED, WITH HEAD AND
    TAIL INTACT
2 TSP. FINELY CHOPPED FRESH
    GINGER
1 TSP. FINELY CHOPPED GARLIC
1 TBSP. CHOPPED SALTED CHILES
1 TBSP. CHILI BEAN PASTE
1¼ CUPS WATER OR EVERYDAY
    STOCK (PAGE 287)
1 TSP. LIGHT SOY SAUCE
½ TSP. DARK SOY SAUCE
½ TSP. CLEAR RICE VINEGAR
A GOOD PINCH RED BELL PEPPER
    SLIVERS FOR COLOR
2 SCALLIONS, GREEN PARTS
    ONLY, CUT INTO SLIVERS
1 TSP. SESAME OIL
½ CUP PEANUT OIL FOR COOKING

1. Make a few deep diagonal slashes into the fleshy part of the fish, on each side, to let the flavors penetrate. Rinse it and then dry thoroughly with a cloth or paper towels.

2. Heat the wok over a high flame until smoke rises, then add the oil and swirl around. When the oil is hot, add the fish and fry, tilting the wok slightly to allow it to cook on both ends, and turning once until golden on both sides; set aside.

3. Drain off all but 3 tablespoons oil from the wok and leave it to cool slightly before returning the wok to the heat. Add the ginger, garlic, chopped chiles, and chili bean paste and stir-fry until richly fragrant, taking care not to burn them. Stir in the water or stock, along with the soy sauces, and bring to a boil.

4. Slide the fish gently into the sauce and return to a boil. Add the vinegar, reduce the heat, and then simmer over a medium flame for about 5 minutes to let the flavours penetrate, spooning the sauce all over the fish as you go. (After 5 minutes the sauce will have reduced by about half.)

5. Gently transfer the fish to a serving dish, and turn up the heat to reduce the sauce to a syrupy consistency. Add the bell pepper slivers to the wok and allow them barely to cook, then add the scallion greens. Stir once or twice, and, off the heat, stir in the sesame oil. Pour the sauce over the fish and serve.

STEAMED SMOKED FISH WITH
BLACK BEANS AND CHILES
zheng la yu

蒸腊魚

The official Chinese Communist Party verdict on Mao Zedong is, bizarrely, that he was seventy per cent right and thirty per cent wrong. In Hunan, as one of my close friends explained to me, it's more like ninety per cent right and ten per cent wrong. Despite the appalling suffering that his policies and political movements inflicted on the Hunanese, most people still revere him as a great local and national hero. Rural houses tend to have a picture of Mao hung in pride of place in the main living room, where pictures of ancestors would have been hung in the past, before which the family eat their meals, drink their tea, and play mah jong. One family I stayed with had an enormous, twice life-size bronze bust of the Chairman beside their television, inscribed with his immortal words "Brightness lies ahead." When I visited another friend on the May Day holiday, the top of his TV was decorated with a statue of Mao, a statue of Father Christmas, and a vase of fake flowers. Even after all this time, I can't pretend to understand.

The following simple peasant dish was one of Mao's favorites, according to his Hunanese cook, Shi Yinxiang. In Hunan it would be made with smoked carp or catfish; I tried the same method with various fish. Kippers (smoked herring), surprisingly, didn't work at all; smoked mackerel were pretty good, but cold-smoked trout were simply magnificent, their moist flesh complemented beautifully by the invigorating spice and the subtle seductive savoriness of the beans.

1 SMOKED TROUT (10 OZ.)

1 TBSP. BLACK FERMENTED
  BEANS, RINSED

DRIED CHILI FLAKES OR CHILI
  OIL WITH SEDIMENT

2 TBSP. PEANUT OIL FOR
  COOKING

1. Cut the trout into bite-size pieces, on or off the bone, discarding the head and skin.

2. Heat the wok over a high flame until smoke rises, then add the peanut oil and swirl around. Add the trout and stir-fry for 1–2 minutes.

3. Place the trout with the oil in a heatproof bowl. Top with the black beans, and chili flakes or chili oil to taste. Place the bowl in a steamer and steam over a high flame for about 15 minutes. Stir everything together before eating.

TANGERINE ISLAND DRY-BRAISED FISH
ju zhou gan shao yu

橘
洲
干
燒
魚

The Hunanese capital, Changsha, is one of China's "furnace" cities, because of its unbearable summer heat. In the soupy midsummer air, the working men of the city strip to the waist for their evening strolls, and walk around fanning themselves in a vain attempt to stir up a breeze. Some people loll on straw mats laid out by the roadside, playing cards, or just falling asleep. Down by the river one night, we descended the steps to the water's edge, where a flotilla of wooden boats decked in bunting and glowing red lanterns bobbed and jostled against the wharf. We hired one, a long boat with a canopy and rows of deck chairs, and headed out across the stream. Around us, the heads of swimmers rose and fell in the gentle swell. As we headed toward the long slip of land called Tangerine Island, the haze of fairy lights on the shore materialized into floating jetties, where people were talking and laughing over their tea.

We had a table set up on the shore of the island, and this is one of the dishes we ate. It was made with a type of small catfish known locally as "yellow quacks" (*huang ya jiao*), allegedly because they quack like ducks (although I've never heard them quack!). They are still occasionally caught in the river by a few fishermen who moor their sampans at the tip of Tangerine Island, but are mostly farmed these days. That evening our fish were dry-braised over a high flame in a hiss of steam and smoke, a method that reduced the sauce to a delicious sticky coating.

I've used the same method here to cook rainbow trout. The fish will have partially disintegrated by the time you serve it, but don't worry, it will taste wonderful. I have tried replacing the hard-to-get perilla leaves with Thai sweet basil, which has a slightly similar licoricelike taste to it—not authentic, but still delicious.

1 RAINBOW TROUT (ABOUT 1 LB.), DRESSED, BUT WITH HEAD AND TAIL INTACT

3 TBSP. CHILI BEAN PASTE

1½ TBSP. FINELY CHOPPED FRESH GINGER

1 TBSP. FINELY CHOPPED GARLIC

SCANT 1 CUP EVERYDAY STOCK (PAGE 287) OR WATER

1 TSP. CLEAR RICE VINEGAR

¼ TSP. DARK SOY SAUCE

1½ TSP. DRIED CHILI FLAKES

A SMALL HANDFUL PURPLE PERILLA LEAVES, ROUGHLY TORN (OPTIONAL)

3 SCALLIONS, GREEN PARTS ONLY, FINELY SLICED

1 TSP. SESAME OIL

½ CUP PEANUT OIL FOR COOKING

TANGERINE ISLAND DRY-BRAISED FISH

1. Make a few diagonal slashes about 1 inch apart into the fleshy parts of both sides of the fish. Dry it as much as possible with a clean cloth or paper towels.

2. Heat the wok over a high flame until smoke rises, then add the peanut oil and swirl around. When the oil is hot, add the fish and fry, tilting the wok slightly to let the fish cook on both ends, and turning once until golden on both sides; set aside.

3. Pour off all but 3 tablespoons oil from the wok, and let it cool down a little bit. Return the wok to a medium flame, add the chili bean paste and stir-fry until the oil is richly red and fragrant. Add the ginger and garlic and stir-fry until they, too, smell wonderful. Pour in the stock or water, add the vinegar, soy sauce, and chili flakes to taste.

4. Return the fish to the wok and then bring the liquid to the boil over a high flame. Continue to cook over a high flame, spooning the sauce over the fish, until the water in the sauce has almost evaporated.

5. Toss in the purple perilla leaves and most of the scallions (save a scattering for the garnish). Stir for a few moments longer until the reduced, sticky sauce clings deliciously to the fish, and only oil remains in the bottom of the wok. Ease the fish onto the serving dish, drizzle with the sesame oil, and scatter with the remaining scallion slivers, and serve.

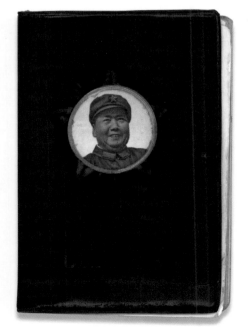

YELLOW-COOKED SALT COD IN CHILI SAUCE
huang men ci ba yu

黄
燜
糍
粑
魚

Fan Qun's family live in a peaceful village in the hills of Yueyang county. A small lake fills the lower valley, and some of the villagers have built their own rowing boats out of local wood. We borrowed one once, on a bright, windy day, and it was terrifyingly unsteady: we scarcely dared move for fear that it would capsize. The lake provides some fish, and on the day we arrived Fan Qun's father went out and caught one for us. Fried in a wok with a little ginger and chili, it was memorably fragrant, sweet, and tender. Another time we ate catfish, salted overnight in the old-fashioned way "to even out its flavours," and then fried golden in home-produced lard. The following recipe is a little more elaborate, and based on the version of the dish that I saw made in the kitchen of the Yuloudong restaurant in Changsha. There they used grass carp, but cod works wonderfully in this recipe.

I've salted the fish for a couple of hours, which gives it a pleasing taste and texture, but some recipe books suggest salting it for up to five days (see Note on the next page). If you can't be bothered with the salting, the same cooking method works very well with fresh fish, too. I've added a little vinegar to the sauce, which I think improves the flavor, but it wasn't in the original recipe.

2 COD FILLETS WITH THEIR SKIN
   (ABOUT 1 LB. TOTAL)

2½ TSP. SALT

1 TBSP. FINELY CHOPPED FRESH
   GINGER

1 TBSP. FINELY CHOPPED GARLIC

½ TBSP. DRIED CHILI FLAKES

2 TSP. SHAOXING WINE

1 CUP EVERYDAY STOCK (PAGE
   287) OR WATER

¼ TSP. DARK SOY SAUCE

1 LONG, FRESH RED CHILI, DE-
   SEEDED AND THINLY SLICED

A HANDFUL CHOPPED PURPLE
   PERILLA (OPTIONAL)

4 SCALLIONS, GREEN PARTS
   ONLY, THINLY SLICED

1. A couple of hours before you want to cook, rub the salt into the cod fillets, then place them in a ceramic or glass bowl and leave in the refrigerator. Rinse well and pat dry before cooking.

2. Heat the oil in a wok or a non-stick skillet over a high flame. Add the fish and fry on both sides until golden, moving the fillets as little as possible so a nice crust develops; set aside. (This step can be done a little in advance.)

3. Heat the wok over a high flame until smoke rises, then add 3 tablespoons peanut oil and swirl around. Add the ginger and garlic and stir-fry until fragrant. Add the chili flakes and sizzle for a few seconds until fragrant, taking care not to burn them. Splash the Shaoxing wine around the edge of the wok and then add the stock or water.

ingredients and method continue on the next page

YELLOW-COOKED SALT COD IN CHILI SAUCE

1 TSP. CHINKIANG VINEGAR
  (OPTIONAL)

1 TSP. SESAME OIL

½ CUP PEANUT OIL FOR COOKING

4. Bring the liquid to a boil, add the soy sauce, and immerse the fish fillets. (If you are using unsalted fish, add a little salt to taste.) Reduce the heat to medium and simmer for a few minutes, spooning the liquid over the fillets from time to time, to allow the fish to absorb the flavors and the sauce to reduce; remove the fish to a serving dish.

5. Add the fresh chili and purple perilla to the remaining sauce in the wok, stir for a few moments, and then add the scallions and vinegar, if using. Give the sauce a few more stirs, then remove from the heat, stir in the sesame oil, and drizzle the liquid over the fish.

NOTE

If you want to salt the fish for five days, cake the fish generously with coarse salt, place it in a ceramic or glass bowl, cover with a heavy weight, and leave in the refrigerator for five days, turning the fillets every day or two, and draining off the liquid that emerges. Before eating, you will need to rinse and soak it overnight in plenty of water, changing the water as many times as possible to get rid of excess saltiness.

YUEYANG SPICY BARBECUED FISH
yue yang shao kao yu

This is an adaptation of a delicious late-night snack from a barbecue stall in Yueyang. They cooked little crucian carp, several of them split open and sandwiched in a grill wire, over a charcoal barbecue, and then served them in a metal pan on a tabletop burner, with a generous scattering of scallion and coriander (cilantro).

1 SEA BASS (ABOUT 1 LB.),
    DRESSED, BUT WITH HEAD
    AND TAIL LEFT INTACT
1 TBSP. SHAOXING WINE
SALT
A SMALL PIECE FRESH GINGER
1 SCALLION, WHITE PART ONLY

For barbecuing:

3 SCALLIONS, GREEN PARTS
    ONLY
A HANDFUL CORIANDER
    (CILANTRO) LEAVES
1 TBSP. LIGHT SOY SAUCE
½ TSP. SWEET BEAN SAUCE
1 TSP. CHINKIANG VINEGAR
1 TSP. SUGAR
PEANUT OIL FOR BRUSHING
GROUND CUMIN
DRIED CHILI FLAKES

1. Make a few deep, diagonal slashes at even intervals into the thickest part of the fish. Rub with the Shaoxing wine and a little salt. Crush the ginger and scallion white with the flat side of your cleaver or a heavy object, and place them in the cavity of the fish; set aside while you preheat the barbecue.

2. Meanwhile, finely slice the scallion greens, and chop or tear the coriander leaves; set both aside.

3. When you are ready to cook the fish, discard the ginger and scallion from the cavity, and pat the fish dry with paper towels. Combine the soy sauce, sweet bean sauce, vinegar, and sugar in a bowl, then brush the mixture over the fish. Finally, brush the fish with peanut oil and sprinkle with a little salt to taste.

4. Brush the hot barbecue grill with a little oil. Place the fish on the barbecue, and grill on both sides until cooked through and a chopstick slides easily into the thickest part of the back. When it is approaching the end of the cooking time, brush the fish with more peanut oil, and scatter it generously with cumin and chili flakes on both sides. Finally, sprinkle the fish with scallion greens, let them feel the lick of the heat, and then transfer to a serving dish, and scatter with coriander.

YUEYANG VELVETED FISH
liu yu pian

Down at the wharf in Yueyang on a misty day, a couple of old men pull small fish in on their lines in a flash of silver. Not far away, the Fish Alley Market sells fresh local produce, including many varieties of fish, although these days they are mostly farmed, and the docks and the wharf have a desolate air. In the past, though, this part of Yueyang was the center of a flourishing fish industry. According to a local historian, Li Peitian, there has been a market on the Fish Alley site for nearly 2,000 years, and by the time of the Tang dynasty it was renowned for its fish traders and restaurants. They sold fish and other aquatic foods from the Dongting Lake, including various types of carp, mandarin fish, catfish, bream, small silverfish, river shrimp, loaches, and eels, and, most exotic of all, the Junshan Island tortoise. Not surprisingly, Yueyang also became known for its fish cooking, and the following elegant dish is one local specialty. It is traditionally made with the snakehead fish (*cai yu*), which has dark snaky scales, but I've substituted halibut in this recipe. I learned to make this at the Everyone Restaurant in Yueyang.

14 OZ. HALIBUT FILLET

½ TSP. SALT, PLUS EXTRA TO
    TASTE

3 DRIED SHIITAKE MUSHROOMS,
    SOAKED IN HOT WATER FROM
    THE KETTLE FOR 30 MINUTES,
    THEN DRAINED

½ RED BELL PEPPER, THIN-
    SKINNED IF POSSIBLE

½ GREEN BELL PEPPER, THIN-
    SKINNED IF POSSIBLE

3 SCALLIONS, GREEN PARTS
    ONLY

3 GARLIC CLOVES, THINLY SLICED

1–1½-IN. PIECE FRESH GINGER,
    PEELED AND THINLY SLICED

½ TSP. LIGHT SOY SAUCE

½ TSP. CLEAR RICE VINEGAR

3 TBSP. EVERYDAY STOCK (PAGE
    287) OR WATER

½ TSP. POTATO FLOUR MIXED
    WITH 2 TSP. COLD WATER

1 TSP. SESAME OIL

1¼ CUPS PEANUT OIL FOR
    COOKING

For the marinade:

1 TBSP. SHAOXING WINE

2 TBSP. EGG WHITE

2 TBSP. POTATO FLOUR

1. Cut the halibut into ½-inch slices, discarding any remaining skin and cartilage. (If you are cutting slices from one piece of fillet on the skin, it is easiest to do this by holding the knife at a steep angle and slicing diagonally.) Put the halibut slices in a bowl, add the marinade ingredients with ½ teaspoon salt and mix well; set aside while you prepare the other ingredients.

2. Drain and squeeze the reconstituted shiitake mushrooms, then remove the stems and slice the caps. Cut the red and green bell peppers into ¾-inch strips, and then diagonally into lozenge shapes (for the most attractive results discard any odds and ends). Cut the scallion greens into bite-sized pieces, or slivers if they are thick. Set aside the prepared vegetables separately.

3. Heat the wok over a high flame until smoke rises, then add the peanut oil and heat until it reaches 275°F. Add the fish, and stir with chopsticks to separate the slices. When they are white but not fully cooked, remove with a slotted spoon and set aside. Drain off all but 3 tablespoons of the oil, and return the wok to the stovetop over a high flame.

4. Add the garlic, ginger, shiitake, and both peppers to the wok and stir-fry until fragrant. Add the fish and toss in the fragrant oil, seasoning with the soy sauce, vinegar, and salt to taste. Add the stock, and then the potato flour mixture, stirring as it thickens the liquid to a glaze. Stir in the scallion greens and then, off the heat, the sesame oil. Serve.

STEAMED FISH WITH HAM, SHIITAKE, AND CHILES
gan zheng xian yu

This simple recipe has echoes of Cantonese cooking, particularly in the use of hot oil at the end to extract the fragrance of the scallions, but the chiles give it a Hunanese twist. In Hunan, they like to steam the Chinese perch or Mandarin fish, among others; at home in England I tend to use sea bass. You might like to finish the dish off with a dash of light soy sauce as they do in the Cantonese south, although the ham and shiitake alone give it a delicious flavor. Vegetarians can, of course, simply omit the ham.

4 OR 5 DRIED SHIITAKE
    MUSHROOMS

1 SEA BASS (ABOUT 1¼ LB.)

1 TBSP. SHAOXING WINE

SALT

2 FRESH RED CHILES

¾-IN. PIECE FRESH GINGER

1 SLICE COOKED HAM (ABOUT
    1½ OZ.)

2 SCALLIONS, WHITE AND GREEN
    PARTS SEPARATED

4 TBSP. PEANUT OIL OR MELTED
    LARD

1. Soak the mushrooms in hot water from the kettle for about 30 minutes before you begin.

2. Meanwhile, make a few neat diagonal slashes into the thickest part of the flesh on each side of the fish to let the flavors penetrate. Splash the fish inside and out with the Shaoxing wine, and rub with a little salt; set aside while you prepare the other ingredients.

3. Discard the stems and seeds of the chiles and cut into fine slivers. Drain the mushrooms, then squeeze dry. Discard the stems and cut the caps into fine slivers. Peel and cut the ginger into fine slivers. Cut the ham and scallion greens into slivers. Combine all the slivered ingredients, except the scallion greens, and mix them with a few pinches of salt.

4. Rinse the fish under cold running water, then pat dry. Place on a heatproof plate that will fit inside your steamer. Smash the white parts of the scallions with the side of a cleaver blade or a heavy object and place into the cavity of the fish. Sprinkle the fish with a little salt. Strew the combined chiles, ginger, ham, and mushroom slivers over, and drizzle 2 tablespoons oil or lard over.

5. Steam the fish over high heat for about 8 minutes, until a chopstick slides easily into the fleshy part of the fish's back. Shortly before the fish is done, heat the remaining 2 tablespoons oil or lard over a high flame until really hot.

6. Remove the plate from the steamer, scatter the scallion greens over the fish, and then drizzle with the sizzling hot oil.

STEAMED FISH WITH CHOPPED SALTED CHILES
duo jiao zheng yu

剁
椒
蒸
魚

Steamed fish heads with chopped salted chiles were all the rage when I was living in Changsha. Waiters would emerge from restaurant kitchens bearing enormous, steaming platters, each one carrying a huge fish head, opened out flat, covered in a colorful scattering of scarlet chili and flecked with black beans and green. Chinese people love to eat foods with what my father would call a "high grapple factor," in other words, that require dexterity with tongue and teeth, and fish heads are a prime example. They are prized for the silkiness of their flesh and their variety of textures, and are easily eaten with chopsticks. The huge fish heads enjoyed in Hunan are those of the bighead carp (*yong yu* in Chinese, or *xiong yu* in Hunan dialect).

I've adapted the recipe for people who might prefer not to eat fish heads, but would nonetheless appreciate the splendid colors and bold flavors of this dish. In testing it, I've used lemon sole, because its silkiness reminds me of the original recipe, but you might prefer other flatfish, or perhaps a whole brill or turbot for a larger party (as long as it will fit into your steamer). And if you want to be as authentic as possible, buy a large salmon head, cleave it nearly in half, and lay it, open and skin-side up, onto a pair of chopsticks on a large serving dish. Season and steam as in the recipe below, and remove the chopsticks before serving.

1 WHOLE LEMON SOLE, GUTTED
  (ABOUT 14 OZ.)

1 TBSP. SHAOXING WINE

¾-IN. PIECE FRESH GINGER,
  UNPEELED AND SMASHED

1 WHOLE SCALLION, SMASHED

½ TSP. BLACK FERMENTED
  BEANS, RINSED

1½ TSP. FINELY CHOPPED FRESH
  GINGER

4 TBSP. CHOPPED SALTED
  CHILES

1. Make several diagonal slashes into the fish at intervals of about 1 inch to let the flavors penetrate. Rub with the Shaoxing wine and set aside. Place the smashed ginger and scallion in the middle of a deep heatproof plate that will fit into your steamer.

2. Heat the wok over a high flame until smoke rises, then add the oil and swirl around. Add the black beans and chopped ginger and stir-fry briefly until fragrant.

3. Drain the wine and juices from the fish, then lay it over the ginger and scallion. (Their purpose is to let the steam circulate around the fish, and to enhance its flavor.) Cover the fish evenly with the chiles, and then scatter with the beans and ginger from the wok.

ingredients and method continue on the next page

2 SCALLIONS, GREEN PARTS ONLY,
FINELY SLICED

2 TBSP. PEANUT OIL FOR COOKING

4. Put the plate in your steamer and steam over a high heat until just cooked and a chopstick easily slides into the thickest part of the fish. A 14-ounce fish should take about 5 minutes.

5. Serve on the steaming plate with a scattering of sliced scallion.

Variations

An alternative to this recipe is one made with pickled green chiles, which looks nice garnished with a sprig of coriander (cilantro). Or you might like to follow the example of some Hunan restaurants and offer a "double-chili" steamed fish head (or fish), half covered in scarlet chopped salted chiles, half in green pickled chiles.

STEAMED SEA BREAM WITH PURPLE PERILLA
zi su zheng bian yu

This is a loose adaptation of a delicious dish I enjoyed with the local police force in Liuyang, after a ride through town in their police car. It was served in a very simple "rustic" restaurant called the Pengjiapo Fanzhuang, just after the Chinese New Year, when the weather was so damply cold we needed to toast our feet over the metal dish of wood embers under our table. The restaurant used dried perilla, but use fresh if you can find it. And feel free to try this with other types of fish (large fish can be cut into chunks and steamed in a bowl with the seasonings). The perilla had an almost tealike flavor, dark and intense.

1 SEA OR FRESHWATER BREAM
  OR SEA BASS (ABOUT 1¼ LB.)
1 TBSP. SHAOXING WINE
SALT
4 FRESH RED CHILES
2 GOOD HANDFULS FRESH
  PURPLE PERILLA LEAVES
2 SCALLIONS
1 TSP. DRIED CHILI FLAKES
1½ TBSP. BLACK FERMENTED
  BEANS, RINSED
¾-IN. PIECE FRESH GINGER,
  PEELED AND FINELY
  CHOPPED
4 TBSP. PEANUT OIL OR MELTED
  LARD

1. Make a few neat diagonal slashes into the thickest part of the flesh on each side of the fish to let the flavors penetrate. Splash the fish inside and out with the Shaoxing wine and rub with a little salt. Set aside while you prepare the other ingredients.

2. Discard the chili seeds and stems and chop finely. Discard the purple perilla stems and finely chop the fresh leaves. Separate the green and white parts of the scallions. Finely chop the green parts and bash the white parts with the flat blade of a cleaver.

3. Rinse the fish under cold running water and pat dry. Sprinkle inside and out with a little salt and place the scallion whites into the cavity. Place the fish on a heatproof plate that fits inside your steamer and scatter the dried chili flakes over.

4. Mix the fresh chili, black beans, ginger, and purple perilla and strew them over the fish. Drizzle 2 tablespoons of the oil or lard over.

5. Put the plate in a steamer and steam the fish over high heat for about 8 minutes, until just cooked and a chopstick slides easily into the fleshy part of the back. Shortly before the fish is done, heat the remaining 2 tablespoons oil or lard over a high flame until really hot.

6. When the fish is ready, remove it from the steamer and scatter with the scallion greens. Drizzle over the hot oil and serve immediately.

JUNSHAN STEAMED FISH IN RICE MEAL
jun shan fen zheng yu

One of the dishes served at "The Baling Fish Banquet" of Yueyang is a kind of catfish (*hui yu*) coated in rice meal and steamed in a section of fresh bamboo, which gives it a delicate bamboo fragrance. As fresh bamboo is hard to come by, I suggest you use a steamer lined with a fragrant lotus leaf instead. The following recipe is based on one taught me by Liu Xiaoming, a chef at a small lakeside restaurant on Junshan Island. He used to be a fisherman, but started cooking when Junshan became a tourist resort, and learned how to cook the fish banquet dishes while working at the main guesthouse on the island.

10 OZ. HAKE OR OTHER WHITE
    FISH FILLETS

1 DRIED LOTUS LEAF, SOAKED IN
    HOT WATER FROM THE
    KETTLE UNTIL SOFT

A LITTLE PEANUT OIL

2 OZ. RICE MEAL (SEE RECIPE
    FOR STEAMED CHICKEN IN
    LOTUS LEAVES ON PAGES
    132–3 FOR METHOD TO MAKE
    RICE MEAL: YOU WILL JUST
    NEED HALF THE QUANTITY IN
    THE RECIPE)

2 SCALLIONS, GREEN PARTS
    ONLY, FINELY SLICED

For the marinade:

2 TSP. SHAOXING WINE

2 TSP. FINELY CHOPPED FRESH
    GINGER

1 TBSP. CHOPPED SALTED CHILES
    OR CHILI BEAN PASTE

1½ TSP. LIGHT SOY SAUCE

A LITTLE WHITE PEPPER

1. Holding the knife at a steep angle and cutting toward the skin, cut the fish fillet into slices about ¼ inch thick, removing the skin as you cut. Place in a bowl, add the marinade ingredients, and mix well (it's easiest to use your fingers for this).

2. Line a bamboo steamer with the drained lotus leaf and brush lightly with oil.

3. Add 2 teaspoons peanut oil to the fish and mix well. Add the rice meal and 6 tablespoons cold water. Mix well so the fish is evenly coated in rice.

4. Lay the fish on to the lotus leaf in a fairly thin layer. Cover the steamer and steam over a high heat for 6–10 minutes, until the rice meal has cooked to a soft and comforting consistency. Serve with a scattering of scallion greens.

VEGETARIAN VERSION
★ STEAMED LOTUS ROOT WITH RICE MEAL
fen zheng ou

Peel 14 ounces lotus root and cut it into bite-size chunks. Sprinkle lightly with salt and leave for 30 minutes or so to draw out some of its water; rinse and shake dry. Add salt and pepper to taste. Mix 1–2 tablespoons peanut oil into the lotus root to help the rice meal to stick, and then add 2 ounces rice meal and 6 tablespoons cold water. Steam over a high heat for 30 minutes. Garnish with finely sliced scallion, if desired.

★ MAOIST CUISINE—*MAO JIA CAI*

Could anywhere but China have a culinary school named after a political dictator? "Mao's homestyle cooking" (*mao jia cai*) is the name given to the kind of food served in dozens of small restaurants in Mao Zedong's home village, Shaoshan, and the branches they have spawned in Beijing, other Chinese cities, and even in London. There is even a Maoist cookbook written under the guidance of Mao's favorite Hunanese cook.

Strictly speaking, Maoist cuisine is just the invention of canny Shaoshan entrepreneurs trying to make a fast buck out of the name of a man who remains, despite everything, a national hero. On the other hand, we do know an unusual amount about Mao's own dietary preferences, partly because of the perennial Chinese fascination with food.

Food has long been at the heart of Chinese life, and it has always been taken seriously. One Shang dynasty cook is said to have impressed a king so much he was made prime minister, and all the great Chinese philosophers have used culinary metaphors. Late imperial and Nationalist officials were the driving force behind the development of regional haute cuisines. And even in the communist period, Chinese leaders have been in the habit of visiting famous restaurants and noodle bars in a blaze of publicity, posing for photographs and recording for posterity their comments on the food.

Above: SMOKED MEAT AND FISH, YUEYANG

In Mao's case, the biography written by his personal physician, Li Zhisui, mentions that the classic Hunanese peasant dish pork with hot peppers was one of the Chairman's favorite foods, and that he always preferred the spicy cooking of his home province to more subtle Cantonese fare. Dr. Li also recounts an unsettling occasion when Mao offered him a taste of bitter melon, and laughed when he appeared to find it unpalatably bitter. Paranoid that Mao was making a jibe about his privileged, upper-class upbringing by testing his ability to "eat bitterness," Dr. Li hastily pretended that he had enjoyed it. (Eating bitterness—*chi ku*—is the universal Chinese metaphor for suffering.)

In Hunan, the master chef Shi Yinxiang was in charge of catering for Mao whenever he returned to his home province. He recalls his nervousness when he first found out he would be cooking for the Chairman, in the spring of 1959. Despite his brilliance as a chef, he was concerned that his food might not meet with Mao's personal approval, so he questioned people close to him about the Chairman's dietary tastes. He learned about Mao's dislike for fancy food and the exotic ingredients that were de rigueur at banquets, and his preference for coarse staples and everyday Hunanese dishes.

According to Shi Yinxiang, Mao liked eating red-braised pork, the dish that now bears his name in countless Hunanese restaurants, and considered it to be good for his memory. He loved simple rustic dishes: steamed bacon and smoked fish with plenty of chili, wild mushrooms, bean curd, and cabbage, and the wild vegetables that were generally disdained as peasant food, such as fiddlehead ferns, purslane, and shepherd's purse. Even more eccentric was his preference for the "coarse grains" that were the traditional foods of poverty and desperation: roasted sweet potato, corncobs, and unpolished rice mixed with beans. Master Shi was accustomed to dazzling his guests with banquet delicacies, but he reverted to simple peasant cooking for Mao. The Chairman was apparently so delighted with his red-braised pork and pickled cabbage that he told the other chefs in his retinue, who came from different regions in China, to learn from Master Shi. It is tempting to suppose that Mao's personal dislike of fine food, one of the foremost trappings of wealth in China, played a part in his willingness to oversee the destruction of elite and bourgeois culture.

At least in this sense, he was not a hypocrite: by all accounts he lived as he preached.

Mao's passion for chiles is legendary. According to the Hunanese food writer Liu Guochu, he loved them so much he even sprinkled ground chiles on slices of watermelon, and, when advised to cut down on his chili consumption for the sake of his health, replied to his doctor: "If you are scared of the chiles in your bowl, how on earth will you dare to fight your enemies?"

TANGERINE ISLAND FISH SOUP
ju zhou qing dun yu

橘
洲
清
炖
魚

Tangerine Island is a long, narrow strip of land that lies between the east and west banks of the Xiang River as it flows through Changsha. At its southern end is a park where the tangerine trees, blooming, make the air sweet and heavy with an intoxicating fragrance; and at the end of the park a promontory teahouse that faces upriver like the prow of a ship. During his time at teacher-training college in Changsha, Mao Zedong liked to swim in the river and relax with his friends among the tangerine trees on the island. In one of his most famous poems, "Changsha" (1925), he describes himself standing at the island's tip, looking out over the boats toward crimson hills, and pondering the destiny of man.

Along the eastern side of the island are a number of modest restaurants serving colorful local fish dishes. One sunny afternoon I sat on a shady terrace there with some friends, drinking beer as the barges and fishing boats went past and a gentle breeze stirred the trees. We ate, among other things, a delicious soup made from a pale, smooth-skinned fish that resembled a small shark. It was a type of catfish known locally as the "white pearl" (*bai zhu zi*). The following recipe is based on that dish, although I have adapted it to be made with conger eel, which has some similar qualities.

1 LB. 10 OZ. CONGER EEL

2 TSP. FINELY CHOPPED GARLIC

1-IN. PIECE FRESH GINGER, PEELED AND SLICED

A FEW THIN SLICES CARROT

1 QT. EVERYDAY STOCK (PAGE 287), BOILING

½ TSP. WHITE VINEGAR

SALT AND WHITE PEPPER

3 SCALLIONS, GREEN PARTS ONLY

DRIED CHILI FLAKES

A HANDFUL PURPLE PERILLA OR CORIANDER (CILANTRO), CHOPPED

3 TBSP. PEANUT OIL FOR COOKING

1. Cut the conger eel, on the bone, into thick slices, then rinse well; set aside.

2. Heat the wok over a high flame until smoke rises, then add the peanut oil and swirl around. Reduce the heat, add the garlic, ginger, and carrot and stir-fry until fragrant. Add the fish slices and gently toss in the hot oil for 1–2 minutes. Pour in the stock and return to a boil. Add the vinegar and a little salt and set at a very slow boil for about 10 minutes.

3. Put the scallions and pepper to taste into a soup tureen or a Chinese clay pot. Season the fish soup with salt and dried chili flakes to taste (the chili should stain the soup slightly orange), then throw in the perilla or coriander, stir once, and pour over the seasonings in the tureen.

FRAGRANT-AND-HOT TIGER PRAWNS
xiang la xia

香
辣
蝦

We drove to Zhuzhou on a damp spring day, when mist had softened the landscape, like the moist brushstrokes of a traditional Chinese painting. I am in the habit of thinking that sunlight is perfection, and was surprised when Sansan told me that she found gray and foggy days more lovely. But, on that day, I could see what she meant. In the damp air and the drizzle, the rust-red earth had deepened in hue, and the shapes of the wooded hills were blotted into ambiguity. The soft greens of grass and trees framed exposed hillsides that seemed to glow wine-dark in the obscurity. In some places the earth was a palette of plum, damson, and deep burgundy, in others paprika, cayenne, and an almost turmeric orange.

A platter of river shrimp studded with ginger, garlic, and chiles was part of the meal we shared that evening. I've adapted the recipe to be made with tiger prawns, but you can also use jumbo shrimp. Leave the shells on for best results. To eat, take a bite of a whole prawn and remove the shell with your teeth and tongue, then spit it gently into your bowl or remove it from your mouth with chopsticks.

1 LB. TIGER PRAWNS OR JUMBO
   SHRIMP, THAWED IF FROZEN

½ TSP. SALT

1 TBSP. SHAOXING WINE

1 TSP. FINELY CHOPPED FRESH
   GINGER

1 TSP. FINELY CHOPPED GARLIC

1 TSP. CHILI BEAN PASTE

1 TSP. CHOPPED SALTED CHILES

3 TBSP. WATER

¼ TSP. DARK SOY SAUCE

2 SCALLIONS, GREEN PARTS
   ONLY, FINELY SLICED

1 TBSP. FINELY CHOPPED RED
   BELL PEPPER

1 TSP. SESAME OIL

1 CUP PEANUT OIL FOR COOKING

1. Cut the heads off the prawns or shrimp, and remove the legs. Poke out as much as possible of their dark veins with a darning needle. (This is fiddly, but I like to do it.) Rinse the prawns, then mix with the salt and Shaoxing wine and set aside.

2. Heat the oil in a wok over a high flame until it reaches 350°F. Shake the prawns dry. Tip them into the wok and deep-fry for less than 30 seconds, until they have turned pink and are partially cooked. Remove with a slotted spoon and set aside.

3. Pour off all but 3 tablespoons of the oil, and return the wok to a medium flame. Add the ginger, garlic, chili bean paste, and chopped salted chiles and stir-fry until the oil is wonderfully fragrant and stained a deep red by the chiles. Add the water and dark soy sauce and bring to a boil.

4. Add the prawns and then cook over a high flame to reduce the sauce, stirring constantly. When the water in the sauce has evaporated, add the scallions and bell pepper to give them a lick of heat. You should smell the fragrance of the onions after a few seconds, at which point remove the wok from the heat, stir in the sesame oil, and serve.

FISHERMAN'S SHRIMP WITH CHINESE CHIVES
yu jia chao xia qiu

This is based on a dish I enjoyed eating in Yueyang, where it was made with small river shrimp, cooked in their shells. I've adapted the recipe to be made with shelled large shrimp, which have a different texture, but are still delicious. (Shrimp and Chinese chives are a particularly happy combination.) If you want a glossy, restaurant-style sauce, add a little stock at the end of cooking, and thicken with a mixture of potato flour and water.

1 LB. FRESH OR FROZEN RAW LARGE SHRIMP, THAWED IF FROZEN

3 OZ. CHINESE CHIVES

2 TSP. FINELY CHOPPED GARLIC

1 TBSP. CHOPPED SALTED CHILES OR 1 TSP DRIED CHILI FLAKES

1 TSP. CHINKIANG VINEGAR

1 FRESH RED CHILI, SEEDED AND THINLY SLICED

SALT

1 TSP. SESAME OIL

1 CUP PEANUT OIL FOR COOKING

For the marinade:

1 TSP. SALT

1 TBSP. POTATO FLOUR

1 SMALL EGG WHITE

1. Shell and devein the shrimp, removing and discarding the heads and legs, if necessary, then rinse and shake dry. Put them in a bowl, add the marinade ingredients, and mix well; set aside.

2. Trim the chives, discarding any tougher or wilted leaves (they should be pert and fresh) and cut into 1¼-inch pieces.

3. Heat the oil in a wok over a high flame until it reaches 300°F. Discard any excess egg white from the shrimp, then add them to the wok and fry briefly until pinkish but not fully cooked. Remove with a slotted spoon and set aside.

4. Drain off all but 3 tablespoons of the oil. Add the garlic and chopped salted chiles and stir-fry briefly until fragrant. Add the shrimp, stirring well, followed by the vinegar.

5. When all is sizzling and delicious, add the chives and fresh chili and stir-fry until they are barely cooked. Season with salt to taste, then remove from the heat, stir in the sesame oil, and serve.

VARIATION

A similar recipe uses finely chopped garlic stems instead of Chinese chives: the method is the same except you stir-fry the garlic stems with the ginger and chopped salted chiles until fragrant, before adding the shrimp.

BEAN CURD 豆腐類
DISHES

★ BEAN CURD DISHES

The soybean is native to China and has been cultivated there for more than 3,500 years. An astonishingly rich source of protein, it is fundamental to Chinese cooking and food culture, and has become one of the defining characteristics of the Chinese way of eating. Soy sauce is considered one of the seven household essentials (alongside salt, oil, vinegar, tea, rice, and firewood), and it can be argued that bean curd, or tofu as it's often known in the West, has a place equivalent to dairy products in European food cultures.

Bean curd is made all over China, often in small neighborhood workshops, by a process that bears some similarity to basic cheese-making. Dried yellow soybeans are soaked, ground with water, and then strained through cheesecloth to make bean milk. The milk is boiled, left to cool slightly, and then mixed with a coagulant, usually gypsum. As it cools, the milk sets to a very delicate curd, which is called "bean flower" (*dou hua*) or "bean curd brain" (*dou fu nao*). At this stage, the curd is often eaten directly, either in a savory soup or, with a sprinkling of white sugar, like a pudding. It is a delightful snack, smooth and silky and comforting. For firm bean curd, the warm milk is poured into cheesecloth-lined wooden molds soon after the gypsum is added, and pressed in a viselike instrument to extract some of its water as it sets.

No one is sure about the origins of bean curd. Legend says it was invented in the second century BC by Liu An, the king of Huainan; some argue that a stone relief excavated from a tomb of the same era depicts a bean curd workshop. The earliest written reference to bean curd, however, is in a tenth-century

Above: BEAN CURD WORKSHOP, ZHANGGUYING

text, and the Liu An legend only dates back a few hundred years, to the Ming dynasty. Some scholars have suggested bean curd was first made by nomads who migrated south and hankered after their customary cheese; others that it was developed by a rural doctor who would have been familiar with soymilk and had gypsum in his medicine chest. All that is certain is that by the Song dynasty it had become a popular food.

"Flower" bean curd and firm white bean curd are just the most basic forms of this most versatile foodstuff. In the markets of Hunan, there are stalls piled high with a dozen different varieties.

There are slices of golden smoked bean curd (*la gan zi* or *xiang gan*); blocks of stewed aromatic bean curd of various kinds (*lu dou fu* or *xiang gan*); deep-fried bean curd puffs (*you dou fu*); "hundred-leaves" sheets of leather-thin bean curd (*bai ye*); wafflelike "dried orchids" that have been cut into trellis patterns and deep-fried (*lan hua gan*); and "bound chickens" (*kun ji*), tightly tied rolls of thin bean curd that are used by Buddhists as a chicken substitute.

Above: FERMENTED BEAN CURD

There is also fermented bean curd (*dou fu ru*), a chili-laced relish that can be as sublimely rich and creamy as a high blue cheese. Fermented bean curd is eaten as a relish with rice congee or noodles for breakfast, or simply nibbled at the start of a meal, to whet the appetite—just a morsel on the tip of a chopstick is enough to send your taste buds wild with *umami* excitement. It is also used as an occasional seasoning in Hunanese cookery. Along with soy sauce, black fermented beans, and winter-sacrifice beans, fermented bean curd brings to Chinese vegetarian food some of the rich and savory tastes that one associates with meat and poultry.

The Hunanese even make use of the dregs that are a by-product of straining the ground soybeans through cheesecloth. In the village of Zhangguying, which specializes in bean curd production, these dregs are packed into molds and left to ferment, before being cut into slices and dried in the sun. Added to soups, they have an intriguing flavor and a pleasant consistency, a bit like brown bread.

Hunan also has its own version of that notorious Chinese snack, stinking bean curd (*chou dou fu*). This is the durian fruit of Chinese street food, its rotten fragrance so pervasive that it invades entire streets and neighborhoods. In the east of China and Taiwan, stinking bean curd is pale in color and looks innocuous, but in Hunan it takes on a distinctive and even sinister aspect. Uncooked, it is smearily purple-black and glistening: after deep-frying it puffs up until it has the dry frizzy blackness of volcanic lava.

Above: FERMENTED BLACK BEANS

Above: BEAN CURD STALL, CHANGSHA

This might sound unappetizing—but, of course, the essence of stinking bean curd is that it *is* unappetizing, but delicious once you have braved its formidable aroma. (Think of it, again, as a Chinese equivalent of a ripe and pungent blue cheese.)

The Hunanese make this unusual delicacy by steeping slices of bean curd in a fermented broth made from, among other things, black fermented beans, winter bamboo shoots, shiitake mushrooms, silken bean curd, and wine. It is then deep-fried and dressed in soy sauce, stock, and a mixture of chili and sesame oils. Street vendors sell it in the center of Changsha, their stalls lurking in a stinky, aromatic haze, but it's most strongly identified with the Huogongdian restaurant, where it has delighted many illustrious visitors including Mao Zedong. The restaurant has a snappy catchphrase to describe its charms: "Smell it and it's stinky; eat it and it's deliciously fragrant." (*wen qi lai chou, chi qi lai xiang*).

When it comes to more formal bean curd cooking, the most celebrated Hunanese dish is *zu'an* bean curd. It takes its title from the assumed name of the Nationalist Premier and fabled gourmet Tan Yankai and is

based on a traditional recipe that Tan adapted in consultation with his private chef, Cao Jingchen. This extravagant concoction is made with the finest bean curd, which is soaked and simmered in several changes of water and chicken stock, and then stewed with dried scallops, chicken, pork belly, rice wine, and seasonings, which imbue it with a marvelous flavor. The chicken and pork are discarded, and the bean curd served in its rich cooking juices, enhanced with the addition of wild *ko mo* mushrooms and a drizzling of fine chicken oil. (See pages 190–1 for a fuller account of Tan Yankai's gastronomic exploits.)

Above: BEAN CURD STALL, ZHANGGUYING

PENG'S HOME-STYLE BEAN CURD
peng jia dou fu

Like General Tso's chicken, this dish is the creation of one of the most famous of all Hunanese chefs, Peng Chang-kuei, who has mostly lived in Taiwan since he fled the Chinese mainland at the end of the civil war (see pages 117–18). Although it was invented in Taiwan, its Hunanese roots are plain to see in its rich, savory taste and the pairing of black fermented beans and chiles, and, of course, because it's a variation of the traditional home-style bean curd recipe on pages 186–7. Mr. Peng, who started making it in the late 1960s or 1970s, never intended to serve such a humble dish in his restaurant. "I used to sit at the front of the restaurant, and although the customers knew my name they didn't recognize me," Mr. Peng told me when I met him in 2004. "One day I was hungry, so I called my chef over and asked him to make me some bean curd, giving him detailed instructions on how to cook it. I ate it with a bowl of rice, mixing them together as I went along. Every customer who entered the restaurant had to pass by my table, and soon someone asked a waiter if they could have the same dish, which wasn't on the menu. The dish arrived, and another customer saw it and wanted some too, and soon it spread like a rash over the whole restaurant. In that one day we sold twenty-three portions of 'Peng's home-style bean curd'!"

Like many of Peng Chang-kuei's dishes, this one has been imitated far and wide: not long ago I saw it on the menu of a fashionable restaurant in Hong Kong. The version below is my attempt to re-create the dish as I was taught it by the head chef of Mr. Peng's current restaurant, the Peng Yuan, in Taipei.

continued on the next page

3 OZ. BONELESS LEAN PORK, THINLY SLICED

1 TSP. SHAOXING WINE

¼ TSP. SALT

1 BLOCK FIRM BEAN CURD, DRAINED (ABOUT 1¼ LB.)

3 SCALLIONS, GREEN PARTS ONLY

2 FRESH RED CHILES

1 TBSP. FINELY CHOPPED GARLIC

3 TBSP. BLACK FERMENTED BEANS, RINSED

1 CUP EVERYDAY STOCK (PAGE 287)

¼ TSP. DARK SOY SAUCE

SALT

¾ TSP. POTATO FLOUR MIXED WITH 1 TBSP. COLD WATER

½ TSP. SESAME OIL

2 TSP. CHILI OIL (OPTIONAL)

1 CUP PEANUT OIL FOR DEEP-FRYING

1. Put the pork in a bowl, add the Shaoxing wine and salt, and mix well; set aside.

2. Cut the bean curd into oblong slices, about ½ inch thick. Cut the scallion greens and chiles into thin diagonal slices, discarding the chili seeds as far as possible.

3. Heat the oil for deep-frying over a high flame until it reaches 350–400°F. Add the bean curd in 3 or 4 batches, and fry until the slices are just tinged with gold; drain and set aside on kitchen paper.

4. Pour off the oil, reserving 3 tablespoons. Clean the wok, then reheat it over a high flame until smoke rises, add the reserved oil, and swirl it around. Add the garlic and chiles and sizzle for a few seconds until fragrant. Add the pork, and as it becomes pale, throw in the black beans, stirring all the time. When all is hot and fragrant, pour in the stock, add the bean curd and dark soy sauce, and bring to a boil.

5. Reduce the heat and simmer for several minutes to let the flavors of the sauce enter the bean curd. Add salt to taste, if necessary.

6. Add the potato flour mixture and stir as the liquid thickens, then stir in the scallion greens. Finally, off the heat, stir in the sesame oil and chili oil, if using, and serve.

VEGETARIAN VERSION

Vegetarians can omit the pork and use a vegetarian stock (page 287).

HOME-STYLE BEAN CURD
jia chang dou fu

When I stay with my friend Fan Qun at her parents' farmhouse in northern Hunan, we sit outside on sunny days, looking out over the narrow fields and gently rising hills. The road is a track, and there is virtually no traffic, but neighbors walk past often, and usually stop for a chat or a cup of tea. One occasional visitor is the local bean curd-maker, an old man in a blue Mao suit, who carries a bamboo slat on his shoulders, from which hangs a basket of freshly made bean curd, and a basket of the bean curd dregs that can be made into soup. Fan Qun's mother sometimes fries the bean curd, and then simmers it in a sauce with chiles and other seasonings.

"Home-style bean curd" is one of the most common everyday dishes in Hunan, and is said to have been a particular favorite of Chairman Mao's. I have recorded many different versions of it, in kitchens all over Hunan, and the one below is my own amalgamation of the most delicious. If you don't have either the chili bean paste or the salted chiles, just use double quantities of the one you do have. To make it really rustic, you should use lard instead of oil for frying, and serve the sauce unthickened.

2 DRIED SHIITAKE MUSHROOMS

1¼ LB. FIRM BEAN CURD, DRAINED
 (ABOUT 1¼ BLOCKS)

3 OZ. BONELESS LEAN PORK, CUT
 INTO FINE SLIVERS

1 TSP. SHAOXING WINE

1 TBSP. CHILI BEAN PASTE

1 TBSP. CHOPPED SALTED CHILES

1 TBSP. FINELY CHOPPED GARLIC

1 TSP. DRIED CHILI FLAKES
 (OPTIONAL)

1 CUP EVERYDAY STOCK (PAGE
 287)

¼ TSP. DARK SOY SAUCE

SALT

¾ TSP. POTATO FLOUR MIXED
 WITH 1 TBSP. COLD WATER

3 SCALLIONS, GREEN PARTS
 ONLY, CUT INTO BITE-SIZE
 LENGTHS

1 TSP. SESAME OIL

⅓ CUP PEANUT OIL OR LARD

1. Put the dried mushrooms in a heatproof bowl, pour over enough hot water from the kettle to cover and leave to soak for 30 minutes. Drain, squeeze dry, discard the stalks, and cut the caps into thin slices; set aside.

continued

2. Meanwhile, cut the bean curd into large squares, and then cut these into triangular slices, about ½ inch thick; set aside. Put the pork in a bowl and mix with the Shaoxing wine.

3. Heat the wok over a high flame until smoke rises, then add 3 tablespoons of the peanut oil or lard and swirl around. Lay slices of bean curd onto the surface of the wok and fry, turning over once, until golden on both sides. Drain on paper towels and set aside. You will need to fry the bean curd in a couple of batches.

4. Clean the wok, if necessary, and reheat over a high flame until smoke rises. Add 3 tablespoons peanut oil or lard and swirl around. Add the pork and stir-fry until the slivers separate. Add the chili bean paste and salted chiles and stir-fry until fragrant. Throw in the garlic and mushrooms and continue stir-frying until they also smell delicious. Add the chili flakes, if using, stir once or twice and then pour in the stock.

5. Return the bean curd to the wok with the dark soy sauce and bring to a boil. Reduce the heat and simmer for several minutes to allow the flavors to penetrate the bean curd, seasoning with salt to taste, if necessary.

6. Add the potato flour mixture and stir to thicken the sauce, then add the scallion greens. Finally, off the heat, stir in the sesame oil and serve

Vegetarian version

Simply omit the pork and use a meat-free stock for a vegetarian version (page 287).

SMOKED BEAN CURD STIR-FRIED WITH CELERY
qin cai chao xiang gan

芹菜炒香干

We were driving out of town to visit a renowned Buddhist monk at a hilltop monastery, when I heard what sounded like a croak coming from the back of the car. I turned around and discovered, to my surprise, that Liu Wei's nephew had brought a sackful of frogs on the trip. "Are they for lunch?" I asked, forgetting that Liu Wei's nephew was a Buddhist and a vegetarian. It turned out he had bought them that morning in the food market, and was planning to release them back into the wild as part of his Buddhist practice. It was an admirable thing to do, particularly as these particular frogs were supposed to be a protected species, although I did wonder if they would simply be rounded up later in the day by a canny peasant and sold again as an exotic delicacy. Anyway, he liberated the frogs, and we sat down to an entirely vegetarian lunch at the monastery.

The following dish is one that I associate with my vegetarian friends in Changsha. It takes just a few minutes to prepare, yet the smoky bean curd, pepped up with chili, goes beautifully with the invigorating sharpness of the celery. Spiced bean curd (firm bean curd that has been simmered in a five-spice broth) can be used instead of smoked bean curd, for a different but also delightful combination of tastes.

9 OZ. FIRM SMOKED OR SPICED
    BEAN CURD

7 OZ. CHINESE CELERY OR 5 OZ.
    WESTERN CELERY

A FEW SLIVERS FRESH RED CHILI
    OR RED BELL PEPPER

½ TSP. DRIED CHILI FLAKES

SALT

1 TSP. LIGHT SOY SAUCE

1 TSP. SESAME OIL

3 TBSP. PEANUT OIL FOR
    COOKING

1. Cut the bean curd into fairly thick slices, and then (if it is firm enough) into strips about 2 inches long. If using Chinese celery, trim and cut the stalks into pieces the same length as the pieces of bean curd, discarding the leaves. If using Western celery, trim and destring the stalks, then cut into pieces to match the bean curd.

2. Heat the wok over a high flame until smoke rises, then add the peanut oil and swirl around. Add the bean curd pieces and spread out across the surface of the wok. Fry for a few minutes until tinged golden, stirring from time to time so they are evenly colored. Remove the bean curd and set aside, leaving as much oil as possible in the wok.

3. Return the wok to the heat. Add the celery, fresh chili or bell pepper slivers, and chili flakes and stir-fry until nearly cooked, seasoning with salt to taste.

4. Add the bean curd to the wok with the soy sauce and more salt, if necessary. Stir a few times more until everything is sizzling, then remove from the heat, mix in the sesame oil, and serve.

SMOKED BEAN CURD STEAMED WITH
BLACK BEANS AND CHILES
zheng xiang gan zi

蒸香干子

In the quiet courtyard of the Kaifu Temple in Changsha, Xiaorong and I met three elderly but sprightly nuns: they were in their seventies but looked at least twenty years younger. They had been at the temple for the past half century, and remember the day in the Cultural Revolution when all its Buddhist statues were smashed in a single hour. For years afterward they had been banned from practicing their religion, and instead set to work producing cloth on machines installed in the temple, until they were allowed to be nuns again in the 1980s.

Like all Buddhist nuns and monks, these three were vegetarians, and also avoided the unclean, pungent seasonings like garlic and chives. (Luckily for Hunanese Buddhists, chiles have never been proscribed.) Hunanese vegetarian cooking is most strongly associated with Nanyue, near the sacred southern mountain of Hengshan, where pilgrims can dine on elaborate fakeries of meat and fish dishes, but everyday Chinese vegetarian food is much more simple. The following dish, served with rice and perhaps a stir-fried green vegetable, makes a delicious and easy supper.

9 OZ. SMOKED BEAN CURD

DRIED CHILI FLAKES

1 TBSP. BLACK FERMENTED
    BEANS, RINSED

3 TBSP. PEANUT OIL

1 SCALLION, GREEN PART ONLY,
    FINELY SLICED

1. Cut the bean curd into thickish slices of a nice eatable size, and place in a heatproof bowl.

2. Sprinkle the chili flakes over, black beans, and oil.

3. Place the bowl in a steamer and steam over a high heat for 15–20 minutes, until the bean curd is heated through and the flavors have infused.

4. Scatter with scallion slices and serve. Stir well before eating.

VARIATION
★ STEAMED WHITE BEAN CURD
zheng bai dou fu

Cut some plain, unsmoked firm bean curd into thick slices and pile into a heatproof bowl. Top with rinsed black fermented beans, dried chili flakes, sliced fresh red chili, and vegetable oil, with light soy sauce and salt to taste. Steam over a medium heat for 20–25 minutes, then scatter with sliced scallion greens, and stir well before eating.

ZHANGGUYING RED-BRAISED BEAN CURD PUFFS
zhang gu ying you dou fu

This is a recipe from a small restaurant by the stream in the old village of Zhangguying, which is famous for its bean curd, and particularly for its golden bean curd puffs. These chunks of deep-fried bean curd soak up flavors like a sponge, which indeed they resemble, and after cooking they have a wonderfully juicy mouthfeel. Vegetarians can use a vegetarian stock, and meat-eaters might like to start the recipe by stir-frying some slices of pork, and then adding the garlic and ginger. You can buy deep-fried bean curd puffs in good Chinese supermarkets.

9 OZ. DEEP-FRIED BEAN CURD
   PUFFS

3 GARLIC CLOVES, SLICED

1-IN. PIECE FRESH GINGER,
   PEELED AND SLICED

3⅓ CUPS EVERYDAY STOCK (PAGE
   287)

¼ TSP. DARK SOY SAUCE

LIGHT SOY SAUCE AND SALT

1 FRESH RED CHILI, THINLY
   SLICED

5 SCALLIONS OR GREEN GARLIC
   LEAVES, CUT INTO
   1½-IN. LENGTHS

1 TSP. POTATO FLOUR MIXED
   WITH 2 TSP. COLD WATER

3 TBSP. LARD OR PEANUT OIL
   FOR COOKING

1. Cut the bean curd puffs in half to expose their spongelike interiors, which will encourage them to absorb the flavors of the sauce; set aside.

2. Heat the wok over a high flame until smoke rises, then add the lard or peanut oil and swirl around. Add the garlic and ginger and stir-fry briefly until fragrant. Add the stock and bring to a boil.

3. Add the dark soy sauce and the bean curd puffs and season with light soy sauce and salt to taste. Reduce the heat and simmer gently for a good 5–10 minutes to *ru wei* ("let the flavors enter"). Add the fresh chili and scallions, allow to barely cook, and thicken with the potato flour mixture. Serve.

★ THE FATHER OF HUNANESE GASTRONOMY: TAN YANKAI

Tan Yankai (1879–1930) was a highly educated scholar-official who began his political career in the dying days of the Qing dynasty, rose through the ranks of the revolutionary Nationalist Party, and in 1928 became president of the Executive Yuan, a position equivalent to that of premier. Although his career took him to cities across China, he came from a Hunanese family and served several times as governor of Hunan. The history books remember Tan mainly for his political and military activities, but in culinary circles he is regarded as the father of modern Hunanese haute cuisine.

Like many high-ranking men of his day, Tan Yankai employed a private chef in his official residence. The delicacy and refinement of the food he served at his dinner parties was legendary. His personal chef, Cao Jingchen, was a master of his craft, and Tan himself also played a crucial part in the development of dishes, issuing instructions and offering detailed criticisms of the final results. (He had a famously discriminating palate.) Local food-writer Liu Guochu recounts how Tan gave his chef meticulous instructions for making a thick fish soup. He told Cao to suspend some crucian carp over a clay pot of simmering chicken stock. As the fish cooked gently in the steam, their flesh fell off the bones and into the soup, where they added an unbelievable richness of flavor.

Tan's kitchen was by all accounts a hothouse of culinary innovation. The dishes he and Cao created had Hunanese roots, but incorporated influences from eastern Huaiyang cuisine, southern Cantonese cuisine, and other schools including those of Zhejiang, Qingdao, Tianjin, and Shanghai. Many of them relied on extravagant ingredients, such as shark's fin, dried scallops, and Yunnan ham. Some of their most celebrated creations have entered the canon of classical Hunanese cuisine, including Zu'an shark's fin, Zu'an bean curd, and Zu'an sliced bamboo shoots, all named after Tan Yankai's *nom de plume*, Zu'an. They and other dishes were so influential that some even talked of a new culinary style, Zu'an cuisine.

Food writer Liu Guochu transcribes the menu from a "suckling pig and shark's fin banquet" held by Tan Yankai in his book on Hunanese cuisine. It begins with four cold dishes (including slivered wild mushrooms and crisp gingko nuts) and four hot dishes (including abalone and "golden-thread chicken cakes"), progresses through eight "great dishes" (including Zu'an shark's fin, deer tendons in lamb soup, and Chinese yam with yellow lump sugar) on the way to the main feast dish, a barbecued suckling pig, and then concludes with four "follow dishes" (including braised *choy sam* and steamed eggs with shrimp).

After his years of service in Tan Yankai's household, Chef Cao opened his own restaurant, the Jianleyuan, in Changsha. There, he continued to cook the dishes he had developed in his master's kitchen for a wealthy and discerning clientele. His successor as chef in the household of Tan Yankai, a man named Tan Xiting, later went on to open the Yuloudong restaurant in Changsha, a place that has survived (with a brief hiatus in the 1980s) to the present day.

CLAY-POT BEAN CURD
sha guo dou fu

The following is a kind, gentle dish, a soup of pale bean curd, dark shiitake, and leafy greens. The bean curd is lovely if fried golden as in the recipe, but you can equally well add it directly to the pot, in which case, it's best to refresh it first by blanching in boiling, salted water.

The clay pot (literally "sand-pot") is a rough earthenware vessel with a lid, glazed only on the inside, which you can find in good Chinese stores. It should be heated very gently at first, over a very low flame or on a diffuser, and before using a new pot for the first time, it should be immersed in water overnight —this, apparently, seals it. The clay is supposed to make food cooked in it especially delicious. In Hunan, the clay pot is usually placed on a tabletop burner, where it bubbles away during the meal— another variation on the popular hotpot theme.

3 DRIED SHIITAKE MUSHROOMS

1 HEAPED TBSP. DRIED SHRIMP

1¼ LB. FIRM BEAN CURD, DRAINED
    (ABOUT 1¼ BLOCKS)

2 OZ. WINTER BAMBOO SHOOT

3½ OZ. UNSMOKED SLAB BACON
    OR LEAN BONELESS PORK

3 OZ. BABY BOK CHOY

1 QT. EVERYDAY STOCK (PAGE
    287)

SALT AND WHITE PEPPER

3 TBSP. PEANUT OIL OR LARD
    FOR COOKING

VEGETARIAN VERSION
Vegetarians can omit the pork (and the shrimp, if necessary), using a vegetarian stock (page 287) and increasing the quantity of shiitakes to enhance the *umami* flavors of the dish.

1. Leave the shiitake and dried shrimp to soak in hot water from the kettle for about 30 minutes. Meanwhile, cut the bean curd into oblong slices, about ½ inch thick. Cut the bamboo shoot into thin slices, then slice the bacon or pork. Trim and wash the bok choy.

2. Heat the wok over a high flame until smoke rises, then add the peanut oil or lard and swirl around. Lay the bean curd pieces in a single layer on the hot metal surface and fry, turning once, until slightly golden on both sides. You might need to do them in a couple of batches.

3. When the bean curd is golden, add the mushrooms and the shrimp to the wok with their soaking water, the pork, the bamboo shoot, and the stock. Bring to a boil, add salt to taste and then transfer to a preheated clay pot.

4. Simmer over a gentle heat for about 30 minutes, until the bean curd is puffy and has absorbed some of the flavors of the soup.

5. At this point, add the bok choy and continue to simmer until just tender. Adjust the seasoning, adding pepper to taste, and serve in the pot. If you have a tabletop burner, place the pot on the table as soon as you've added the bok choy, and let it cook at the table.

POCK-MARKED WOMAN'S BEAN CURD
ma po dou fu

This is originally a Sichuanese dish, named after a smallpox-scarred woman who ran a restaurant in the north of the provincial capital, Chengdu, and was renowned for her spectacular braised bean curd. The dish is so popular that it has migrated to other parts of the country. This version comes from the northern Hunanese city of Yueyang. It uses the same cooking method as the original, but substitutes pork for the traditional beef, and adds shiitake mushrooms and the quintessentially Hunanese chopped salted chiles.

3 OZ. GROUND PORK

½ TSP. DARK SOY SAUCE

2 TSP. SHAOXING WINE

1¼ LB. FIRM BEAN CURD, DRAINED
(ABOUT 1¼ BLOCKS)

1 TSP. FINELY CHOPPED GARLIC

2 SOAKED, DRAINED, AND
SQUEEZED DRIED SHIITAKE
MUSHROOMS, FINELY CHOPPED
WITH THE STEMS DISCARDED

1 TBSP. CHOPPED SALTED CHILES

1 TBSP. CHILI BEAN PASTE

1 TSP. DRIED CHILI FLAKES

1 POINTY FRESH RED CHILI,
SLICED

⅔ CUP EVERYDAY STOCK (PAGE
287) OR WATER

1 TSP. POTATO FLOUR MIXED
WITH 1 TBSP. COLD WATER

3 SCALLIONS, GREEN PARTS
ONLY, FINELY SLICED

1 TSP. SESAME OIL

½ TSP. GROUND ROASTED
SICHUAN PEPPER (PAGE 28)

3 TBSP. PEANUT OIL FOR
COOKING

1. Place the pork in a bowl, add the dark soy sauce and Shaoxing wine, and mix well; set aside. Cut the bean curd into bite-size cubes and refresh for a few minutes in a saucepan of simmering lightly salted water over a gentle heat; drain and set aside.

2. Heat the wok over a high flame until smoke rises, then add the peanut oil and swirl around. Add the pork and stir-fry until it has broken up and changed color. Add the garlic, mushrooms, salted chiles, and chili bean paste and stir-fry until fragrant. Add the chili flakes and fresh chili and stir a few times more.

3. Add the bean curd to the wok along with the stock or water and bring to a boil. Reduce the heat and simmer for 5–10 minutes until the bean curd has absorbed the flavors of the sauce.

4. Turn up the heat and add just enough of the potato flour mixture to thicken the sauce to a gravylike consistency. Throw in the scallion greens, stir a few times, and then, off the heat, add the sesame oil. Spoon into a deep bowl and serve with a scattering of ground roasted Sichuan pepper.

6

VEGETABLE
DISHES

植物類

★ VEGETABLE DISHES

In ancient China, the rich were known as "meat-eaters" (*rou shi zhe*), and eating meat remains a minor mark of wealth. For despite the prominence of meat and fish in most famous Chinese dishes, the majority of the Chinese population has lived, for most of the country's history, on a largely vegetarian diet. Within recent memory, in the hard years of the 1960s and 70s, people were so deprived of meat that many tell me they actually dreamed and fantasized about it. These days, although meat is widely available and even the rural poor eat more than they used to, most people exist on a daily diet based on grains, legumes, and vegetables. And, especially in the south of China, with its warm and hospitable climate, the variety of vegetables eaten and the ingenuity with which they are cooked is amazing.

Above: DRIED RADISHES, YUEYANG COUNTY

In Hunan province, with its fertile soil and plentiful rain, the markets abound with fresh, seasonal produce. There are glorious greens: water spinach, with its snaking, hollow stems; trembling bunches of purple amaranth; bold hearts of bok choy; crisp Chinese leaf cabbages; and "winter-cold vegetable" (*dong han cai*), with rounded, fleshy leaves that are pleasantly silken and juicy when eaten in soup. The Hunanese, like their neighbors in Sichuan, also make great use of one of the vegetables I miss most when I am away from China, a swollen lettuce stem (*wo sun*), whose jade-green flesh has a most delicate taste and a delightful texture.

At the start of the year, the juicy young "red" or "white" hearts of a variety of baby cabbage (*hong cai tai, bai cai tai*) appear in the markets for a brief, delicious season, during which they are eaten at almost every meal. The "red" ones have deep purple stems, dark green leaves, and brilliant yellow flowers, and are magnificent stir-fried with a little dried chili and a dash of brown vinegar. (Their purple stems stain the cooking juices a startling cornflower blue.) The "white" ones have lighter green leaves and yellow flowers, and a sweet taste enlivened by just a hint of bitterness.

Fresh, pungent vegetables related to garlic and onion are ubiquitous in Hunanese cooking. Green garlic leaves (*da suan*), garlic stems (*suan miao*), and Chinese chives, fresh and green or blanched hothouse-yellow, serve as accompaniments to meat, poultry, or other vegetable ingredients. Buddhist and Daoist monks traditionally avoid such vegetables on account of their pungency, which some say is a distraction from meditation, and others swear has the ability to stir up the carnal passions.

Beans are dried and made into starchy jellies and pastas, but are also eaten fresh. Many gourds feature in the local diet, including the giant winter melon, its dark-green skin frosted with white. The most important root vegetable is perhaps the white Asian radish (*luo bu*), often known in the West by its Japanese name, *daikon*, which has been grown in China since the ancient past. Eaten fresh in soups, salads, and stir-fries, it is also sun-dried or pickled as a winter preserve.

Of the New World crops that transformed Chinese agriculture during the late Ming and early Qing dynasties, chiles and peppers of various kinds are eaten as vegetables, while sweet potatoes are made into a kind of translucent starch jelly (*hong shu fen*), delicious stir-fried with chili and garlic. Regular potatoes, so familiar in the West, play only a minor role in Hunanese cooking, and are usually stir-fried and eaten when barely cooked and still crunchy.

Bamboo shoot is another common vegetable, highly nutritious and especially prominent in vegetarian cooking. The bamboo plant itself is one of the loveliest and most distinctive features of the southern Chinese landscape, its smooth, upright trunks contrasting with quivering, plumelike leaves. The edible part of the plant is the tender shoots that grow out of the mulch of old leaves in a bamboo grove. Some are as slender as pencils, others weigh several pounds. Various types of bamboo shoot are eaten; one of the best is the "hairy bamboo shoot" (*mao sun*), also known as "cat's head," named for the downy hairs that cover its papery sheath. It can be eaten in spring, but is at its finest in winter, when its plump shoots have not yet emerged from the ground.

Different areas of Hunan province are known for their local produce. In the lake-city of Yueyang, market stalls are piled high with the strange, segmented stems of the lotus root, and, in the appropriate seasons, the same plant's spearlike stems, supple leaves, and fresh juicy seeds. Yueyang is also known for an exotic wild vegetable that is traditionally harvested for only two months a year, *lou hao* (or *ni hao* in Hunan dialect). A kind of artemisia, its deep-green, segmented stems have a

Right: FRESH LOTUS SEED PODS

juicy texture somewhat reminiscent of samphire, a strange, herbal taste, and an almost pinelike fragrance. It is usually stir-fried with aromatic smoked bacon and a little chili. So seasonal is this delicacy that a local rhyme says after the second month of the year it has grown so tough it's only good for fodder or firewood (*yi yue ti, er yue hao, san yue si yue zuo chai shao*).

Above: PICKLED CHILES, CHANGSHA

For China's modern "meat-eaters," the thrill of eating meat is wearing a little thin, as China starts to face the consequences of dietary excess that are so familiar in the West. People talk of the historical progression from "eating your fill" (*chi bao*), the main concern of the past, through "eating well" (*chi hao*), which refers to the nouveau riche habit of guzzling lots of rich, meaty food, to "eating skilfully" (*chi qiao*), describing the emerging demand for food that is healthy, elegant, and environmentally sustainable. So while Chinese peasants flock to the cities to earn enough to eat meat, the urban middle classes flock to the countryside to eat wild ferns and homegrown cabbage.

Wild vegetables are becoming increasingly popular with educated city-dwellers. For the rural poor, they just recall the sorrows of the famine years. The father of my friend Fan Qun, for example, has an encyclopedic knowledge of everything edible that grows in the hills and valleys around his home, but few of them now feature on the family dinner table. Now that times are better, many of these wild foods, like the fiddlehead fern (*jue cai*), are neglected by those who live among them, and sold instead to dealers serving city restaurants.

Most Chinese cookbooks, both in China and the West, emphasize recipes for meat, poultry, and expensive seafood, to the neglect of more humble, vegetarian ingredients. On overseas Chinese restaurant menus, too, you'll find scant attention paid to vegetables beyond the offering of a "monk's vegetable" mixture of bamboo shoots and water chestnuts, or a "seasonal vegetable" that is usually bok choy. Yet, simple, everyday vegetable dishes are one of the great, unsung joys of Chinese cooking: delicious, colorful, easy to prepare, and rich in nutrition. I've deliberately included a good selection of them in this book, partly because I love them so much myself, and partly because most of them are so easy to make they take much of the strain out of cooking a Chinese meal.

Many of the recipes use produce you can find in a normal supermarket; others will require a trip to Chinatown. I've also included a few made with more unusual vegetables that I've found from time to time in Chinese stores in London, where the selection of fresh foods available is growing all the time. If you are cooking for vegetarians, most of the recipes that include small amounts of meat can be adapted by its simple omission; look out also for vegetarian versions of many of the recipes in other chapters of this book.

STIR-FRIED VEGETABLES
SOUNDING RADISH SLIVERS
xiang luo bu si

The unusual name of this traditional dish refers to the delicious crunchy sound the salted and barely cooked radish slivers make when you bite them. It's amazingly simple to make, but delightful in the mouth and on the palate. The silky, yet crisp, strands of radish, threaded with wisps of green and red, have a gentle, refreshing sourness. I owe this recipe to Tong Huiru, my friend Sansan's mother. The addition of potato flour at the end to give the slivers a silky gloss is a restaurant method: feel free to omit this step for a simpler home-cooked dish.

1 LB. ASIAN WHITE RADISH
   (DAIKON)

SALT

1 FRESH RED CHILI

2 SCALLIONS, GREEN PARTS
   ONLY

1 TSP. LIGHT SOY SAUCE

1½ TSP. CLEAR RICE VINEGAR

¾ TSP. POTATO FLOUR MIXED
   WITH 2 TBSP. COLD WATER
   (OPTIONAL)

1 TSP. SESAME OIL

3 TBSP. PEANUT OIL OR LARD
   FOR COOKING

1. Peel the radish and cut into 2½-inch sections. Cut each section first into very thin slices, and then into fine slivers (a mandolin will make this easier). Combine with ¾ teaspoon salt, then set aside for 15 minutes or so.

2. Discard the stem and seeds of the chili, and cut into fine slivers to match the radish. Cut the scallion greens into similar slivers.

3. Before cooking, drain the radish slivers and squeeze dry; set aside.

4. Heat the wok over a high flame until smoke rises, then add the oil or lard and swirl around. Add the chili and sizzle for a few seconds before adding the radish slivers. Stir-fry vigorously for a couple of minutes, adding the soy sauce and salt to taste, if necessary.

5. When the radish slivers are hot, add the scallions and vinegar and stir well to combine. Then add the potato flour mixture to the middle of the wok, stirring rapidly as it thickens to a gloss. Finally, remove the wok from the heat, stir in the sesame oil, and serve.

STIR-FRIED GREEN PEPPERS WITH GROUND PORK AND PRESERVED GREENS
qing jiao suan cai rou ni

青椒酸菜肉泥

One of the curiosities about the revolutionary generation in China is that many of them were given revolutionary names by parents fired up with revolutionary zeal (or perhaps just revolutionary political correctness). In one restaurant kitchen where I spent many days, the head chef was called "Innovation" Xia—he was born in 1967, just a year into the Cultural Revolution. Among his colleagues was a man whose grandfather, a famous anti-Japanese fighter, had given him the name "Red Army" Tong in a fit of patriotism, and a woman called, incredibly, "Cultural Revolution" Lin, who had been renamed by her schoolteacher during a political campaign.

The following is a simple, but delicious, dish I ate with this revolutionary crew after their midday shift. It is a typical example of the kind of home-style food that is good for "sending the rice down" (*xia fan*), because it is well-salted and intensely flavored.

9 OZ. GREEN BELL PEPPERS

7½ TBSP. PRESERVED MUSTARD GREENS (ABOUT 3 OZ.)

3 OZ. MINCED PORK

1 TSP. SHAOXING WINE

SALT

1 TSP. FINELY CHOPPED GARLIC

½ TSP. DRIED CHILI FLAKES

3 TBSP. PEANUT OIL OR LARD FOR COOKING

VEGETARIAN VERSION
Simply omit the pork and stir-fry the peppers with the preserved mustard greens, adjusting the seasonings to taste.

1. Discard the stems and seeds of the peppers and cut, first into ½-inch strips, then into small dice. Give the preserved mustard greens a thorough rinse to get rid of excess saltiness, then squeeze dry; set aside.

2. Return the wok to a medium flame with just a smear of oil. Add the peppers and stir-fry for a few minutes until they have lost some of their water content and start to smell dry and fragrant; set aside.

3. Return the wok to a high flame with the remaining oil or lard. Add the pork and stir-fry until it has changed color and lost some of its water content, adding the Shaoxing wine and a little salt. Add the garlic and preserved vegetable and stir-fry until fragrant. Scatter in the chili toward the end of this time. Return the pork and peppers to the wok and stir-fry for a little while, until all the ingredients smell delicious. Season with salt to taste, if necessary, although you probably won't need any as the preserved vegetable will remain very salty. Serve.

STIR-FRIED PEPPERS WITH BLACK BEANS AND GARLIC
dou chi chao la jiao

It was a gloriously sunny May Day holiday, and we drove out of town to the farmhouse of Wang Junqi. The children pottered around near the pond, while the rest of us chatted, drank endless tea, drew pictures of each other, and played mah jong. Toward lunchtime, we prepared a meal together. I sat on the steps shelling peas, a job that I've loved since childhood, while Mr. Wang chopped up a duck and a fish in the kitchen. We brought the dishes out one by one, and laid them on a large round table in the yard. There were stir-fried paddy eels with garlic stems; braised duck with beer and spices; pork slivers with flowering chives; stir-fried peas; salty duck eggs; steamed bacon with black beans and chili; stir-fried water spinach; red chiles with black beans and garlic; stir-fried amaranth leaves; smoked bean curd with green chiles; fish-fragrant eggplant; dry-fried green beans (the latter two were Sichuanese interlopers made by me); and a whole grass carp stewed and served in a clay pot. About eighteen of us sat around the table to lunch, and later, dinner, and we drove back to Changsha after nightfall, filled with light and laughter.

This is just one of the recipes Mr. Wang made for lunch. You can use either red or green bell peppers, or a mix of both.

1 RED AND 1 GREEN BELL PEPPER

3 GARLIC CLOVES, THINLY SLICED

1 TBSP. BLACK FERMENTED
    BEANS, RINSED

½ TSP. CLEAR RICE VINEGAR

SALT

2 TBSP. EVERYDAY STOCK (PAGE
    287) OR WATER

1 TSP. SESAME OIL

1 TBSP. PEANUT OIL FOR
    COOKING

1. Cut the bell peppers in half, discard the seeds and stems and cut into large squares.

2. Heat the oil in the wok over a medium flame. Add the peppers and stir-fry for 5–6 minutes, until they are tender and their skins puckered and a little golden. (You can deep-fry them, if you wish, for speed.) Remove the peppers with a slotted spoon and set aside.

3. Return the wok to a high flame. Add the garlic and black beans and stir-fry until fragrant. Return the peppers to the wok and season with the vinegar and salt to taste. When everything is sizzling and delicious, stir in the stock or water, and then, off the heat, the sesame oil. Serve.

POUNDED EGGPLANTS WITH GREEN PEPPERS
qing jiao lei qie zi

The exact geographical origins of the eggplant are lost in the mists of history. It is generally believed to be of Indian origin, although the earliest surviving written reference to it is in the *Essential Skills for the Life of the Common People (qi min yao shu)*, a sixth-century Chinese agricultural treatise. Curiously, one is occasionally asked to say "eggplant" while posing for a photograph in China—because *qie zi* sounds a little like "cheese."

Chinese eggplants tend to be long and thin, a pale purple in color. They have delicate flesh and thin skins, so they are not usually peeled. You can sometimes find them in Asian supermarkets, but the more common, dark-skinned Mediterranean type can also be used in Chinese recipes.

Eggplants and green bell peppers are a particularly happy combination in cooking. The two are stir-fried together in many parts of China, and are a regular feature of meals cooked by my friend Fan Qun's mother in their farmhouse in northern Hunan. I am an eggplant addict, and I love the following simple, home-style version of this dish, in which the eggplants are cooked slowly and then pounded or mashed (*lei*) into a delicious sludge, enlivened by the robust flavor of the peppers.

1 LB. EGGPLANTS

SALT

5 OZ. GREEN BELL PEPPER, THIN-
SKINNED IF POSSIBLE

LIGHT SOY SAUCE

4 TBSP. PEANUT OIL FOR
COOKING

1. Peel the eggplants and slice thickly. Sprinkle with salt, toss to coat evenly, and then set aside for 30 minutes.

2. Meanwhile, cut the pepper in half, discard the seeds and stem and thinly slice; set aside.

3. When the eggplants are ready, rinse them to get rid of excess salt, and shake dry; set aside.

4. Stir-fry the peppers in a dry wok over a medium flame until soft and fragrant, pressing them against the sides of the wok; set aside.

5. Heat the oil in a wok over a medium flame. Add the eggplants and stir-fry for a good 10 minutes or so, until they are very tender but not colored. As they soften, mash them up with a wok scoop, until you have a sludgy paste that is about half the volume of the original eggplant slices.

6. Add the bell peppers and stir-fry until both ingredients are fragrant and well-mixed, seasoning with a little soy sauce to taste. Serve.

STIR-FRIED LOTUS ROOT SLICES
chao ou pian

炒
藕
片

Hunan is a water province, threaded by rivers and streams that flow toward the Dengting Lake, and the lotus is one of its most favored water vegetables. This versatile plant emerges from the mud at the bottom of ponds and lakes, spreads its leaves like a carpet over the water's surface, and sends its delicate flowers into the air. The ethereal purity of its blooms, despite their mucky origins, have made the lotus an important symbol of Buddhism, and one seventeenth-century Chinese herbal suggests that the plant might be called "root of the soul" (*ling gen*).

The Chinese make culinary use of almost every part of the lotus. Its seeds are used in tonic soups and sweetmeats, its leaves wrap meat and fish for steaming, and its stems and roots (or, strictly speaking, rhizomes) are added to stir-fries and soups. I've even eaten lotus petals, served like the most delicate tempura, in the dining room of the radical Sichuanese chef Yu Bo.

When you buy lotus root, it has a weird appearance, with pale brown, bulbous sections linked together like a string of sausages. But peel and slice it, and you'll end up with circles ornamented with a delicate pattern of holes. Lotus root cooking has ancient origins in China: one of the magnificent lacquerware vessels unearthed in the Han dynasty tombs at Mawangdui, just outside Changsha, was a tripod in which floated many lotus root slices, still intact after more than 2,000 years.

continued on the next page

There are two main types of lotus root, which have different culinary uses. The first, which seems to be more often available in my local Chinatown, is known in Hunan as "lake lotus" (*hu'ou*). When you break it, fine strands of fiber will appear as you pull the pieces apart. Cooked, it acquires a pinkish tinge, and has a crisp, yet slightly starchy, texture. This variety is most suitable for cooking in soups, like the one on page 245. The other type, known as "sweet lotus'" (*tian'ou*) or "vegetable lotus" (*cai'ou*), has more delicate, crisper flesh, and is white with a pale purplish tinge after cooking. This variety is wonderful in stir-fries, as in the recipe below. Lotus stems, a spring delicacy in Yueyang, can be cooked in a similar way, although I've never seen them sold fresh in a Chinese store in the West. They are about half an inch in diameter and threaded with the same lacy pattern of holes, so they look lovely cut on the slant.

13 OZ. LOTUS ROOT (ABOUT 2
SECTIONS)

SALT

2 TSP. CHOPPED SALTED CHILES
OR FINELY CHOPPED FRESH
RED CHILI

2 TSP. CLEAR RICE VINEGAR

2 TSP. WHITE SUGAR

2 SCALLIONS, GREEN PARTS
ONLY, THINLY SLICED

1 TSP. SESAME OIL

3 TBSP. PEANUT OIL FOR
COOKING

1. Break apart the sections of lotus root and peel them (you can use a potato peeler for this), then slice thinly, discarding the knobby bits at each end of each section; set aside in a bowlful of lightly salted water.

2. When you are ready to cook, shake the lotus slices dry and set aside. Heat the wok over a high flame until smoke rises, then add the oil and swirl around. Add the chiles and sizzle briefly until fragrant. Add the lotus slices and stir-fry, adding the vinegar, sugar, and salt to taste as you go. When the lotus slices lose their flouriness but remain delectably crisp, add the scallion greens and stir once or twice. Remove the wok from the heat, stir in the sesame oil, and serve.

POTATO SLIVERS WITH VINEGAR
cu liu tu dou si

醋熘土豆絲

One late night Liu Wei took Xiaorong and me to visit an eighty-one-year-old monk in a local Buddhist monastery. He welcomed us into his study, a large room lined with bookcases and dominated by an enormous golden statue of the Buddha, and offered us tea. It was hard to believe he was in his eighties, so robust and fit he seemed in mind and body, and we all felt soothed by his kind and gentle presence. As we drank our tea, he told us of the importance of diet in maintaining a healthy mind and body, reminding us of the old Chinese maxim "sickness enters through the mouth" (*bing cong kou ru*). He had been vegetarian since the age of nineteen, when he entered a monastery, and also avoided the pungent vegetables in the garlic family that are regarded as unclean by many practicing Buddhists. He explained to us a few simple vegetarian recipes, and said that he often used ginger "to disperse cold," and vinegar to soften his joints and ward off rheumatism.

In the following recipe, very finely cut potatoes are blanched and then bathed in vinegar, which gives the crunchy slivers a gentle and appetizing sourness. It's an unusual way of eating potatoes for Westerners, used to seeing the potato as a starchy staple food. In southern China, the potato is just another vegetable, to be eaten as an accompaniment to rice. In restaurants, they tend to add a mixture of starch and cold water at the end to give the potatoes a silky gloss, but home cooks usually omit this step.

2 LARGE POTATOES (ABOUT 1 LB.)

SALT

¼ RED BELL PEPPER, OR 1 OR 2 FRESH LONG RED CHILES

3 SCALLIONS, GREEN PARTS ONLY

3 TBSP. CLEAR RICE VINEGAR

3 TBSP. PEANUT OIL FOR COOKING

1. Bring a large saucepan of water to a boil.

2. Meanwhile, peel the potatoes, and cut them into the thinnest possible slices, then cut the slices into very fine slivers. Soak the finished slivers in lightly salted cold water as you work. Cut the bell pepper and scallion greens into very fine slivers; set aside.

3. When the water has boiled, add the drained potatoes and blanch just until the water returns to a boil; drain and set aside.

4. Heat the wok over a high flame until smoke rises, then add the oil and swirl around. Add the potatoes and red pepper slivers and stir-fry for a couple of minutes. Add the vinegar and salt to taste and continue to stir-fry for a short time until the potatoes are cooked, but still a little crunchy.

5. Add the scallion slivers, toss a few times until you can smell their fragrance, and then serve.

FRIED CUCUMBER WITH PURPLE PERILLA
zi su jian huang gua

This is a truly extraordinary way of cooking cucumber, which brings out a most unexpected side to the vegetable. It is sizzled in oil with garlic and chili, seasoned with soy sauce and vinegar, and then scattered with leaves of purple perilla. The cucumber is both fragrant and juicily tender, and the perilla gives it a delightful sour herbiness. If you can't find perilla, the dish will work without it, but the herb lifts it into another culinary dimension. Because perilla is difficult to find, I have also tried this recipe using Thai sweet basil as a substitute—its flavor is different, but in some way akin to perilla, and the dish is magnificent. Although this is cooked in a wok, it is not strictly a stir-fry: the cucumber pieces are colored by laying them more-or-less flat against the surface of the wok, a method known in Chinese as *jian* (pan-fry), rather than *chao* (stir-fry).

1 CUCUMBER

1 FRESH RED CHILI, SEEDED AND
   FINELY CHOPPED

2 TSP. FINELY CHOPPED GARLIC

1½ TSP. LIGHT SOY SAUCE

1 TSP. CLEAR RICE VINEGAR

A SMALL HANDFUL PURPLE
   PERILLA LEAVES, FINELY
   CHOPPED

1 TSP. SESAME OIL

3 TBSP. PEANUT OIL OR LARD
   FOR COOKING

1. Cut the cucumber in half lengthwise, and then, with the knife at an angle, cut each half into slanted, almost semicircular slices about ¼ inch thick.

2. Heat the wok over a high flame until smoke rises, then add the oil or lard and swirl around. Add the cucumber and fry for a few minutes until the slices are tinged a little golden. Spread the slices out so they cover as much as possible of the bottom of the wok, turning from time to time.

3. Add the chili and garlic to the wok and stir-fry until fragrant, adding the soy sauce as you go. Splash the vinegar around the side of the wok and mix well. Add the perilla and stir a few times. Then, off the heat, stir in the sesame oil and serve.

STIR-FRIED BITTER MELON WITH CHINESE CHIVES
jiu cai chao ku gua

韭菜炒苦瓜

By a series of strange coincidences, within twenty-four hours of arriving in Mao Zedong's home village, Shaoshan, I was invited out to lunch by his nephew Mao Anping, now an official in the local government. Mao the younger is a laid-back, affable, chain-smoking sixty-year-old who is blasé about the attention paid to him as one of the Chairman's closest surviving relatives. He brushes aside any suggestion that he looks like his legendary uncle, but, seen in profile or from behind, the resemblance is quite unnerving. We lunched on local specialties that included Mao Zedong's own favorites, peasant dishes now smartened up for a tourist clientele: among them, naturally, was the Shaoshan dish de rigueur, a plateful of rich, fatty, aromatic red-braised pork (see page 78). While we ate, Mao Anping confessed that he was a dab hand at cooking himself, and loved most of all a meal of rice, soup, and simple stir-fried vegetables. This is his recipe for bitter melon, a fresh and radiant stir-fry of jade-green melon, dark green chives, and brilliant scarlet chili.

Bitter melon, a light green vegetable with a tightly gnarled skin, is commonly available in Chinese and Indian food stores. Its bitter flesh is an acquired taste, but it's thought to be excellent for cooling the body during the humid heat of summer. In Hunan, it is most commonly stir-fried, although it can also be sun-dried and mixed with purple perilla, and eaten as a snack.

1 BITTER MELON (ABOUT 1 LB.)

SALT

2 FRESH RED CHILES, SEEDED
   AND FINELY CHOPPED

3 OZ. CHINESE CHIVES

1 TSP. SESAME OIL

3 TBSP. PEANUT OIL OR LARD
   FOR COOKING

1. Wash the bitter melon and cut into 2-inch sections. Cut these in half and scrape out the seeds and pithy center. Then cut lengthwise into thin rectangular slices. Sprinkle with the salt and then scrunch the salt in with your fingers. Set the melon slices aside for about 20 minutes to drain out some of the bitterness.

2. Rinse the melon slices to remove the salt, then shake them dry.

3. Heat the wok over a high flame until smoke rises, then add the oil or lard and swirl around. Add the chiles and sizzle briefly until fragrant. Add the sliced melon and stir-fry for 2–3 minutes until almost tender and fragrant.

4. Add the chives and stir-fry vigorously for another minute or so until barely cooked, adding salt to taste as you stir. Finally, off the heat, stir in the sesame oil and serve.

STIR-FRIED FAVA BEANS WITH CHINESE CHIVES
jiu cai can dou

Fava beans have many intriguing names in Chinese. The Sichuanese call them *hu dou* ("foreign" or "barbarian" beans), because they are one of the crops said to have been brought back from the barbarian West by the envoy Zhang Qian in the Han dynasty, some 2,000 years ago. Other names include Buddha beans (*fo dou*), Arhat beans (*luo han dou*), fairy beans (*xian dou*), and even king's grave beans (*wang mu dou*)—the latter on account of some especially fine beans that grew at the side of ancient imperial graves near Hangzhou. Interestingly, these names echo a long-standing association between the fava bean and the spirit world in Western cultures, which the *Oxford Companion to Food* suggests might have grown out of their mysterious tendency to cause wind, and to provoke the disease of favism in susceptible people. Their most common Chinese name is less esoteric: they are simply known as "silkworm beans" (*can dou*), as their pods are thought to resemble silkworms.

The following recipe is for a vibrant and most pleasing spring stir-fry of tender fava beans and pungent chives, which I learned to make at the Everyone Restaurant (*ren ren cai guan*) in Yueyang. Both the beans and the chives should be sparklingly young and fresh to make the most of this dish.

3 OZ. FRESH CHINESE CHIVES

1½ CUPS SHELLED FAVA BEANS
(ABOUT 1¾ LB. IN THE POD)

2 TSP. CHOPPED SALTED CHILES
OR FINELY CHOPPED FRESH
RED CHILI

2 TSP. FINELY CHOPPED FRESH
GINGER

SALT

2 TBSP. PEANUT OIL FOR
COOKING

1. Wash and trim the chives, then cut the green parts into 1¼-inch pieces; set aside.

2. Blanch the beans in boiling water for about one minute, until barely cooked, drain and set aside.

3. Heat the wok over a high flame until smoke rises, then add the oil and swirl around. Add the chiles and ginger and stir-fry briefly until fragrant. Add the beans and stir-fry until hot and sizzly, adding salt to taste (you might not need extra salt if you are using the salted chiles). Throw in the chives and stir-fry a little while longer until they are just tender. Serve immediately.

STIR-FRIED FAVA BEANS WITH MINCED PORK
can dou chao rou ni

蚕
豆
炒
肉
泥

In China, dried legumes are made into all kinds of sweetmeats, porridges, starches, and jellies, but they are also eaten fresh as seasonal vegetables. Young French beans (*si ji dou*) and yard-long beans (*dou jiao)* are stir-fried in their pods. Mung beans and dried soybeans are sprouted and then stir-fried. Fresh green soybeans (*qing pi dou*) have a particularly lovely, vibrant color, and are delicious not only boiled and squeezed out of their pods as a snack, but also stir-fried with a splash of chili. And in this recipe, young fava beans are wok-cooked with a smattering of spices and tasty cooked pork, or salted mustard greens if you are vegetarian.

1½ CUPS SHELLED FAVA BEANS
    (ABOUT 1¾ LB. IN THE POD)
2 LONG RED FRESH CHILES, CUT
    CROSSWISE INTO THIN SLICES
2 GARLIC CLOVES, SLICED
3 OZ. GROUND PORK
1 TSP. SHAOXING WINE
1 TSP. LIGHT SOY SAUCE
SALT
½ TSP. DRIED CHILI FLAKES
    (OPTIONAL)
1 TSP. SESAME OIL
3 TBSP. PEANUT OIL FOR
    COOKING

1. Heat the wok over a high flame until smoke rises, then add 2 tablespoons of the oil and swirl around. Add the beans and stir-fry for 1–2 minutes, until just tender; set aside.

2. Return the wok to the heat with the remaining tablespoon of oil. Add the red chiles and garlic and stir-fry briefly until fragrant.

3. Add the pork and continue to stir-fry until it has changed color and lost some of its water content, splashing the Shaoxing wine around the edge of the wok and seasoning with the soy sauce and salt to taste. Add the chili flakes, if using.

4. When the pork is sizzly and delicious, return the beans to the wok and stir-fry briefly to allow the flavors to marry. Remove the wok from the heat, stir in the sesame oil, and serve.

VEGETARIAN VERSIONS
This version is extremely delicious. Simply omit the pork, Shaoxing wine, and soy sauce, and use instead 6 tablespoons (about 2 ounces) well-rinsed and dried preserved mustard greens. Stir-fry the greens with the sliced chili and garlic, then add the chili flakes and fried beans, adding extra salt, if necessary. Finish with sesame oil as in the recipe above.

Peas can be cooked in the same manner, either with pork or with preserved mustard greens.

STIR-FRIED MIXED MUSHROOMS
chao za jun

炒雜菌

A number of varieties of fresh fungi are sold in the markets of Hunan, including white button mushrooms (*mo gu*), shiitake (*xiang gu*), slippery wood ears (*mu'er*), and golden enoki (*jin zhen gu*), and, in the colder months, the saffron milk cap (*han jun*). Other fungi, especially shiitake and a number of expensive varieties known collectively as *ko mo*, are used in their dried form to add rich *umami* flavors to all kinds of dishes. In the following recipe, you can use a selection of the more commonly available fresh fungi, including shiitake, button mushrooms, oyster mushrooms, and enoki, to make this dish, enhancing them if possible with more exotic wild mushrooms.

3 OZ. SMOKED BACON, IN ONE PIECE

1 LB. MIXED MUSHROOMS (SEE INTRODUCTION ABOVE)

2 GARLIC CLOVES, SLICED

AN EQUIVALENT AMOUNT FRESH GINGER, SLICED

DRIED CHILI FLAKES

4 TBSP. EVERYDAY STOCK (PAGE 287)

SALT AND PEPPER

2 SCALLIONS, GREEN PARTS ONLY, FINELY SLIVERED

3 TBSP. PEANUT OIL OR LARD FOR COOKING

1. Steam the bacon over a high flame until cooked through, then cut into slices; set aside.

2. Meanwhile, clean the mushrooms and cut into thickish slices; set aside.

3. Heat the wok over a high flame until smoke rises, then add the oil or lard and swirl around. Add the bacon and stir-fry until fragrant and tinged with gold. Add the garlic and ginger and stir-fry until their aromas have developed, scattering in chili flakes to taste towards the end.

4. Tip all the mushrooms into the wok and stir-fry for a few minutes until they are cooked through and tender. Add the stock and salt to taste, and stir as the liquid evaporates. Finally, season with pepper to taste, garnish with scallions, and serve.

STIR-FRIED ZUCCHINI WITH SALTY DUCK EGG YOLKS
xian dan huang chao xiao nan gua

咸蛋黃炒小南瓜

Salted duck egg yolks are a fabulous ingredient with a rich *umami* taste that enhances the most mundane of vegetable ingredients. You can salt your own (see page 286) or simply buy them in Chinese or Vietnamese groceries. I love the strategy used in the following recipe, which involves precooking a chopped vegetable or a kind of seafood, and then coating it in a sizzly egg-yolk paste. The frizz of yellow egg-yolk morsels has led many restaurants to call such dishes after "golden-sand" (*jin sha*)—so look out for "golden-sand corn" and "golden-sand shrimp" on restaurant menus.

The same basic method can be applied to scrumptious effect in cooking many different foods. Green bell peppers and corn kernels work particularly well, as does bitter melon. Try also shrimp in the shell, cucumber, eggplant, and pumpkin (dust the latter in potato flour), and deep-fry, rather than dry-fry, if you are in a hurry. As I write this I'm thinking asparagus might also be spectacular—one to try.

4 VERY SMALL ZUCCHINI

3 SALTED DUCK EGG YOLKS, COOKED (SEE NOTE BELOW)

SALT

3 TBSP. PEANUT OIL FOR COOKING

1. Trim the zucchini and cut them into even slices about ¼ inch thick. You can cut on an angle into elliptical slices, or cut into sections and then rectangular slices. Chop or mash the cooked egg yolks into fragments; set aside.

2. Heat a wok over a medium flame with just a smear of oil. Add the zucchini and dry-fry for several minutes, until they have lost some of their water content and are floppy and fragrant; set aside.

3. Return the wok to a high flame until smoke rises, then add the remaining oil and swirl around. Add the egg yolks and stir-fry briefly: they will rise up in a marvelous froth. Return the zucchini to the wok and stir-fry until all the pieces are scattered with golden egg yolk, adding salt to taste. Serve.

NOTE

There are two ways of cooking the egg yolks. Either break the eggs, set aside the runny whites and place the yolks, which will be hard and spherical, in a small, heatproof bowl, cover, and then put into a steamer for 10–20 minutes over a high heat until cooked through (the whites can be drizzled into a soup of leafy greens if you don't want to waste them); or hard-boil the eggs, leave to cool, and then remove the yolks. The second method is easiest, but you tend to end up with little bits of egg white sticking to the yolks. Some Chinese supermarkets sell the salted yolks alone, in vacuum packs.

SLENDER BAMBOO SHOOTS WITH GROUND PORK
xiao sun zi chao rou mo

小笋子炒肉末

One splendid spring day, I walked with Fan Qun through the park on the edge of the South Lake in Yueyang. The water glittered with silver in the blazing sunlight, and a strong breeze stirred in the tall camphor trees and feathery bamboo. Fan Qun knew the names and useful properties of many of the plants we saw that day. She pointed out camellia oil seeds, fiddlehead ferns, and a kind of wild raspberry with sour, grapefruit-pink lobes. And we gathered ourselves some bamboo shoots, pencil-thin and tenderly green, which Fan Qun cooked as part of our supper.

One of the delights of living in China is the easy availability of fresh bamboo shoots, and there are several different kinds. The larger shoots are generally cut into slices or slivers, while the slender ones are simply sliced in half to expose their laddered insides, and then cut into pieces. There are various ways of cooking these slender shoots: they can be blanched and served as a salad; steamed with chili and black fermented beans; or stir-fried with the crinkly black leaves of preserved mustard greens. Canned bamboo shoots don't really compare with fresh ones in terms of taste and texture, but my friends loved the following dish, pepped up with pork and spices, which I made in London with some brine-preserved shoots. If you are lucky enough to be cooking near a source of fresh bamboo shoots, look out for slim ones that will be about the thickness of a finger, and twice as long, when dehusked.

14 OZ. PACKAGED OR FRESH
    SLENDER BAMBOO SHOOTS

SALT

2 GARLIC CLOVES, FINELY
    CHOPPED

1 FRESH RED CHILI, SEEDED AND
    FINELY CHOPPED

½ TSP. DRIED CHILI FLAKES

3 OZ. GROUND PORK

1 TSP. SHAOXING WINE

2 TSP. CLEAR RICE VINEGAR

2 TSP. LIGHT SOY SAUCE

3 TBSP. EVERYDAY STOCK (PAGE
    287) OR WATER

3 SCALLIONS, GREEN PARTS
    ONLY, THINLY SLICED

1 TSP. SESAME OIL

3 TBSP. PEANUT OIL OR LARD
    FOR COOKING

1. Cut the bamboo shoots in half lengthwise and then into ½-inch pieces. If you are using fresh shoots, husk them, if necessary, and blanch in boiling water until tender; if you are using packaged shoots, add some salt to boiling water and just blanch to heat through. Refresh the shoots under cold water; set aside.

2. Heat the wok over a medium flame with just a smear of oil or lard. Add the blanched shoots and stir-fry for a few minutes until they are dry and a little fragrant; set aside.

3. Return the wok to a high flame with the remaining oil or lard. Add the garlic and fresh and dried chiles and stir-fry briefly until fragrant. Tip in the pork and continue to stir-fry until it is cooked through and changes color, splashing in the Shaoxing wine as you go and adding salt to taste.

4. Return the bamboo shoots to the wok, and when everything is hot and sizzly, add the vinegar, soy sauce, and more salt to taste. Add the stock or water and stir for 1–2 minutes longer to allow the flavors to penetrate the shoots. Toss in the scallions at the end of the cooking time. Finally, off the heat, stir in the sesame oil and serve.

STIR-FRIED CHINESE LEAF CABBAGE WITH CHOPPED SALTED CHILES
duo jiao chao ya bai

On a slow, sleepy day in Mao Zedong's home village of Shaoshan, I hopped on to the back of a young man's motorbike, and we wound our way up into the hills. The valleys were terraced with rice paddies, intensely green; the higher slopes planted with food crops; and the hilltops thickly wooded with pine. Black mountain goats grazed here and there; scrawny chickens dawdled and pecked. Fish ponds glinted among the fields. After a while, we stopped at an old adobe farmhouse, where an elderly lady invited us in. She gave us homegrown green tea made with water that tasted of charcoal, poured out from a blackened kettle suspended over a dying fire. As we sat, she reminisced about the time in 1957 that she'd seen Chairman Mao, walking through a rapturous crowd on the streets of Shaoshan, trailing clouds of revolutionary glory on one of his rare visits home. Like most inhabitants of Shaoshan, the old lady revered Mao as the man who restored the dignity of the Chinese nation after a century of humiliation. She brushed aside memories of the bitter years of the early 1960s, when his mad economic policies left the people of Shaoshan without any grain to eat, forcing them to go foraging in the hills for wild roots and leaves. But then the people of Shaoshan have much to thank Mao for in the post-reform era: many now make their livings from the revolutionary tourist industry, selling Mao memorabilia and feeding tour groups with the Chairman's favorite dishes.

When we'd finished our tea, the old lady took us for a stroll on her small patch of land, where she was growing soybeans, potatoes, garlic, pumpkins, chives, and cabbages. A cabbage dish, then, in honor of the old lady, her fields, her memories, and her tea.

The Hunanese name for the Chinese leaf cabbage is *ya bai*, "sprout white," and they like to eat it stir-fried with salted chiles, as in the following simple recipe.

1 LB. CHINESE LEAF CABBAGE (A SMALL HEAD, OR ½ A LARGE ONE)

1½ TBSP. CHOPPED SALTED CHILES

SALT (OPTIONAL)

1 TSP. SESAME OIL

3 TBSP. PEANUT OIL OR LARD FOR FRYING

1. Cut the cabbage leaves in half, down the spine, and then chop into large squares; set aside.
2. Heat the wok over a high flame until smoke rises, then add the oil or lard and swirl around. Add the chiles and stir-fry until fragrant. Toss in the cabbage and stir-fry vigorously until just tender, seasoning with extra salt, if necessary. Off the heat, stir in the sesame oil and serve.

HAND-TORN CABBAGE WITH VINEGAR
shou si bao cai

手撕包菜

The Cultural Revolution was not only a time of infamously bad food, but also of bizarre displays of political correctness in every aspect of life. One of my teachers recalls lining up for lunch in a work-unit canteen, where you had to recite a saying from Chairman Mao before you could collect your meal. The man in front of him, who clearly had a black sense of humor, insisted on reciting passage after passage of the Chairman's works. No one dared laugh as the political maxims flowed, and no one dared interrupt him for fear of being labeled a counterrevolutionary. So the food got cold, everyone in the line seethed with silent fury, and the man got away with his bitter joke.

No doubt the menu consisted of everyday vegetables with a meager portion of grain. The following is the kind of inexpensive, simple vegetable dish that might have been on the menu. Despite its modesty, it's rather nice. The round white cabbage is known in Hunan as "wrapped vegetable" (*bao cai*), and its leaves are wrapped slightly more loosely than the more common green cabbages in the West. You can use the same method to cook Chinese leaf cabbage.

14 OZ. GREEN OR CHINESE
    CABBAGE

3 DRIED RED CHILES

SALT

2 TBSP. CHINKIANG VINEGAR

4 TBSP. PEANUT OIL FOR
    COOKING

1. Use your hands to divest the cabbage of its leaves, and to tear them into bite-size pieces, or you can shred the cabbage if you'd rather; set aside. Cut the dried chiles in half lengthwise and discard seeds as far as possible.

2. Heat the wok over a high flame until smoke rises, then add 3 tablespoons of the oil and swirl around. Add the cabbage and stir-fry for a few minutes, until tender but still a little crunchy, reducing the heat to medium if necessary to avoid singeing.

3. When the cabbage is approaching tenderness, push the cabbage to the side and pour the remaining tablespoon oil into the space at the bottom of the wok. Add the chiles and sizzle briefly in the hot oil, before mixing it into the cabbage. Season with salt to taste.

4. When the cabbage is ready, add the vinegar and stir for a few moments to let the flavors fuse, then serve.

STIR-FRIED PEA LEAVES WITH GARLIC
chao dou miao

炒豆苗

The southern Chinese eat an astonishing array of leafy green vegetables, often simply stir-fried on their own or with garlic. Aside from Chinese cabbage, bok choy and all their botanical relatives, the Chinese also make use of the nutritious young sprouts (*miao*) of many legumes and root vegetables. In my travels across China, I've eaten sweet potato sprouts, peanut sprouts, Asian radish sprouts, and even the young leaves of the Chinese wolfberry. Most of these were once considered peasant food, but have come into vogue as part of the craze for back-to-nature dining.

Pea leaves are one of the Chinese leaf vegetables that have become more commonly available in western Chinatowns, and even more mainstream food stores. Sometimes known as "dragon's whiskers" because of their delicate fronds, they have a bright pea flavor and a juicy texture. They can be used to add a splash of green to a delicate broth, and are also delicious stir-fried, particularly with lashings of garlic.

7 OZ. FRESH, TENDER PEA LEAVES

2 TBSP. FINELY CHOPPED GARLIC

SALT

3 TBSP. PEANUT OIL OR LARD FOR COOKING

1. Wash the pea leaves and discard any coarse stems and wilted leaves; set aside.

2. Heat the wok over a high flame until smoke rises, then add the oil or lard and swirl around. Add the garlic and sizzle for a few seconds before adding the pea leaves. Stir-fry briskly for a couple of minutes until just wilted, adding salt to taste. Serve.

TWO WAYS WITH WATER SPINACH

Water spinach is an everyday southern Chinese vegetable with a pleasant taste and a delightful mouthfeel: its stems become juicily crisp after cooking, its leaves soft and silky like regular spinach. There are two main varieties with different-shaped leaves; the one with long, slender leaves reminiscent of bamboo is most commonly available in the UK. It is particularly good cooked with strong flavors such as black fermented beans, fermented bean curd, and, in Malaysia, dried shrimp. The common Hunanese name for water spinach is "hollow-heart vegetable" (*kong xin cai*) because of its tubular stems.

Many people stir-fry the stems and leaves together, but I like this Hunanese method of separating them to make the most of their contrasting textures. You will need one large bunch of water spinach, about 1 pound, to make both these recipes, cut approximately in half to separate leaves and stems.

STIR-FRIED WATER SPINACH LEAVES WITH GARLIC
chao kong xin cai

LEAVES FROM 1 LB. WATER
   SPINACH (ABOUT
   8 OZ.)
2 TBSP. FINELY CHOPPED GARLIC
SALT
3 TBSP. PEANUT OIL OR LARD
   FOR COOKING

1. Cut the bunch of leafy spinach sections in half, which will make the pieces easier to move around the wok.
2. Heat the wok over a high flame until smoke rises, then add the oil or lard and swirl around. Add the garlic and sizzle until fragrant, then add the spinach leaves and stir-fry until just-cooked, adding salt to taste.

STIR-FRIED WATER SPINACH STEMS WITH BLACK BEANS AND CHILES
dou la chao kong xin cai geng

STEMS FROM 1 LB. WATER
   SPINACH (ABOUT
   10 OZ.)
1 TBSP. FINELY CHOPPED GARLIC
2 FRESH RED CHILES
2 TBSP. BLACK FERMENTED
   BEANS, RINSED
1 TSP. CLEAR RICE VINEGAR
SALT
1 TSP. SESAME OIL
3 TBSP. PEANUT OIL OR LARD
   FOR COOKING

1. Cut the water spinach stems into ¾-inch pieces; set aside. Cut the chiles on a steep angle into thin slices, discarding the stems and seeds as far as possible.
2. Heat the wok over a high flame until smoke rises, then add the oil or lard and swirl around. Add the garlic, chiles, and black beans and sizzle until fragrant.
3. Add the spinach stems and stir-fry for a few minutes until barely cooked, adding the vinegar and salt to taste as you go. When the stems are tender, remove the wok from the heat, stir in the sesame oil, and serve.

STIR-FRIED PURSLANE
chao ma si han

炒
馬
齒
莧

Purslane is a wild vegetable that grows around the fields in many parts of China, and is known to have been used as a food for more than 2,000 years. Like many wild vegetables, it is traditionally regarded as peasant fare, but has recently regained favor with the middle-class vogue for "green," rustic ingredients. It is often blanched, which helps to reduce its sourness, and then dressed like a salad, or sun-dried after blanching and then steamed with pork belly. The following recipe offers a simple and lovely way of cooking it as a vegetable. The stems become fabulously juicy, and the ginger and chili help to tease out their delicate, sweet-sour flavor. I buy mine in generous, paper-wrapped bunches in my local Turkish supermarket.

1 LB. FRESH PURSLANE

1 FRESH RED CHILI, SEEDED AND
   FINELY CHOPPED

1 TSP. FINELY CHOPPED FRESH
   GINGER

SALT

1 TSP. CLEAR RICE VINEGAR

3 TBSP. PEANUT OIL FOR
   COOKING

1   Trim the ends of the purslane, and remove any wilted leaves. Blanch the purslane in a generous saucepan of boiling water until just tender, then quickly refresh under cold running water. Shake dry, and then cut into 2-inch lengths.

2. Heat the wok over a high flame until the smoke rises, then add the oil and swirl around. Add the chili and ginger and sizzle briefly until fragrant.

3. Add the purslane and stir-fry until piping hot, adding salt to taste and splashing the vinegar in toward the end of the cooking time. Serve.

STIR-FRIED WATER CELERY
chao shui qin cai

炒水芹菜

Water celery has a magical, transporting scent: fresh and green, a little herbal, gently reminiscent of pine. It has long, segmented stems that are hollow inside, and narrow, serrated leaves, although these are usually stripped off before it is sold. I've never found it in a Chinese store, but buy mine from a Vietnamese trader, who calls it *rau cân*. If you are trying it for the first time, crush a section of the raw stem between your fingers and deeply inhale.

"Dry celery" entered China some 2,000 years ago, and water celery was the original Chinese celery, mentioned in texts dating back to the third century BC. It might have an ancient connection with the Hunan region, since one of its Chinese names is *chu kui*, Chu being the name of the long-lost state that embraced the area now called Hunan province. These days it's not widely cultivated, but is a common, everyday vegetable in Hunan in winter and spring, when it is usually stir-fried or cooked with paddy eels. Its forest taste is unusual and a little strange on first encounter.

9 OZ. WATER CELERY STEMS,
    TRIMMED WITH THE LEAVES
    DISCARDED

1 TBSP. FINELY CHOPPED GARLIC

2 FRESH RED CHILES, SEEDED
    AND FINELY CHOPPED

1 TBSP. BLACK FERMENTED
    BEANS, RINSED

1 TSP. DRIED CHILI FLAKES

SALT

1 TSP. CLEAR RICE VINEGAR

3 TBSP. PEANUT OIL OR LARD
    FOR COOKING

1. Rinse the celery well and cut into 2-inch sections; set aside.
2. Heat the wok over a high flame until smoke rises, then add the oil or lard and swirl around. Add the garlic, fresh chiles, and black beans and stir-fry briefly until fragrant. Add the chili flakes and stir once or twice more.
3. Add the water celery and stir-fry vigorously until barely cooked, adding salt to taste and splashing in the vinegar toward the end of the cooking time. Serve.

STEAMED VEGETABLES
STEAMED TARO WITH CHOPPED SALTED CHILES
duo jiao zheng yu tou

Taro is an extraordinary-looking vegetable: purple-brown corms ringed by ridges and covered in hairs. Some varieties produce smaller, subsidiary cormels, which are known rather charmingly in some Chinese sources as "sons," "grandsons," and even "great-grandsons," depending on their relationship with the "mother" corm. The most commonly used variety in Hunan has small corms or cormels with chalk-white flesh that cook to a texture a little like potato, but with a silkier mouthfeel. The Hunanese favor the smallest ones, about the size of new potatoes, which are typically boiled into a soup or steamed with chiles and oil as in the following recipe.

Traditionally, taro is regarded as poverty food, an unwelcome substitute for rice when times are hard, but these days it has come back into fashion. I love its comforting texture, and the following taro concoction is one of my favorite Hunan dishes. Don't be deceived by its simplicity—it's really wonderful.

Look out for taro in Chinese and Caribbean or African stores. If you can find them, use tiny young corms; otherwise, larger ones will do. And do make sure you wear rubber gloves to peel the taro; their hairy skins contain a mild toxin that can otherwise make your wrists and arms itch like crazy for an hour or so. (It's helpful to retain the gloves for cutting, as the peeled taro are slippery and can try to escape across the kitchen.)

1¼ LB. TARO

¼ TSP. SALT

5 TBSP. PEANUT OIL OR MELTED LARD

2 TBSP. CHOPPED SALTED CHILES

1 TSP. BLACK FERMENTED BEANS, RINSED

2 TSP. FINELY CHOPPED GARLIC (OPTIONAL)

1. Wear rubber gloves to peel the taro. If they are tiny, you can leave them whole; otherwise slice them, or for really large ones, cut into batons. Place in a heatproof bowl with the salt and 2 tablespoons of the oil or lard, and use your hands to mix thoroughly; set aside.

2. Heat the wok over a high flame until smoke rises, then add the remaining 3 tablespoons oil or lard and swirl around. Add the salted chiles, black beans, and garlic, if using, and stir-fry briefly until they are fragrant.

3. Pour the chili mixture over the taro. Place the bowl in a steamer and steam over a high flame for about 30 minutes, until tender. Serve in the bowl, giving everything a good stir before eating.

BOWL-STEAMED EGGPLANT WITH WINTER-SACRIFICE BEANS AND SALTED GREENS
kou qie zi

扣
茄
子

This is a vegetarian version of the classic Chinese dish, bowl-steamed pork belly with salted mustard greens, and is equally, if not more, delicious. The strong, salty flavors of the beans and preserved vegetable work beautifully with the lazy richness of the eggplant, and it's best eaten with plain steamed rice. The yellowish winter-sacrifice beans are not easy to find, so I've included an alternative version using the more commonly found black fermented beans. I find it hard to decide which I like best.

In Hunan, this dish is made with long, pale purple Asian eggplants, but you can also use the dark purple ones. You will need a heatproof bowl deep enough to hold the eggplants and the other ingredients. In cooking this dish for the photograph on page 225, I used a clay bowl about six inches in diameter and two-and-a-half inches deep. See page 29 for information about winter-sacrifice beans.

1 LB. 5 OZ. EGGPLANTS

SALT

5 TBSP. PRESERVED MUSTARD
GREENS (ABOUT 1¼ OZ.)

¼ CUP WINTER-SACRIFICE BEANS

3 TBSP. CHILI OIL, OR TO TASTE

1 SCALLION, GREEN PART ONLY,
FINELY SLICED

½ CUP PEANUT OIL FOR COOKING

1. Cut off and discard the stems of the eggplants. Cut each eggplant in half lengthwise, and then cut each half, again lengthwise, into even slices about ½ inch thick. Sprinkle liberally with salt and leave to drain for 30–60 minutes.

2. Give the preserved mustard greens a thorough rinse under cold water to get rid of excess saltiness, then shake them dry and stir-fry in a dry wok to help them lose the rest of the water. When they are more-or-less dry, add a little oil and stir-fry briefly until fragrant; set aside.

3. Heat the remaining oil in a wok until it reaches 350°F. Add the eggplant slices, a few at a time, and fry until soft and tinged with gold; set aside on folded paper towels.

VARIATION

Follow the same recipe, but omit the winter-sacrifice beans and the chili oil. Stir-fry the preserved mustard greens with 1 tablespoon rinsed black fermented beans until fragrant, adding chili flakes to taste. Place this mixture on top of the eggplants and steam as above.

4. Layer the neatest slices of eggplant, skin-side down, in a heatproof bowl. Mix the rest of the eggplants, including any odds and ends, with the beans and lay on top of the tidy slices. Scatter with the prepared mustard greens and then drizzle over chili oil to taste.

5. Place the bowl in a steamer and steam over a high heat for about 20 minutes to fuse the flavors. To serve, turn into a deep serving dish and scatter with the scallion.

A FEW OTHER IDEAS FOR STEAMED VEGETABLES

Many vegetables can be steamed to delicious effect. They are generally seasoned with salt, a little oil or lard, and some *umami*-rich ingredient, such as everyday stock (page 287), rinsed black fermented beans, or good chicken stock. Feel free to experiment!

★ SIMPLE STEAMED EGGPLANT   *zheng qie zi*

Cut eggplants into thickish slices. If you are using dark purple eggplants, sprinkle them with salt and leave to drain for 30 minutes. (If you are using pale Chinese eggplants, there is no need to do this.) Place the eggplants in a steaming bowl, top with rinsed black fermented beans, dried chili flakes or sliced fresh chiles, a dash of oil or lard, and salt to taste. Steam until the eggplants are meltingly tender. Alternatively, steam the eggplants on their own, and then dress with finely chopped garlic and fresh ginger, soy sauce, Chinkiang brown vinegar, salt, sesame oil, and finely sliced scallion greens.

★ STEAMED ITALIAN FRYING PEPPERS WITH BLACK BEANS   *dou chi zheng jian la jiao*

Discard the pepper stems and cut the flesh into bite-size sections. Place in a steaming bowl, top with rinsed black fermented beans, finely chopped fresh ginger, a dash of chicken stock, a dash of oil or lard, and salt to taste. Steam until tender.

★ STEAMED WINTER MELON WITH SALTED DUCK EGG YOLKS   *xian dan huang zheng dong gua*

Peel a 1-pound chunk of winter melon, discard the pith and seeds and cut into bite-size slices. Lay these in a shallow heatproof dish and scatter with 2 finely chopped cooked salty duck egg yolks (page 286), a little oil (I prefer olive oil for this—not very Hunanese, but very good), and salt to taste, if necessary. Steam for 20 minutes over a high heat, then scatter with finely sliced scallion greens to serve. The translucent melon looks best when cooked in a colored dish, perhaps blue or green to set off the yellow egg yolk.

★ STEAMED PEAS WITH GINGER   *zheng chuan dou*

Place podded peas in a heatproof bowl. Top with slivers of fresh ginger, salt to taste, a little lard or vegetable oil, and a slug of good chicken stock. Steam until tender.

★ STEAMED SOYBEANS WITH CHILI   *zheng qing pi dou*

Place podded fresh soybeans in a heatproof bowl. Top with sliced fresh red chili, salt to taste, a little lard or vegetable oil, and a slug of good chicken stock. Steam until tender.

★ STEAMED BEETS (A COMPLETELY NON-CHINESE EXPERIMENT)

Boil, peel, and slice some beets, then steam them with chopped red onion, a little salt, and generous sloshes of balsamic vinegar and olive oil. This is delicious, especially when left to cool and marinate overnight.

BOILED VEGETABLES
BOILED AMARANTH WITH PRESERVED DUCK EGGS
pi dan zhu han cai

左侧竖排：皮蛋煮莧菜

Purple amaranth is one of my favorite Chinese greens. The variety I find in my local Chinese supermarket has very soft, rounded green leaves with a splash of bright purple in the middle of each. The easiest way to cook it is simply to stir-fry it with garlic and a little salt (see below), but I also love this Hunanese variation, in which preserved duck eggs lend a rich savory taste to a stock colored pinkish by the amaranth juices. Use your chopsticks to pluck pieces of egg and strands of silky amaranth from the stock, and then a spoon and rice bowl to take some of the liquid like a soup.

7 OZ. AMARANTH

2 PRESERVED DUCK EGGS

1 CUP PLUS 2 TBSP. EVERYDAY
    STOCK (PAGE 287)

2 GARLIC CLOVES, SLICED

SALT

3 TBSP. PEANUT OIL FOR
    COOKING

1. Discard any thick, tough stems and wilted leaves from the amaranth; set aside. Peel the preserved duck eggs, then rinse them under cold water and cut each egg into 6–8 segments. Bring the stock to a boil, then set aside.

2. Heat a wok over a high flame until smoke rises, then add the oil and swirl around. Add the garlic and sizzle briefly until fragrant. Add the amaranth and stir-fry until the leaves wilt and the stems are tender.

3. Add the stock and bring rapidly to a boil. Add the eggs and boil for a minute or so until just heated through, adding salt to taste. Serve in a deep bowl.

VARIATIONS
★ STIR-FRIED AMARANTH WITH GARLIC
chao han cai
Heat a wok over a high flame until smoke rises, then add 3 tablespoons peanut oil and swirl around. Add a few sliced garlic cloves and sizzle briefly until fragrant. Add the amaranth (perhaps 10 ounces) and stir-fry until the leaves wilt and the stems are tender, and pink juices have gathered on the bottom of the wok. Add salt to taste as you go.

★ BOILED AMARANTH
shui zhu han cai
This is exactly the same as the main recipe above, but made without the preserved duck eggs. Asian radish (*daikon*) tops and *dong han cai* (page 196) are also cooked in this way.

FAVA BEANS WITH PICKLED MUSTARD GREENS
pao cai zhu can dou

泡菜煮蠶豆

Brine-pickled mustard greens, with their pale, gentle sourness, and fresh fava beans are a delightful combination that will make you sigh with pleasure. It is definitely worth taking the time to peel the beans after shelling them, not only because of their superior taste and mouthfeel, but also because their springlike greenness brightens up the appearance of the dish. The following recipe is my attempt to re-create a beautiful dish I ate at the Yuloudong restaurant in Changsha.

ABOUT 1½ CUPS/1 LB. 7 OZ. FAVA
 BEAN PODS

3 OZ. PICKLED MUSTARD GREENS

A FEW SLICES PEELED FRESH
 GINGER

1 CUP WATER

SALT

A FEW SLICES FRESH RED CHLLI

2 TBSP. PEANUT OIL FOR STIR-
 FRYING

1. Shell and peel the fava beans; set aside.
2. Cut the thicker, paler parts of the mustard greens into ½-inch strips and then into squares. Rinse them well in cold water; set aside.
3. Heat a wok over a high flame until smoke rises, then add the oil and swirl around. Add the mustard greens and ginger and stir-fry until the greens have lost some of their water and are fragrant.
4. Add the beans, stir a few times, and then add enough water to immerse them and simmer for a few minutes, adding salt to taste if necessary, until the beans are tender and the liquid reduced by about two-thirds (the dish should remain very juicy). Toward the end of the cooking time, add the chili slices. Serve.

BRAISED VEGETABLES
BOK CHOY WITH CHESTNUTS
ban li shao cai xin

Around Mao Zedong's ancestral village of Shaoshan, the road winds among gentle, wooded hills, the flat valleys among them a mosaic of paddy fields and vegetable crops. Spring Festival couplets, painted in black ink on scarlet paper, are pasted around the door frames, a splash of color amid the green. One afternoon I sat drinking homegrown tea with the wife of the local communist party secretary, surveying the family's fields and little orchard, blue-gray hills rising gently in the distance. She pointed out the fruit trees that would bear their crops later in the year, including tangerines and oranges, pomelos, loquats, and pears. There were also chestnut trees, whose starchy nuts are most delicious in the following recipe, a Hunanese equivalent of the English Christmas concoction of brussels sprouts and chestnuts.

5 OZ. CHESTNUTS

1¼ LB. BOK CHOY OR BABY BOK CHOY

SALT AND PEPPER

3 TBSP. EVERYDAY STOCK (PAGE 287) OR WATER

¼ TSP. POTATO FLOUR MIXED WITH 1 TBSP. COLD WATER

1 TSP. SESAME OIL

3–5 TBSP. LARD OR PEANUT OIL FOR COOKING

1. If you are using packaged, cooked chestnuts, simply cut them into thick slices. If using fresh chestnuts, make a slash in the shell of each, put them in a saucepan with cold water to cover, and bring to a boil. Then turn off the heat and, taking the chestnuts out of the water one at a time, peel off their shells and skins. (As the water cools, this will become more difficult, so you might need to reheat it.) Cut the chestnuts into thick slices, place in a heatproof bowl, and steam over a high heat for about 10 minutes until tender; set aside.

2. Meanwhile, trim the bok choy, then cut them in half or quarter lengthwise, depending on size.

3. Heat the wok over a high flame until smoke rises, then add 3 tablespoons lard or oil and swirl around. Add the chestnuts and fry until golden, seasoning with salt to taste; set aside.

4. Return the wok to the heat with a little more lard or oil, if necessary. Add the bok choy and stir-fry until tender, seasoning with salt to taste. Return the chestnuts to the wok with the stock, and season with pepper to taste, stirring vigorously. Finally, add the potato flour mixture and stir as it thickens to a gloss.

5. Remove the wok from the heat, drizzle the sesame oil over, and serve. For best results, use a pair of chopsticks to lay the bok choy in a neat pile on your serving dish, and then place the chestnuts neatly in the middle or over the leafy ends.

SPICY EGGPLANT POT
qie zi bao

茄
子
煲

Although the culinary regions of China have their own notional borders, in reality these borders have always been porous. Hunanese haute cuisine brings together influences from all the great Chinese cooking regions, spurred on by the inventiveness of chefs and the tastes of high officials who served in different parts of the country. But even at the level of domestic and everyday cooking, there is a blurring of regional boundaries, and a constant cross-fertilization of ideas. This humble, but delicious, dish comes from a restaurant in Yueyang in northern Hunan. The cooking method and the use of chili and fava bean paste with ginger and garlic, have an affinity with the cooking of Sichuan to the northwest, while the serving, in a *bao* clay pot, is southern Cantonese in style. The addition of a little fresh scarlet chili gives it a final, Hunanese stamp.

1 LB. 7 OZ. EGGPLANTS

SALT

2 DRIED SHIITAKE MUSHROOMS,
   SOAKED IN BOILING WATER
   FOR 30 MINUTES

3 OZ. GROUND PORK

2 TBSP. CHILI BEAN PASTE

2 TSP. FINELY CHOPPED FRESH
   GINGER

2 TSP. FINELY CHOPPED GARLIC

1 FRESH RED CHILI, FINELY
   SLICED

⅔ CUP EVERYDAY STOCK (PAGE
   287) OR WATER

½ TSP. DARK SOY SAUCE

2 SCALLIONS, GREEN PARTS
   ONLY, FINELY SLICED

1 TSP. SESAME OIL

PEANUT OIL FOR DEEP-FRYING

1. Peel the eggplants, then cut them in half lengthwise and then crosswise. Cut each quarter into chunks, sprinkle with salt and leave to drain for about 30 minutes. Meanwhile, drain the shiitakes and squeeze dry. Finely chop them and set aside.

2. Rinse and pat dry the eggplants. Heat the oil for deep-frying in the wok over a high flame until it reaches 350°F. Add the eggplants and fry for a few minutes until they are tender and faintly tinged with gold. Use a slotted spoon to remove the eggplant, shaking off the excess oil; set aside on folded paper towels. You might wish to do this in several batches.

3. Drain off all but 3 tablespoons of the oil and return the wok to a high flame. Add the pork and stir-fry as it separates and loses its water content. Add the chili bean paste and stir-fry until the oil is red.

4. Add the ginger, garlic, shiitakes, and chili and sizzle until they are wonderfully fragrant. Pour in the stock, add the dark soy sauce, return the eggplants, and simmer for a few minutes over a medium heat to let the flavors penetrate the eggplants. Season to taste with salt, if necessary.

5. Finally, turn up the heat, if necessary, to reduce the sauce. Add the scallions and stir-fry until barely cooked. Remove the wok from the heat, stir in the sesame oil, and serve, preferably in a small clay pot.

RED-BRAISED WINTER MELON
hong shao dong gua

紅燒冬瓜

The winter melon is the blue whale among Chinese vegetables, a vast gourd that can weigh up to fifty pounds. The dark skin of less enormous varieties can be carved into intricate patterns and its flesh scooped out, transforming it into an elegant soup tureen for a banquet, but for home use it is generally bought in more manageable chunks. This is how you will usually see it in Chinese supermarkets in the West. Winter melon flesh is firm when raw, but pulpy and translucent after cooking, so it's usually eaten in soups and stews. It can also be candied as a Spring Festival sweetmeat. The following dish has a satisfying flavor and comforting texture, perfect for eating on rice, curled up on the sofa.

1¾ LB. WINTER MELON

3 OZ. GROUND PORK

1 TBSP. FINELY CHOPPED GARLIC

1 TBSP. CHOPPED SALTED CHILES
    OR FINELY CHOPPED FRESH
    RED CHILI

½ CUP EVERYDAY STOCK (PAGE
    287)

½ TSP. DARK SOY SAUCE

LIGHT SOY SAUCE

SALT

2 SCALLIONS, GREEN PARTS
    ONLY, FINELY SLICED

1 TSP. SESAME OIL

4 TBSP. PEANUT OIL FOR
    COOKING

1. Peel the winter melon, then cut out and discard the seeds and pith. Cut the flesh into bite-size slices.

2. Heat the wok over a high flame until smoke rises, then add 3 tablespoons of the oil and swirl around. Add the melon slices and fry without moving them around too much, so they become a little golden; set aside.

3. Return the wok to the flame with the remaining oil. Add the pork and stir-fry until it has changed color and lost some of its water content. Add the garlic and chiles and stir-fry until they are fragrant.

4. Return the melon to the wok with the stock, dark soy sauce, a dash of light soy, and salt to taste. Bring to a boil, then turn the heat down, and simmer until the winter melon is tender. Stir in the scallions, and, off the heat, the sesame oil. Serve.

RED-BRAISED WINTER-COLD MUSHROOMS
hong shao han jun

紅燒寒菌

The forests of western Hunan are host to a wealth of wild fungi, and perhaps the most highly prized is the "winter-cold mushroom" (*han jun*), known in English as the saffron milk cap because of the pale orange milk that oozes from its cut flesh. The mushrooms emerge around the time of the "double-ninth festival" (*chong yang*), which falls on the ninth day of the ninth lunar month. This date traditionally marked the start of winter, when fires would be lit to warm the house, which is why the mushroom is known as the "winter-cold mushroom." Other folk names include "fragrant in the ninth month"(*jiu yue xiang*).

I've never found the saffron milk cap on sale in England, but it is a delicacy in Spain, where it can be seen piled up in the markets of Barcelona, late in the year, during the wild mushroom season. (It is known there as *rovelló*.) Its flesh is pale orange, tinged with green, and has a firm texture and a slightly peppery flavor. In London, I have used the same method to cook Portobello mushrooms, which worked rather well.

1 LB. SAFFRON MILK CAP
    MUSHROOMS OR PORTOBELLO
    MUSHROOMS

¾-IN. PIECE FRESH GINGER,
    PEELED

2 SCALLIONS, WHITE AND GREEN
    PARTS SEPARATED

3 OZ. PORK BELLY OR BACON,
    THICKLY SLICED

1– 1¼ CUPS EVERYDAY STOCK
    (PAGE 287)

½ TSP. DARK SOY SAUCE

SALT AND PEPPER

½ TSP. POTATO FLOUR MIXED
    WITH 2 TSP. WATER

1 TSP. SESAME OIL

3 TBSP. PEANUT OIL OR LARD
    FOR STIR-FRYING

1. Clean the mushrooms and, if they are large, cut into bite-size slices or chunks. Bash the ginger and scallion whites with the flat side of a cleaver or a heavy object to release some of their flavors. Cut the scallion greens into 1½-inch pieces or, if they are thick, into slivers.

2. Heat the wok over a high flame until smoke rises, then add the oil or lard and swirl around. Add the ginger and scallion whites and stir-fry until they smell delicious. Add the pork and mushrooms and continue to stir-fry for a few minutes, until fragrant.

3. Add the stock, dark soy sauce, and salt to taste and bring to a boil, then turn down the heat and simmer over a very low flame for 10–15 minutes to let the flavors meld. (Hunanese cooks transfer the mushrooms to a clay pot or bowl for the simmering, to "enhance the fragrance.")

4. Finally, discard the pork or bacon, ginger, and spring onion, and turn up the heat under the wok to reduce the sauce. Add just enough of the potato-flour mixture to thicken the sauce, stir in the scallion greens and pepper to taste, and then turn into a serving bowl, or return to the clay pot if you are using one. Drizzle the sesame oil over and serve.

7

SOUP DISHES 湯菜類

★ SOUP DISHES

Like the people of neighboring Sichuan province, the Hunanese take their soup at the end of the meal, to refresh the palate after the rich and spicy flavors of the other dishes. Some soups are made quickly in the wok, but the most characteristically Hunanese are those simmered slowly in clay pots. In some restaurants, small clay pots are arranged on rungs around the interior of waist-high jars that contain a dish of glowing wood embers and mimic the gentle cooking of the farmhouse range. They are often tonic soups, simple but nourishing concoctions like black chicken with medicinal herbs, lotus seeds, and silver ear fungus, or spare ribs and corn, and are brought to the table in their cooking pots.

In the winter months, the Hunanese, especially in the north of the province, love to eat hotpot. It's a different style of hotpot from those of Sichuan and Beijing. The Sichuanese hotpot is a meal in itself, a great potful of fiendishly spicy broth into which you dip all the other ingredients to cook or heat them. The "Mongolian hotpot" (known in Chinese as "scalded mutton," *shuan yang rou*) of Beijing also dominates the table. But the Hunanese tend to enjoy their hotpot as part of a more general meal, where it takes the place of the regular soup. It might be a simple mutton stew, or radish slivers in chicken soup (see page 243), although it is usually served in a fairly large pot. Toward the end of the meal, when everyone has eaten their fill of the other dishes on the table, someone will tip a few platefuls of simple vegetarian ingredients into the broth: some leafy green vegetables, sweet potato noodles, or plain white bean curd. As they cook, everyone uses their chopsticks to help themselves to the solid ingredients, and then a ladle to take the broth.

The hotpot is one of a whole family of dishes that continue to bubble away on the dinner table. There are "dry woks" (*gan guo*), small woks filled with food that is already cooked. These dishes are not soups, but often spicy concoctions of meat, fish, or crisp vegetables that come in a little sauce and won't spoil with longer heating. The most Hunanese of all, however, is the "clay-bowl" (*bo zi*), also, confusingly, sometimes

Above: RED-BRAISED FISH HOTPOT, YUEYANG

Right: TONIC SOUPS, CHANGSHA

called a hotpot, that is closely associated with the northern city of Changde. It too contains a precooked dish that can simmer away for some time. In the Hunan winter, steam drifts up from almost every restaurant table, sometimes from a single hotpot bubbling away in the middle, sometimes from an assortment of clay pots and small iron woks on separate burners.

In recent years this style of eating has been fashionable throughout Hunan, but its roots lie in the north, in Changde and the surrounding Dongting Lake region. A local rhyme sends up the northerners for their obsession with hotpot, saying they "don't want to go to court to be the emperor's son-in-law, they just want a hotpot bubbling away on its burner." Some say that the Changde hotpot has roots in the ancient cooking culture of China's central plains, others that it was born out of the necessity for fishermen to eat one-pot meals cooked on a single stove when they lived on their boats for long periods of time. Either way, it is seen as perfectly suited to the climate of the region.

To return to the subject of soups: although many Hunanese soups are light and refreshing, legend has it that the brilliant founder of the Hunan Army, Zeng Guofan, leading his soldiers to war in the nineteenth century, often let them eat a robustly spicy soup made from ox blood, ox tripe, beef, and plenty of chiles and pepper. According to food writer Liu Guochu, it helped treat the rheumatism they suffered after long periods of sleeping out of doors, and fired them up for their military campaigns.

"BAMBOO TUBE" CHICKEN SOUP
zhu jie ji zhong

This subtle soup is one of the creations of the Hunanese exile chef Peng Chang-kuei (see pages 117–18), although you can find versions of it in restaurants run by his apprentices and those they taught, including the Hunan restaurant in London. It was originally cooked and served in individual sections of bamboo, one for each diner, which imparted to the meat a gentle bamboo fragrance, although Peng himself now uses little china pots (*zhong*) in his restaurant in Taiwan.

The banquet version of this dish is made with squab meat, enhanced by the rich flavor of dried scallop, but chicken breast and ground pork work very well, too. The finely ground meat rises to the surface of the pot during cooking, and gathers into a soft mass that floats in a clear broth. At table, use your spoons to break up the meat and eat it with the soup.

4 DRIED SHIITAKE MUSHROOMS

7 OZ. CHICKEN OR SQUAB
    BREAST MEAT

2 OZ. PORK BELLY (I SUSPECT
    PANCETTA WILL WORK WELL
    HERE, TOO)

12 WATER CHESTNUTS, FRESH OR
    CANNED

2 SCALLIONS, GREEN PARTS
    ONLY

2 TSP. VERY FINELY CHOPPED
    FRESH GINGER

4 TSP. SHAOXING WINE

SALT AND WHITE PEPPER

2½ CUPS FINE STOCK (PAGE 288)

1. Soak the shiitake mushrooms in hot water from the kettle for about 30 minutes to reconstitute.

2. Meanwhile, finely grind the chicken or squab with the pork to make a smooth paste. (This can be done in a food processor.) Chop the water chestnuts, and finely slice the scallion greens; set aside separately.

3. When the mushrooms are soft, drain them and squeeze dry, then remove and discard the stems and chop finely.

4. Combine all the ingredients, except the stock and scallion greens, seasoning with salt and pepper to taste; mix well. Add the stock and mix to a very runny paste.

5. Divide the mixture between 4 little heatproof pots or bowls and place in a steamer. Steam for 15 minutes over a high heat. Serve one pot to each guest, with a scattering of scallion greens.

LILY FLOWER, CLOUD EAR, AND SLICED PORK SOUP
huang hua cai rou pian tang

This is a beautiful soup made with two of the traditional Chinese "mountain treasures," a name given to faintly exotic ingredients like flowers and wild mushrooms. The dried day lily flowers, known in Chinese as "yellow flower vegetable" (*huang hua cai*) or "golden needle vegetable" (*jin zhen cai*), can easily be found in Chinese supermarkets. They are long and thin, and a dark gold in color. The strands of lily and the silky pieces of cloud ear have a particularly lovely mouthfeel. The Yueyang restaurant where I learned to make this, added a dash of lard just before serving; you might like to use olive oil instead, which is not authentic but works very well.

A SMALL HANDFUL DRIED
   CLOUD EAR MUSHROOMS
   (ABOUT ¼ OZ.)

A SMALL HANDFUL DRIED LILY
   FLOWERS (ABOUT ¾ OZ.)

¼ LB. LEAN BONELESS PORK

1-IN. PIECE FRESH GINGER

3 SCALLIONS, GREEN PARTS
   ONLY

¼ QT. EVERYDAY STOCK (PAGE
   287)

1 TBSP. SHAOXING WINE

LIGHT SOY SAUCE

SALT AND WHITE PEPPER

2 TBSP. LARD (OR OLIVE OIL)

3 TBSP. PEANUT OIL FOR
   COOKING

1. Set the cloud ears and the lily flowers to soak in separate bowls with hot water from the kettle for at least 30 minutes. When the mushrooms are soft, drain, squeeze dry, discard the stems, and cut the caps into bite-size pieces; set aside. Drain the lily flowers and add to the mushrooms.

2. Meanwhile, slice the pork thinly and evenly; set aside. Peel and slice the ginger. Cut the scallions into bite-size pieces.

3. Bring the stock to the boil and then set it to rest on a back burner while you prepare the rest of the soup.

4. Heat the peanut oil in a wok over a medium flame. Add the ginger and stir-fry until fragrant. Turn up the heat, add the pork and stir-fry until it has changed color and lost some of its water content, splashing in the Shaoxing wine as you do so.

5. Add the cloud ears and lily flowers and stir-fry for a couple of minutes until everything is hot and sizzly. Pour in the heated stock and return to a boil.

6. Skim off any froth that rises to the surface, and then season with light soy sauce and salt to taste. Simmer for about 5 minutes to let the flavors meld. Add a little lard, if you wish.

7. Place the scallions and a scattering of pepper to taste in a soup tureen. Pour the hot soup over, and finish with a dash of olive oil, if desired.

SILVERFISH AND MEATBALL SOUP
yin yu rou wan tang

This is a wonderful soup, a gentle melee of tender meatballs, richly savory fish and mushrooms, with a flash of soft egg yellow. Although it is called a *tang*, the name given to the thinner, brothlike kind of soup, it is so thick with floating ingredients that it recalls the *geng* stews of meat with vegetables or grains that were one of the principal dishes in ancient China. This kind of thick fish soup is traditionally offered to guests in the Yueyang area.

6 DRIED SHIITAKE MUSHROOMS

¾ OZ. DRIED SILVERFISH (PAGE 86)

1 EGG

¾-IN. PIECE FRESH GINGER, PEELED AND SLICED

1 QT. EVERYDAY STOCK (PAGE 287)

SALT

3 SCALLIONS, GREEN PARTS ONLY, CUT INTO PIECES ABOUT 1½ IN.

WHITE PEPPER

2 TBSP. LARD (OR OLIVE OIL)

4 TBSP. PEANUT OIL FOR COOKING

For the meatballs:

1 EGG, BEATEN

½ LB. MINCED PORK

½-IN. PIECE FRESH GINGER

1 TBSP. SHAOXING WINE

2 TBSP. POTATO FLOUR

1. Set the shiitake mushrooms to soak in hot water from the kettle for at least 30 minutes. When they are soft, drain, squeeze dry, discard the stems, and slice the caps; set aside.

2. Rinse the silverfish under cold running water, then put them in a bowl and cover with cold water. Squeeze them a few times in your hand, and then leave to soak for 5–10 minutes while you prepare the other ingredients, by which time they should be soft and supple.

3. Heat a skillet over a medium flame, then pour in 1 tablespoon of the oil and swirl it around. Pour the egg into the pan in a single, thin layer, tilting the pan to make it spread as much as possible. When the egg is set on one side, flip it over and cook on the other side, taking care not to let it brown. When the egg is cooked, turn it onto a plate and, when cool, cut into strips about ¼ inch wide; set aside.

4. To make the meatball mixture, smash the ginger with the flat blade of a cleaver or a heavy object, place in a little bowl and just cover with cold water. Combine the other meatball

SILVERFISH AND MEATBALL SOUP
continued

ingredients in a bowl, and then add enough of the strained ginger-fragrant water to make a soft paste; set aside.

5. Heat the wok over a high flame until smoke rises, then add the peanut oil and swirl around. Add the sliced shiitake and stir-fry for another minute or so, until the mushrooms smell delicious. Pour the stock into the wok with the silverfish and bring to a boil. Skim the surface, then season with salt to taste.

6. Remove the pan from the heat. Take a small handful of the meatball mixture, make a fist and then squeeze the mixture up through the hole between your thumb and index finger. When a large cherry-size blob of mixture has been squeezed up, use your other hand or a teaspoon to scoop it off and drop it into the soup. Repeat with the rest of the meatball mixture.

7. Return the pan to the heat and bring to a boil again. Reduce the heat and simmer for a few minutes until the meatballs have cooked through; cut one open to test.

8. Place the scallions and pepper to taste in a soup bowl or tureen. Pour the soup with the meatballs over, add a dash of melted lard (or olive oil), and then top with the ribbons of cooked egg.

TARO AND WATERCRESS SOUP
yu tou wa wa cai

芋
頭
娃
娃
菜

The name of this dish in Chinese is "taro and baby vegetable soup"—*wa wa* is the charmingly onomatopoeic Chinese word for baby, and *wa wa cai* is the common name for the tender young leaves of the Asian radish (*daikon*). This is humble peasant food, but it's one of my favorite Hunanese soups. The taro gives the liquid a soothing, silky consistency, and it has a delicate flavor from the leaves. If by any chance you have Asian radishes growing in your garden, you can use the tops in this dish. Otherwise, watercress is a delightful substitute. Vegetarians can make the soup with water, or with "rice soup," the liquid left over from making rice in the traditional manner (see page 254).

Taro is thought to have originated in India or Southeast Asia, although some Chinese sources claim it as a native plant. Its cultivation is mentioned in the *Guanzi*, a philosophical work dating back to the Warring States period, 475–221 BC.

1¼ LB. TARO

3⅓ CUPS CHICKEN STOCK OR WATER

3 SCALLIONS, GREEN PARTS ONLY

3 OZ. WATERCRESS

SALT AND WHITE PEPPER

3 TBSP. PEANUT OIL

1. Wash the taro, place in a saucepan, cover with cold water, and bring to a boil. Reduce the heat and simmer for about 20 minutes, until tender. Let the taro cool, then peel, rinse, and slice them.

2. Put the taro slices in a saucepan with the chicken stock or water and bring to a boil. Reduce the heat and simmer for 20–30 minutes, until they have almost dissolved. (This step can be done some time in advance of your meal.)

3. Just before you are ready to eat, finely slice the scallion greens; set aside.

4. Heat the wok over a high flame until smoke rises, then add the peanut oil and swirl around. Add the watercress and stir-fry until just wilted. Pour in the soupy taro mixture, bring to a boil and season with salt to taste. Reduce the heat and simmer for a couple of minutes to let the flavors meld, then pour into a serving bowl or tureen. Scatter with the scallions and pepper to taste.

"FLOWER" BEAN CURD SOUP WITH PRESERVED MUSTARD GREENS
suan cai dou hua tang

We left the main road in a village and walked for a couple of hours up a rutted track, still muddy in places after the previous day's rain. The valley was terraced with rice paddies that shone brilliantly green in the late spring sun. A few mud-brick farmhouses stood in the languid embrace of tall, billowing plumes of bamboo. Colorful butterflies flitted around, grasshoppers chirruped in the undergrowth, and small, urgent tweets could be heard emanating from swallows' nests under the eaves. At the top of the hill and the long, winding track was a monastery, where an ancient monk was giving a teaching that day. We lunched there, all of us, on a few simple vegetarian dishes, including this one.

This delightful soup is easy to make, and the tender bean curd is soothing on the tongue. It's perfect for vegetarians, although meat-eaters might also like to make it with a pork- or chicken-based stock. (I've made it with the stock leftover from cooking my Christmas ham—the spices added an interesting dimension.) I suspect it would work well, too, with a miso soup base.

7½ TBSP. CHOPPED PRESERVED
   MUSTARD GREENS (ABOUT
   3 OZ.)

DRIED CHILI FLAKES
   (OPTIONAL)

1 QT. VEGETARIAN STOCK, SUCH
   AS QING QING'S VEGETARIAN
   BLACK BEAN STOCK (PAGE
   287)

14 OZ. VERY SOFT SILKEN BEAN
   CURD

SALT AND WHITE PEPPER

2 SCALLIONS, GREEN PARTS
   ONLY, FINELY SLICED

2 TBSP. PEANUT OIL OR LARD
   FOR COOKING

1. Place the preserved mustard greens in a sieve and rinse thoroughly under cold water, to get rid of excess salt. Squeeze as dry as possible; set aside.

2. Heat the wok over a high flame until smoke rises, then add the oil or lard and swirl around. Add the mustard greens and stir-fry until fragrant, adding dried chili flakes to taste, if desired.

3. Pour in the stock and bring to a boil, skimming the surface, if necessary. Add the silken bean curd and break it up into the soup so it is evenly distributed. Reduce the heat and simmer for a couple of minutes, seasoning with salt and pepper to taste.

4. Pour into a serving bowl and scatter with the scallions.

PURPLE SEAWEED AND EGG "FLOWER" SOUP
zi cai dan hua tang

While living in Changsha I was lucky enough to meet one of the really great chefs of the older generation, Shi Yinxiang, then in his late eighties and still overseeing a restaurant bearing his name in the middle of town. Master Shi was born in 1917, the third generation of chefs in his family. He told me he had begun cooking at home at the age of ten, and five years later had started his apprenticeship under a famous chef who had worked in the household of a government official before opening his own restaurant in Changsha. There he learned the subtle arts of Hunanese haute cuisine, and by the 1950s he was working for the government, and in charge of the catering for the visits of national leaders, including Mao Zedong, Zhou Enlai, Liu Shaoqi, and Jiang Zemin. Shi became known for his brilliant and innovative cooking, and in the 1980s he published a comprehensive Hunanese cookbook that brought together his more than fifty years' experience. He is an enchanting man, with a kindly manner and a face that creases up frequently into a beatific smile. He is still riding on a crest of glory as the man who managed to delight Chairman Mao with his cooking, and the first Hunanese chef to be awarded "special first-grade" status.

The following recipe is a humble one, but it's a soup that I ate at Master Shi's restaurant as he told me about his life. The dried seaweed, which is sold in thin disks about eight inches in diameter, and looks black and frizzy before soaking, can be found in good Chinese supermarkets.

1 QT. EVERYDAY STOCK (PAGE 287), OR A VEGETARIAN STOCK

1 DISK DRIED PURPLE LAVER SEAWEED (*NORI* IN JAPANESE)

¾-IN. PIECE FRESH GINGER, PEELED AND SLIVERED

SALT AND WHITE PEPPER

1 EGG, BEATEN

1 SCALLION, GREEN PART ONLY, FINELY SLICED

1. Heat the stock with the seaweed and ginger and simmer gently as the seaweed reconstitutes itself. Tease the tightly massed disk apart with a pair of chopsticks, so the seaweed drifts in strands in the liquid. Season with salt and pepper to taste.

2. Beat the egg well. Turn the heat down to a minimum, drizzle in the egg into the soup in a thin spiraling stream across the surface. Turn off the heat, cover the pan tightly, and leave for a minute to allow the egg to set into little flakes or "flowers."

3. Serve immediately with a sprinkling of scallion greens.

CHICKEN SOUP WITH RADISH SLIVERS
luo bu si ji tang

This is a delicate soup that I came across at a dinner at one of the largest restaurants I have ever been to, the Good Luck on the southern outskirts of Changsha. The Good Luck is a vast, three-storied building, arranged around a quiet courtyard garden, and looks more like an apartment complex than a restaurant. Inside, two large public dining halls can seat 550 guests apiece, and, upstairs, sixty luxurious private rooms lead off corridors decorated like old-fashioned lanes. The restaurant can seat more than 2,000 guests simultaneously, but amazingly, given its vast scale, it offers freshly prepared and often delicious food. That evening, we dined on about twenty dishes, including duck simmered with bamboo shoots and dark wind-dried ham, spicy lamb ribs, wind-dried carp, and this soup, which simmered away on its own tabletop burner.

The soup is best made with winter radish, which is sweet and crisp. You can treat this soup as a hotpot if you wish, serving it on a burner and using it to cook other ingredients such as greens and bean curd.

14 OZ. ASIAN RADISH (*DAIKON*)

1¼ QT. RICH CHICKEN STOCK

SALT AND WHITE PEPPER

To serve:

1 THIN SLICE DARK PINK
  COOKED HAM (ABOUT 1½ OZ.)

2 SCALLIONS, GREEN PARTS
  ONLY, FINELY SLIVERED

1 TBSP. LARD OR CHICKEN FAT
  (OR OLIVE OIL)

1. Bring a large saucepan of water to a boil. Peel and cut the radish into very thin slices, and then into very fine slivers. Drop them in the boiling water and allow it to return to a boil, then drain well and squeeze dry. Cut the ham and the scallions into very fine slivers; set aside.

2. Bring the chicken stock to a boil in a large saucepan or wok over a high flame. Add the radish slivers and simmer for a couple of minutes to let the flavors meld. Season with salt to taste.

3. Place the lard or chicken fat (or olive oil) and pepper to taste in a serving bowl or tureen. Pour the radish sliver soup over. Garnish with the ham and scallion slivers.

DUN SOUPS

Hunanese soups are often very simple, savory broths made by simmering meat, fish, or poultry in water, usually with a little ginger and one or two supplementary ingredients. Salt and pepper are added later, just before serving. These soups are usually cooked in clay pots, most typically the kind of tall pot with a handle on one side you occasionally come across in a Chinese supermarket in the West. Such soups make a refreshing conclusion to a meal of strong and spicy flavors, and are very easy to make. The following are three variations on a spare-rib theme.

SPARE RIB AND CORN SOUP
yu mi dun pai gu

This soup has a delicate, but sumptuous, corn flavor, a hint of yellow in its color and a slightly milky mouthfeel. It is based on a soup of corn and pork bones made by my friend Fan Qun's mother, who brought it to a boil over the fire and then let it stew gently in the embers. Corn is another rustic ingredient, which is often served, steamed or grilled, as a snack at street fairs and railroad stations. Roasted corncob is said to have been one of Chairman Mao's favorite snacks.

14 OZ. SPARE RIBS AND/OR BELLY
    PORK
1 EAR OF FRESH CORN
1-IN. PIECE FRESH GINGER,
    PEELED AND SLICED
1 TBSP. SHAOXING WINE
1½ QT. PORK BONE STOCK OR
    WATER
SALT

To serve:

2 SCALLIONS, GREEN PARTS
    ONLY, FINELY SLICED
WHITE PEPPER

1. Cut the ribs into bite-size chunks (it's easier to ask your butcher to do this for you). Use a heavy cleaver to chop the ear of corn into bite-size chunks.

2. Bring a large saucepan of water to a boil. Add the ribs and blanch just until the water returns to the boil; drain and discard the blanching water.

3. Place the ribs into the rinsed pan or clay pot with the corn, ginger, wine, and stock or water and bring to a boil (very slowly and gently if you are using a clay pot), skimming the surface, as necessary. Reduce the heat, partially cover the pan and leave to simmer for a couple of hours, topping up with boiling water occasionally, if necessary.

4. Toward the end of the cooking time, season the broth with salt to taste. (Leave it unsalted or very lightly salted if drinking with a strongly flavored Hunanese meal.)

5. Serve with the scallion slices and a sprinkling of pepper to taste.

玉
米
炖
排
骨

SPARE RIB AND LOTUS ROOT SOUP
hu ou dun pai gu

This soup is made with the variety of lotus root that is most commonly available in Chinese supermarkets in the West. It produces hairlike fibers when cut or pulled apart, and develops a pale pinkish color during cooking, which it lends to the broth in the following recipe. (See pages 203–4 for more information about the lotus.)

8 OZ. FRESH LOTUS ROOT

14 OZ. SPARE RIBS AND/OR PORK
    BELLY

1-IN. PIECE FRESH GINGER,
    PEELED AND SLICED

1 TBSP. SHAOXING WINE

1½ QT. PORK BONE STOCK OR
    WATER

SALT

To serve:

2 SCALLIONS, GREEN PARTS
    ONLY, FINELY SLICED

WHITE PEPPER

1. Peel and trim the sections of lotus root. If they are fairly thin, cut them into 1¼-inch slices so you can see their beautiful cross sections. If they are plump, cut them into chunks of a size that can be picked up easily with chopsticks.

2. Proceed as in the previous corncob recipe, replacing the corncob with the lotus root.

SPARE RIB AND KELP SOUP
hai dai dun pai gu

Kelp, or "sea ribbon" (*hai dai*) is one of two types of seaweed that are used in Hunanese soups. (The other is laver, as in the recipe on page 242.) It is sold in stiff, dark green sheets that are covered in a frostlike deposit of (natural!) monosodium glutamate.

14 OZ. SPARE RIBS AND/OR PORK
    BELLY

1-IN. PIECE FRESH GINGER,
    PEELED AND SLICED

1 TBSP. SHAOXING WINE

1¼ QT. PORK BONE STOCK OR
    WATER

1–2 SHEETS DRIED KELP (*KOMBU*
    IN JAPANESE)

SALT

To serve:

2 SCALLIONS, GREEN PARTS
    ONLY, FINELY SLICED

WHITE PEPPER

1. Cut the ribs into bite-size chunks (it's easiest to ask your butcher to do this for you).

2. Bring a large saucepan of water to a boil. Add the ribs and blanch just until the water returns to the boil; drain well, discarding the blanching water. Place the ribs into the rinsed pan or a clay pot with the ginger, wine, and stock or water. Bring to a boil (very slowly and gently if you are using a clay pot), then reduce the heat to very low, partially cover, and leave to simmer for a couple of hours, topping up with boiling water occasionally, as necessary.

3. Set the kelp to soak in hot water from the kettle. When it is soft, drain and rinse it and use scissors or a knife to cut into thin ribbons.

4. Toward the end of the cooking time, add the kelp to the soup and continue simmering until it has lent its flavor to the broth and given it a slightly greenish tint. Season with a little salt to taste.

5. Serve with scallion slices and a sprinkling of pepper to taste.

VARIATIONS

Chunks of Asian radish (*daikon*) are another delicious addition to a basic spare rib broth—for best results first blanch them in boiling water to remove any hotness, add them to the ribs towards the end of the cooking time and simmer until tender. Winter melon can be added in a similar way, as can saffron milk cap mushrooms (*han jun*).

CHICKEN SOUP WITH CLOUD EARS AND GINGER
lao jiang yun er dun ji

老姜雲耳炖鷄

Chinese city-dwellers often wax lyrical about the flavors of rustic food. One elderly man I know went to work as a communist propagandist in the remote mountains of Hunan in the early 1970s. The local farmers felt obliged to treat him and his revolutionary delegation like officials of the old dynastic regime, so they plied them with bacon and rice. He remembers them taking a chunk of bacon down from the smoking rack above the fire, washing it, steaming it, and then slicing it, and says he has never since eaten such delicious bacon. And their everyday greens were so sweet and so delicious, he says, grown without pollution or artificial fertilizers.

I had my own rustic food epiphany while staying with my friend Fan Qun's family over the Chinese New Year. Her mother made a soup from one of their home-reared chickens, simmered with ginger and a tonic tuber (*tian ma*) in a blackened pot suspended over the kitchen fire, and finally seasoned with scallion and bell pepper. It was a chicken soup to dream about, the most delicious chicken soup I have ever tasted.

The following is a basic recipe for a Chinese chicken soup. Its flavor will obviously depend on the quality of the bird—for best results you should use an old female chicken, traditionally reared, although I've suggested using only the thighs for an easier version.

½ OZ. DRIED CLOUD EAR
    MUSHROOMS

1¼ LB. CHICKEN THIGHS ON THE
    BONE

1½-IN. PIECE FRESH GINGER,
    PEELED AND SLICED

2 TBSP. SHAOXING WINE

1¼ QT. WATER

SALT

2 TBSP. PEANUT OIL

To serve:

3 SCALLIONS, GREEN PARTS
    ONLY, CUT INTO BITE-SIZE
    PIECES

WHITE PEPPER

1. Set the cloud ears to soak in plenty of hot water from the kettle for at least 30 minutes. When they are tender, pluck out their knobby bottoms, squeeze dry, and cut them into bite-sized pieces; set aside.

2. Use a heavy cleaver to chop the chicken into bite-size pieces on the bone. Blanch them in boiling water just until the water returns to a boil, then drain, pat dry, and set aside.

3. Heat the wok over a high flame until smoke rises, then add the peanut oil and swirl around. Add the ginger and stir-fry until fragrant. Add the blanched chicken and stir-fry in the fragrant oil for a few minutes. Splash the Shaoxing wine around the edge of the wok, cover with cold water, and bring to a boil, skimming the surface.

4. Reduce the heat to very low, partially cover the wok, and leave to simmer for 30–40 minutes, until the chicken is tender. (In China, you would transfer the soup to a clay pot (*sha guo*) for the simmering, but you can simmer it in the wok, if you prefer.)

5. When the chicken is tender, add the cloud ears, season with salt to taste, and simmer for 10–15 minutes longer.

6. Place the scallions and pepper to taste in a serving bowl or soup tureen. Pour the chicken soup over and serve.

VARIATIONS

★ CHICKEN WITH PAPAYA
mu gua dun ji
Omit the cloud ears and add chunks of peeled and seeded papaya toward the end of the cooking time.

★ CHICKEN WITH GASTRODIA ELATA
tian ma dun ji
Omit the cloud ears and cook the chicken (or duck) with a small handful of the Chinese medicinal tuber *tian ma* (*Gastrodia elata*).

TONIC SOUPS:
Chinese supermarkets sell packages of tonic herbs for various ailments. They are normally stewed with chicken, duck, or pork for a couple of hours. You will usually find detailed instructions on the packages.

8

RICE
AND NOODLES

米飯面條

★ RICE AND NOODLES

Above: GLUTINOUS RICE CONES (ZONGZI)

Hunan is part of the fertile region that once belonged to the great state of Chu. Rice is the staple grain, and eaten at almost every meal. Wheat is very much a secondary staple, used in noodles, steamed breads, and dumplings. (One restaurant manager I know groans at the mere mention of the wheaten diet of the northern Chinese: "Their steamed buns are so solid and stodgy you could use them to knock someone out!" he told me.)

Both rice and wheat have been eaten in the region since ancient times, although in the distant past they were supplemented with other grains that are now hard to find: barley, millet, broomcorn millet, and hemp seeds were all unearthed in the Han dynasty tombs at Mawangdui. And in the desolate years of famine and food rationing in the 1960s and 1970s, people attempted to bulk out their staple grains with sweet potatoes and taro, and in the worst of times with barely edible wild plants.

Plain steamed rice (*bai mi fan*) is the background to dishes made from all kinds of other ingredients: traditionally parboiled and then steamed or cooked gently over the kitchen fire, these days it is most commonly made in an electric rice cooker. Rice is also used in sweetmeats, like the eight-treasure glutinous rice served at the New Year, and in various kinds of dumplings. Different varieties of rice are sold in the markets, some of them with beautiful names such as "silver-needle rice" (*jin zhen mi*), "cat's tooth rice" (*mao ya mi*), and "jade pearl rice" (*yu zhu mi*).

The Hunanese also specialize in rice *fen*, pasta made from rice in a variety of shapes. Most typically, soaked rice is ground with water to a paste, and the paste is steamed in thin layers until it sets. The set pasta is hung over bamboo poles until it is leather-dry, and then cut into ribbons with a knife. Because it is already cooked, it simply needs to be reheated in boiling water, usually in a deep ladle made from metal or woven bamboo. Rice *fen* is eaten for breakfast all over Hunan. Some people buy the freshly made *fen* and take it home, where they serve it in a bowlful of broth, topped perhaps with a fried egg, some sliced scallions, and a dollop of chopped salted chiles. Others stop at a street stall or café, where

the *fen* will be topped with a spoonful of rich meat stew or another topping.

Though *fen* is the most characteristic Hunan pasta, wheat noodles are also eaten, especially at the venerable Yangyuxing chain of restaurants. The original Yangyuxing was founded in 1893 by a man named Yang Xintian, and his son took over the business in the 1930s. Yangyuxing is famous for its own-made egg noodles and great variety of noodle toppings, which were traditionally written out on strips of wood and hung on the walls like a menu. Some are *wei ma*, stews that simmer away, and are simply spooned over a bowlful of noodles when a customer places an order. Others are *chao ma*, stir-fries that are cooked to order. There are also steamed dishes, served in the clay steaming bowl with a separate bowl of noodles. And for two people, you can order *guo mian*, a double portion of noodles served in large bowl with a couple of fried eggs, some blanched greens, and a generous spoonful of your preferred noodle topping. Chopped salted chiles, dried chili flakes, soy sauce, and brown rice vinegar are placed on each table and added to the noodles according to taste. Specialist rice *fen* restaurants offer a similar variety of toppings, served in the same way.

The quality of the stock used in noodle restaurants is vital to the taste of their dishes: as they say, "stock is to the cook what pitch is to the opera singer" (*chu zi de tang, xi zi de qiang*). In the kitchen of

the Huangchunhe *fen* restaurant in Changsha, an enormous pot of stock simmers away at a gentle heat. In it are whole chickens, pork bones, shiitake stems, and an exotic secret ingredient that is a specialty of the house, and that I am forbidden from mentioning in print!

Left: A MONASTERY LUNCH OF RICE AND VEGETABLES

RICE
POT-STICKER RICE
guo ba fan

The old-fashioned Hunanese way to cook rice is to parboil the grains, drain them, and then place them in a pot with a tightly fitting lid and set them to cook very slowly in the embers of the fire. This method produces fragrant rice with a layer of golden crust on the bottom of the pan. Families would traditionally squabble over who would eat this delicious *guo ba*. Although people in rural Hunan still use this method, it has been usurped in the cities by the electric rice cooker, but such is popular nostalgia for the golden *guo ba* that many "rustic" restaurants now advertise it as a special delicacy.

In times of hardship and famine, rural people were forced to rely on poverty staples, such as sweet potatoes, when there wasn't enough rice to go around. Their pathetic rice rations were bulked out by the addition of such starchy vegetables, not to mention, in the most desperate times of all, notorious "food substitutes" such as bark and clay. These days, when rice and everything else is plentifully available, some cooks still like to mix a few pieces of potato, taro, or sweet potato into their pot-sticker rice. It tastes good, and for the generation of urbanites who were sent down to the countryside to labor as peasants during the Cultural Revolution, evokes bittersweet memories of their youth.

A side-product of *guo ba fan* is the starchy rice liquid drained off after the parboiling. It has a silky texture that is richly comforting, and was drunk as a soup by poor peasants who couldn't afford to waste the nutrients it held. In the worst years, people tell me, they didn't even wash the rice, for fear of losing some of its starch in the water. Some neorustic restaurants offer vegetarian soups that make use of this "rice broth" (*mi tang*) instead of stock—and my Hunanese vegetarian friends adore it, as do I. Coarse, cheap rices make better *mi tang*—the more clean and polished the rice, the less starchy the soup.

If by any chance you happen to be cooking over a fire, just leave the pot of drained rice nestling in the edge of the embers as you prepare the other food, turning occasionally for an even rice crust.

POT-STICKER RICE

continued

A FEW POTATOES, TAROS, OR

SWEET POTATOES

(OPTIONAL)

1½ CUPS THAI FRAGRANT RICE

OR SIMILAR

PEANUT OIL OR LARD

1. Peel the vegetables and cut into bite-size chunks, if using.

2. Place the rice in a heavy-bottomed saucepan, along with the vegetables, if you are using them, and cover with plenty of water. Bring to a boil over a high flame, stirring occasionally to prevent sticking, then continue to boil for 5–7 minutes, until the rice is partially cooked but still *al dente* (each grain should still be hard in the middle). Drain off the cooking water, reserving it for a soup, if you please.

3. Rub the surface of the pan with a little oil or lard, add the rice and vegetables, and cover with a tight-fitting lid. (If your saucepan lid is not tight-fitting, cover the pan with a damp dish towel, place the lid on top, and then draw the edges of the cloth up into a knot over the lid so the edges don't trail on the stovetop.) Set the pan to cook over the lowest possible heat for about an hour. The *guo ba* will start to form after 30 or 40 minutes, but needs a little longer to become thick and golden.

4. Either serve the rice from the pan, scraping the *guo ba* from its bottom with a metal spatula as you go, or invert the whole lot into a serving bowl, with the *guo ba* in appetizing pieces on top. Make sure you portion out the *guo ba* fairly, or there might be trouble.

SERVES 4–6, DEPENDING ON APPETITE

TRADITIONAL STEAMED RICE
zeng zi fan

瓹
子
飯

The other traditional way of cooking rice is to parboil the grains and then steam them until they are fully cooked and fragrant, usually in a wooden steamer lined with cheesecloth. The old-fashioned rice steamer is known as a *zeng zi*. It's a cooking vessel that has really ancient roots in China: an earthenware *zeng zi* is on display at the New Stone Age Banpo site in northern Shaanxi province, and one of the finds in the Han dynasty tombs at Mawangdui, in Hunan, was a steaming set of a pottery cauldron (*fu*) and its matching *zeng zi*.

Some restaurants steam portions of rice in individual clay bowls, and serve them with a spoonful of a spicy pickled relish. My first meal in Hunan consisted of a clay bowl of steamed rice and another one of steamed pork and preserved mustard greens, which I bought on the railroad station platform in Huaihua. To my amazement, my fellow passengers, when they had finished their meals, threw the bowls out of the window of the train: they were the local equivalent of the disposable carryout carton (but biodegradable!).

¼–½ CUP THAI FRAGRANT RICE OR SIMILAR PER PERSON, DEPENDING ON APPETITE

1. Line a bamboo steamer with a piece of clean cheesecloth.
2. Place the rice in a saucepan, cover with plenty of cold water and bring to a boil. Reduce the heat and simmer 5–7 minutes, until nearly cooked but still *al dente* (each grain of rice should still be hard in the very middle).
3. Drain off the water, spread the rice in the steamer, cover, and steam over a high heat for about 10 minutes, until it smells wonderful and is fully cooked.

NOTE
The parboiling water (*mi tang*) can be used as the base for a rustic soup. (See the introduction for Pot-sticker rice on page 254.)

MUNG BEAN AND RICE PORRIDGE
lü dou zhou

★

Some of the snack restaurants in Changsha serve their food from carts, Cantonese style: there are dumplings and buns, cold meats and vegetables, tonic soups, and pickles. Local specialties include *shao mai* steamed dumplings that look like little money bags, stuffed with glutinous rice and small pieces of meat (*nuo mi da shao mai*), and "silver-silk rolls," steamed buns that fall apart into delicate threads when you pick them up with your chopsticks (*yin si juan*). There are also congees and porridges, including the following recipe, which I find most satisfying. In Hunan, this is normally eaten as a snack, with other "small eats" or a late-night barbecue, and most people sweeten it with sugar. I prefer, however, to eat it unsweetened with pickles for breakfast, or as a substitute for rice with a Chinese meal. This porridge reminds me of an extraordinarily delicious stew my friend Fan Qun's mother made during one of our visits: she simmered the mung beans with the bone from her home-smoked bacon, and added lard and scallion greens before serving.

1 CUP DRIED MUNG BEANS, SOAKED OVERNIGHT IN WATER TO COVER

¼ CUP THAI FRAGRANT RICE OR SIMILAR

SUGAR (OPTIONAL)

1. Drain the beans, then place them and the rice in a saucepan with plenty of fresh cold water. Place over a high flame and bring to a boil, then boil rapidly for 10 minutes, after which turn the heat down and simmer gently for at least an hour until the beans are tender and have split open (literally *kai hua*, "burst into flower").
2. To eat in the Hunanese manner, add sugar to taste.

SERVES 4

STIR-FRIED RICE WITH PORK AND SHIITAKE MUSHROOMS
rou si chao fan

Fried rice never has the prominence in China that it does in Chinese restaurants in the West. Plain steamed rice is the daily staple in Hunan, while fried rice is offered as a snacky meal in noodle bars. It is thought to be uncomfortably dry on its own, so is always served with a small bowlful of a very simple soup, perhaps a stock with some seaweed and egg, or pork slivers and chiles. (Japanese miso soup would be an appropriate substitute if you want a short cut.) Don't worry about precise quantities in the following recipe, because this is casual cooking. Use chicken slivers if you'd rather, and perhaps add other ingredients you have left in the refrigerator.

6 DRIED SHIITAKE MUSHROOMS

7 OZ. LEAN BONELESS PORK OR
    GROUND PORK

2 SCALLIONS, GREEN PARTS
    ONLY

1 TBSP. SOY SAUCE

1 TBSP. SHAOXING WINE

SALT AND PEPPER

DRIED CHILI FLAKES
    (OPTIONAL)

2½ CUPS COOKED RICE (ABOUT
    1¼ CUPS RAW RICE)

1 TSP. SESAME OIL

3 TBSP. PEANUT OIL FOR
    COOKING

1. Soak the shiitake mushrooms for at least 30 minutes in hot water from the kettle. When they are soft, trim off and discard their stems and thinly slice the caps.

2. Meanwhile, if you are using a piece of pork rather than ground meat, cut it into thin slices, and then into fine slivers. Finely slice the scallion greens; set aside.

3. Heat the wok over a high flame until smoke rises, then add the peanut oil and swirl around. Add the pork and stir-fry until it has changed color, adding half the soy sauce, all the Shaoxing wine, and a little salt to taste. Add the sliced mushrooms and stir-fry until fragrant, adding a few chili flakes, if desired.

4. Tip in the rice and continue to stir-fry, seasoning with the remaining soy sauce and salt to taste. When the rice is fragrant and delicious, add the scallion greens and stir a few times until you can smell them. Off the heat, season with the sesame oil and pepper to taste, and serve.

SERVES 2

STIR-FRIED RICE WITH EGG AND PRESERVED MUSTARD GREENS
suan cai dan chao fan

This is another easy way to use up leftover rice, and the rich, sour-salty taste of the preserved mustard greens goes particularly well with the yellow richness of the egg. Like the previous recipe, this will always be served with a small bowlful of soup in Hunan.

6 TBSP. CHOPPED PRESERVED
   MUSTARD GREENS (ABOUT
   2 OZ.)

4 EGGS

SALT AND PEPPER

2 SCALLIONS, GREEN PARTS
   ONLY

2½ CUPS COOKED RICE (ABOUT
   1¼ CUPS RAW RICE)

1 TSP. SESAME OIL

3 TBSP. PEANUT OIL FOR
   COOKING

1. Rinse the preserved mustard greens thoroughly to get rid of excess salt; shake dry. Beat the eggs together with a little salt. Finely slice the scallion greens.

2. Heat the wok over a high flame until smoke rises, then add the peanut oil and swirl around. Add the preserved mustard greens and stir-fry briefly until fragrant. Add the beaten eggs and stir to scramble them.

3. When the eggs are half-cooked, throw in the rice and continue to stir-fry until it is fragrant (it will make crisp, popping noises and taste delicious). Add salt if you wish, although you may not need to because of the remaining saltiness of the mustard greens.

4. Finally, add the scallion greens and stir a few times until you can smell their aroma. Off the heat, season with the sesame oil and pepper to taste, and serve.

SERVES 2

SOUP NOODLES
HUNANESE SOUP NOODLES
hu nan tang mian

湖
南
湯
面

Most Chinese food stores sell a great variety of noodles, fresh and dried, and made from both rice and wheat. All the following recipes can be made with either wheaten egg noodles or rice pasta (often sold as *ho fun*), whichever you prefer.

GENERAL BLUEPRINT FOR SERVING HUNANESE SOUP NOODLES

Whether you are serving rice *fen* or wheaten noodles, and whether you are serving them with a stew, a stir-fry, or a steamed topping, the basic method is the same. First, you need to prepare the base seasonings in each bowl, and then to add some hot stock—everyday stock (page 287), fine stock (page 288), or vegetarian stock, as you please. You then add the cooked noodles, some blanched greens, if you like, and finally spoon the topping over. Allow your guests to mix everything together at the table, and to add chopped salted chiles, chili sauce, dried chili flakes, soy sauce, and/or vinegar to taste.

Depending on the appetites of your guests, use about 3–4 ounces dried or 11 ounces fresh noodles per person.

STEP 1: PREPARE THE BOWLS

1. Place in each serving bowl:

A DASH LIGHT SOY SAUCE TO GIVE THE STOCK
A NICE COLOR

SALT AND PEPPER TO TASTE

A GOOD SCATTERING FINELY SLICED
SCALLION GREENS

A DASH PEANUT OIL OR LARD (I OFTEN USE
OLIVE OIL, ACTUALLY)

STEP 2: HEAT THE STOCK, BLANCH THE GREENS (IF USING), COOK THE NOODLES

1. Bring a saucepan of water to a boil, and bring 1¼ cups soup stock per person to a boil in a separate pan at the same time.

2. Blanch any greens in the boiling water, then remove with a slotted spoon and set aside.

3. Return the water to a boil, then cook or reheat the noodles until tender. (See the note below on cooking noodles.)

4. When the noodles are nearly ready, add a portion of the boiling stock to each serving bowl.

5. Add a portion of cooked noodles to each serving bowl and lay the greens alongside the noodles.

STEP 3: ADD THE TOPPING

1. If you are using a stew or a steamed topping, simply spoon one portion over each bowlful of noodles.

2. If you are using a stir-fried topping, cook it quickly now and spoon it over the noodles.

STEP 4: SERVE, WITH TABLE CONDIMENTS

1. Allow your guests to add any or all of the following to their noodles, to taste:

CHOPPED SALTED CHILES

CHILI SAUCE OF YOUR CHOICE

DRIED CHILI FLAKES

LIGHT SOY SAUCE

CHINKIANG VINEGAR

A NOTE ON COOKING THE NOODLES OR *FEN*

1. If you are using fresh rice *fen*, which are often available in larger Chinese food stores, they simply need reheating in boiling water, and then draining.

2. Dried rice *fen* should be soaked in hot water for about 30 minutes until supple, and then reheated in boiling water when you want to eat them.

3. Fresh and dried wheaten noodles should be cooked according to the directions on the package.

Each topping that follows serves 4. And don't forget you can easily use the same method to eat up leftovers of stews from other culinary traditions: how about topping Chinese noodles with navarin of lamb or stewed brisket?

CHANGDE RICE NOODLES WITH RED-BRAISED BEEF
jin shi niu rou fen

This recipe is particularly associated with the Hui, the ethnic Chinese Muslims who are scattered the length and breadth of China, and who have traditionally run noodle restaurants in the northern Hunanese city of Changde. This version of red-braised beef was taught to me by a noodle restaurant owner called Zhu Qingyan, and is traditionally served over round rice noodles a little thicker than spaghetti, but it's equally delicious over flat *ho fun* or any other Chinese noodles. Mr. Zhu makes this topping in large pots and seasons it with more than forty spices. The essentials are cassia bark, star anise, and ginger, and I've suggested adding Sichuan pepper, fennel seeds, and *cao guo* if you have them on hand. If you wish to cook for a large party and are feeling adventurous, you can add some or all of the other spices listed in the recipe for spiced aromatic broth (*lu shui*) on pages 54–5.

1 LB. BRAISING BEEF STEAK

2 TBSP. BEEF DRIPPING OR
    PEANUT OIL

2½ TBSP. CHILLI BEAN PASTE

A FEW SLICES FRESH GINGER,
    UNPEELED

2 PIECES CASSIA BARK

1 STAR ANISE

1 TBSP. SHAOXING WINE

1 TBSP. DARK SOY SAUCE

1 SCALLION

¼ TSP. WHOLE SICHUAN PEPPER

¼ TSP. FENNEL SEEDS

1 *CAO GUO* OR 3 CARDAMOM
    PODS

1. Cut the beef into bite-size cubes. Place in a saucepan with cold water to cover and bring to the boil over a high flame, skimming off the froth that rises to the surface. Remove the beef with a slotted spoon and set aside. Skim the cooking liquid again if necessary, then strain into a jug; set aside.

2. Heat the dripping or oil in a clean pan or a wok over a medium flame. Add the chili bean paste and stir-fry until the oil is red and fragrant. Add the ginger, cassia, and star anise and continue to stir-fry until you can smell their wonderful aromas.

3. Tip in the beef and toss in the fragrant oil and spices. Add enough of the cooking liquid to cover generously, along with the other ingredients. (The seeds can be tied in a piece of cheesecloth if you have some to hand.) Bring to a boil, then reduce the heat, partially cover the wok or pan, and simmer for 2–3 hours over a very low flame, until tender.

ingredients and method continue on the next page

To serve:

NOODLES, STOCK, AND BASE
    SEASONINGS (SEE GENERAL
    DIRECTIONS ON PAGES 260–1)
CHOPPED CORIANDER LEAVES

4. Serve the noodles according to the general directions on pages 260–1, adding a little chopped coriander to the seasonings in each bowl.

NOTE

The beef topping on its own makes a magnificent winter stew, which in Hunan would normally be served with rice and other dishes, but which goes equally well with mashed potato. If you wish to eat it as a stew, I suggest doubling the quantities, and perhaps cutting the meat into slightly larger pieces: this will serve four as a western main course, six as part of a Chinese meal. A delicious addition is chunks of Asian radish (*daikon*), blanched to remove any sharpness, and then added to the stew about 30 minutes before you wish to eat and simmered until tender. You might need to add a little more water or stock to the pot to accommodate them. The soft, translucent flesh of the radish is a wonderful foil for the beef. You might also like to garnish the stew with coriander.

SPICED PORK NOODLES
jiang zhi mian

酱汁面

Sansan and I rose early, and were greeted with the spectacular vista of the Fenghuang riverside stirring in a blazing dawn. Slanting sunlight caught the wooden facades of overhanging buildings, and a few fishermen pottered around. A cluster of people in brightly colored clothes were doing their washing on stone slabs jutting out into the water. Fragments of their conversations and the whack of wooden batons on wet cloth sounded along the river in the still morning air. We breakfasted in a small café, on rice noodles in soup with stewed pork and chiles, and then hitched a lift out into the countryside to explore the villages. The terraced rice paddies were in their full flush of green, stirred silver by small gusts of wind, and the shallow, peacock-blue river tumbled over stones as it coursed through a valley of gentle hills. Later, there were steeper slopes as the road, now precipitous, wound up into the mountains. In a desolate country town we bought straw hats to shield us from the searing heat, and hitched a lift on the back of a rattling truck that jostled and jumped over a steep rutted track.

The following is a recipe for the spiced stewed pork that is common all over the province, and according to waiting staff is the most popular noodle topping in the famous old Changsha restaurant, Yangyuxing.

1¼ LB. PORK TENDERLOIN

¾ TSP. SALT

1 TBSP. SWEET BEAN SAUCE

1 TBSP. SHAOXING WINE

2 TBSP. CRUSHED YELLOW ROCK
   SUGAR

1 STAR ANISE

2 SLICES FRESH GINGER,
   UNPEELED

To serve:

NOODLES, STOCK, AND BASE
   SEASONINGS (SEE GENERAL
   DIRECTIONS ON PAGES 260–1)
CHOPPED SALTED CHILES

1. Cut the pork evenly into bite-size cubes. Cover with cold water and bring to a boil over a high flame, skimming the froth that rises to the surface. Remove the pork with a slotted spoon and set aside. Add the salt to the boiling cooking liquid, then strain the liquid into a jug.

2. Return the pork to the pan with the sweet bean sauce, Shaoxing wine, sugar, star anise, and ginger, and pour enough of the cooking liquid over to cover. Bring to a boil, half-cover the pan, and then leave to simmer very gently for 2–3 hours, until the pork is very tender, topping up with a little more liquid as necessary. (If you happen to have an Aga, leave it to stew in the bottom oven—it's ideal!) Add a little more salt before serving, if necessary.

3. Serve the noodles according to the general directions on pages 260–1. If you add a good spoonful of chopped salted chiles and a scattering of scallion greens to the base seasonings in the bowl, a stir of the chopsticks will make the dish satisfyingly colorful.

SOUR-AND-HOT NOODLES
suan la mian

This recipe is based on one from the Huangchunhe rice noodle restaurant on Liberation Street in Changsha. Huangchunhe prides itself on the quality of its fresh rice *fen*, which are delivered daily in great bamboo baskets.

6 OZ. BAMBOO SHOOTS (EITHER BRINED OR DRIED AND RECONSTITUTED BY SOAKING IN HOT WATER FROM THE KETTLE)

3 TBSP. CHOPPED PRESERVED MUSTARD GREENS (ABOUT 1 OZ.)

¼ LB. GROUND PORK

1 TBSP. SHAOXING WINE

1 TBSP. DRIED CHILI FLAKES

2 CUPS EVERYDAY STOCK (PAGE 287)

1½ TBSP. LIGHT SOY SAUCE

¼ TSP. DARK SOY SAUCE

SALT AND PEPPER

3 TBSP. PEANUT OIL FOR COOKING

1. Cut the brined or soaked bamboo shoots into slices and then slivers and blanch them in lightly salted boiling water just until the water returns to the boil; shake dry and set aside. Rinse the preserved mustard greens to get rid of excess saltiness, then shake and squeeze dry.

2. Heat the wok over a high flame until smoke rises, then add the peanut oil and swirl around. Add the pork and stir-fry until it has changed color, splashing in the Shaoxing wine as you go. Add the mustard greens and bamboo shoots and continue to stir-fry until everything is sizzly and fragrant. Add the chili flakes, stir a few times to bring out their aroma, and then pour in the stock. Bring to a boil, add the soy sauces, and season with salt to taste.

3. Reduce the heat, partially cover, and simmer for about 20 minutes until the pork is tender. Serve the noodles according to the general directions on pages 260–1.

NOODLES WITH SHIITAKE MUSHROOMS
AND BABY GREENS
xiang gu cai xin mian

The shiitake mushrooms give this dish a fabulously smoky and savory taste. This topping is perfect for vegetarians if you serve the noodles in a vegetable stock.

20 SMALL DRIED SHIITAKE
    MUSHROOMS, OR 8 LARGER
    ONES
10 BABY BOK CHOY
1-IN. PIECE FRESH GINGER,
    PEELED AND SLICED
LIGHT SOY SAUCE
SALT AND WHITE PEPPER
½ TSP. POTATO FLOUR MIXED
    WITH 2 TSP. COLD WATER
1 TSP. SESAME OIL
3–4 TBSP. PEANUT OIL FOR
    COOKING

SERVES 2

1. Soak the dried mushrooms in hot water from the kettle for 30 minutes or so until soft.
2. Trim the bok choy, and if their stems are thick, make a cross-shaped cut into them to help them cook more quickly, as you might when preparing brussels sprouts.
3. Heat the wok over a high flame until smoke rises, then add 2 tablespoons of the peanut oil and swirl around. Add the bok choy and stir-fry briskly until barely cooked; set aside.
4. Strain the mushrooms, reserving the soaking liquid. Squeeze the mushrooms dry, and if they are large slice each into 3 or 4 bite-size pieces, discarding the stems.
5. Return the wok to the high flame with a little extra oil. Add the ginger and stir-fry until fragrant. Tip in the mushrooms and continue to stir-fry until they smell wonderful. Then add about ¼ cup of the soaking water, bring to a boil and season with soy sauce and salt to taste. Add the bok choy and a good pinch of pepper, mix well, and then stir in just enough of the potato flour mixture to give the sauce a glossy thickness.
6. Off the heat, stir in the sesame oil and then divide between 2 prepared bowls of soup noodles.

VARIATION

Use the same recipe to cook fresh mushrooms of your choice, but stir-fry them until they are tender before you add the other ingredients.

OTHER IDEAS:

Other recipes in this book work very well as noodle toppings, for example the chicken soup with cloud ears and ginger (see pages 248–9) and the steamed chicken with chopped salted chiles (see page 123).

NOODLES WITH FRESH SHRIMP AND BABY GREENS
xia ren cai xin mian

蝦
仁
菜
心
面

The noodles at Yangyuxing are served in traditional Hunan style. Bowls of steaming-hot soup noodles are stacked along wooden serving boards (*ban zi*), each deeply engraved with crosses to stop the bowls from slipping. Each layer of bowls can be topped with another board, and another layer of bowls, and so a single waiter bearing one of these double-decker trays can serve several people at a time.

This recipe is inspired by one of the specialties of the Yangyuxing noodle restaurant in Changsha. It serves 2–4 people as a noodle topping in the Hunanese manner, depending on greed. If you can't find baby greens, use regular choy sam or bok choy, cutting bok choy lengthwise into bite-size pieces.

20 FRESH JUMBO SHRIMP

SALT AND WHITE PEPPER

1 TBSP. POTATO FLOUR

1 EGG WHITE

5 SCALLIONS

8 BOK CHOY OR BABY CHOY SAM

2 TSP. FINELY CHOPPED GARLIC

2 TSP. FINELY CHOPPED FRESH
    GINGER

2 TSP. CHOPPED SALTED CHILES
    OR FINELY CHOPPED FRESH
    RED CHILI

½ CUP EVERYDAY STOCK (PAGE
    287)

½ TSP. POTATO FLOUR MIXED
    WITH 2 TSP. COLD WATER

1 TSP. SESAME OIL

SALT AND WHITE PEPPER

1 CUP PEANUT OIL FOR COOKING

To serve:

CHINKIANG VINEGAR

CHOPPED SALTED CHILES OR
    CHILI SAUCE OF YOUR CHOICE

1. Shell and devein the shrimp, then rinse thoroughly and shake dry. Place in a bowl, stir in ½ teaspoon salt and then the potato flour and egg white and mix well; set aside.

2. Separate the green and white parts of the scallions, and cut them into 1½-inch pieces. Discard any wilted leaves from the greens and, if you are using bok choy, cut a cross into each stem as you might with brussels sprouts, so they will cook quickly.

3. Heat the peanut oil in a wok until it reaches 300°F. Strain any excess egg white from the shrimp, and then fry them briefly, stirring to separate, until they just turn pink; remove and set aside. Drain off all but 2 tablespoons of the oil.

4. Add the scallion whites, garlic, ginger, and chili to the oil in the wok and stir-fry until fragrant. Add the shrimp and stir a few times. Pour in the stock and season with salt to taste. Add the bok choy or choy sam and the scallion greens, and continue to stir until they are cooked but still crunchy. Give the potato flour mixture a stir and pour into the middle of the wok, stirring briefly as the liquid thickens. Off the heat, stir in the sesame oil and pepper to taste, then spoon over your prepared bowls of noodles (see the general directions on pages 260–1). Give the noodles a good stir before eating. At the table, add vinegar and extra chopped salted chiles or chili sauce to taste.

STIR-FRIED NOODLES

STIR-FRIED RICE NOODLES WITH CHICKEN SLIVERS
ji si chao fen

★

The Heji restaurant in northern Changsha, which dates back to the 1920s, specializes in rice *fen*. The vast majority of *fen* dishes at the Heji are served in a soup, but they also offer some delicious stir-fried versions, including this one. Like fried rice, fried noodles are always served with a small bowlful of soup, because they are thought otherwise to be uncomfortably dry.

2 BONELESS CHICKEN BREAST
  HALVES (12 OZ. TOTAL)

4 DRIED SHIITAKE MUSHROOMS,
  SOAKED FOR 30 MINUTES IN
  HOT WATER FROM THE KETTLE

1½ LB. SOAKED *HO FUN* RICE
  NOODLES (ABOUT 5 OZ. DRY)

3 SCALLIONS, GREEN PARTS
  ONLY

2 TSP. FINELY CHOPPED FRESH
  GINGER

2 TSP. FINELY CHOPPED GARLIC

2 TSP. CHOPPED SALTED CHILES

2 TSP. SOY SAUCE

SALT AND WHITE PEPPER

5 OZ. FRESH BEAN SPROUTS

1 TSP. SESAME OIL

5 TBSP. PEANUT OIL FOR
  COOKING

For the marinade:

½ TSP. SALT

2 TSP. LIGHT SOY SAUCE

1½ TSP. POTATO FLOUR

1 TSP. SHAOXING WINE

1 TBSP. WATER

1. Cut the chicken breasts along the grain of the meat into fine slivers. Place in a bowl with the marinade ingredients and mix well; set aside.

2. Drain the mushrooms, squeeze dry, and remove the stems, then cut into fine slices. Cut the scallion greens into thin slivers about 1½ inches long; set aside.

3. Heat the wok over a high flame until smoke rises, then add 3 tablespoons of the oil and swirl around. Add the drained noodles and stir-fry until hot and fragrant; set aside. (If you have deep-frying oil at hand, you can deep-fry instead, which is faster.)

4. Rinse the wok if necessary, then reheat with 2 tablespoons fresh oil. Add the chicken slivers and stir-fry until they separate. Add the ginger, garlic, salted chiles, and mushrooms and stir-fry until fragrant. Add the hot noodles and continue to stir-fry, adding the soy sauce and salt and pepper to taste.

5. Stir in the bean sprouts and stir-fry until they are piping hot. Finally, add the scallion greens, stir-fry a few times, then remove from the heat, and stir in the sesame oil. Serve immediately.

VARIATIONS

The same dish can be made with egg noodles, and you can use pork slivers instead of chicken if you prefer, or a mixture of mushrooms if you are vegetarian.

9

SWEET DISHES 甜品類

★ SWEET DISHES

Sweet foods play almost no part in the everyday Hunanese meal. There is no local equivalent to the dessert course of the West, and Hunanese people do not, as a rule, like to mix their sweet and savory tastes. However, as in many parts of China, banquet cooking tends to blur the boundaries of regional tastes, incorporating elements from other culinary schools, and this is where you might encounter sweet dishes like the apples trailing golden threads in this chapter. Sweet snacks are also part of the street food tradition, and you will find some of these described in the Appetizers and Street Food chapter beginning on page 44. The only sweet dish I can remember being offered as part of a meal in a Hunanese home was the eight-treasure glutinous rice (see page 279), and that was served during the New Year holiday, when every household stocks up on sweets and fruits to offer to well-wishing visitors.

Above: ROCK HONEY FROM
WESTERN HUNAN

Interestingly, honey tends to be eaten on its own, as a tonic drink. When I was staying with Liu Wei and Sansan, Sansan's father returned from a trip to the remote west of Hunan with an extraordinary chunk of rock honey (*shi mi*) that he said had been found in a mountain cave. It was a rare find, a great, pale yellow rock, pitted and holey like volcanic lava, embedded with wisps of lichen and other vegetation. Some papery honeycomb bee chambers were still visible in places, and it had a breathtakingly sweet and intoxicating fragrance. We dissolved chunks of it in hot water, strained off the golden liquid and drank it like nectar.

Right: EIGHT-TREASURE GLUTINOUS
RICE, LIUYANG

APPLES TRAILING GOLDEN THREADS
ba si ping guo

拔
絲
苹
果

This variation on the "toffee banana" theme is a delightful combination of juicy apple rich batter, and chewy golden toffee, and it looks amazing with its halo of golden threads.

The only trick is to make sure you heat the syrup to the right temperature, and then move quickly: if you boil it for too long it will caramelize. The Chinese name of the dish literally means "apples trailing silken threads," a reference to the hairlike strands made by the toffee when you pick up a piece of apple in your chopsticks. You can use exactly the same method to make toffee bananas. (Curiously, "banana" has acquired a mildly insulting meaning in modern China: if you call someone a banana, you suggest they are "yellow on the outside but white on the inside," in other words, that they might look Chinese but their heart and soul are in the West. A similar insult, "radish," which sounds outdated in these capitalist times, would imply someone was a fake communist, "red on the outside, white on the inside.")

1 LB. CRISP APPLES

2 EGGS, BEATEN

6 TBSP. POTATO FLOUR

5 TBSP. ALL-PURPOSE FLOUR

1 CUP GRANULATED SUGAR

¼ CUP COLD WATER

PEANUT OIL FOR DEEP-FRYING
    (AT LEAST 2 CUPS)

1. Lightly oil a serving dish; set aside. Peel, quarter, and core the apples, and then cut each quarter in half lengthwise.

2. Beat the eggs together. Mix 4 tablespoons of the potato flour and all the all-purpose flour with enough beaten egg to make a thick batter, about the consistency of raw cake batter.

3. Set 2 bowls of iced water on the serving table.

4. Heat the oil for deep-frying until it reaches 350°F. Dust the apple segments with the remaining dry potato flour, and then mix them into the batter, taking care to cover them completely. When the oil is hot enough, tip in the apples, using a pair of chopsticks to separate the pieces. Deep-fry until golden, then drain and set aside. (If you use a wok with only 2 cups oil, it's best to fry the apple slices in 2 batches.)

continued on the next page

5. Pour off all the oil and give the wok a quick rinse. Place the dry wok over a gentle flame with the sugar and water. Heat gently to dissolve the sugar, then turn up the heat and boil for about 10 minutes until the syrup reaches 275°F. You don't actually need a thermometer for this: just keep stirring the syrup with chopsticks, and lifting the chopsticks out. The syrup will become very frothy as it approaches the right temperature, and at 275°F, a raised chopstick will produce a hairlike, floating strand of sugar, and the syrup will be just turning yellow. When this temperature has been reached, turn off the heat, move swiftly to tip the apples into the syrup, and stir briskly to coat them.

6. Tip the apples onto the serving dish. Now use a pair of chopsticks to move a few segments of apples around: this will produce lots of hairlike strands trailing over the golden mound of apples, which look fabulous. Serve immediately.

7. Invite your guests to use chopsticks to pick up pieces of apple and dip them into the iced water, where the toffee will solidify immediately.

甜
酒
冲
蛋

HUNANESE EGGNOG
tian jiu chong dan

Dilute sweet glutinous rice wine (see opposite) with roughly 2 parts water and bring to a boil in a saucepan. Break an egg into each person's bowl or mug, and beat well. Pour plenty of the boiling wine mixture over, stirring with chopsticks as you do. The egg will set into wisps in the hot liquid. Season with sugar and pepper to taste.

SWEET GLUTINOUS RICE WINE
tian jiu

甜
酒

One misty, moisty morning, my friend Fan Qun and I picked our way among the paddy fields in her village, and climbed a hill. At the top, an ancient evergreen spread its branches over a Buddhist shrine and a tumbledown house built of earth and wood. There we found an old lady who Fan Qun remembered from her childhood. She invited us in, and offered us low wooden chairs by the kitchen fire. She toasted sesame seeds in a pan in the embers and scattered them, hot and fragrant, into mugs of homegrown tea. And as the rain pattered down outside, she told us about her life in the 1930s, when she and other villagers fled to the mountains to escape attack by Japanese soldiers, who looted houses and stole their food. "We never had enough to eat," she said. "Just boiled wild vegetables mixed with a little rice." Perhaps her memories made her hungry, because she roused herself to make us mugfuls of a delicious Hunanese "eggnog." She ladled some homemade glutinous rice wine from an earthenware pot into an enameled mug with a lid, which she set in the embers to boil. Off the heat, she stirred in some beaten eggs, sugar, and ground pepper. And it was wonderful, warm and nourishing in the damp spring weather.

Glutinous rice wine, or "sweet liquor" in Hunanese dialect, is an ingredient used to add a gentle, boozy fragrance to many sweet dishes, and sometimes to enhance the taste of savory foods. The clear liquid can be strained off, but it is often used with the whole rice grains. *Tian jiu* is easy to make at home, but you might be able to find it in jars in your local Chinese supermarket. (Look for rice grains in a slightly cloudy, but colorless, liquid). In Hunan, it is sold in markets, and by street vendors who set their large earthenware tubs of *tian jiu* on small wooden platforms, suspended from each end of a shoulderpole.

Wine yeast balls (*jiu qu*) can be found in good Chinese supermarkets.

1¼ CUPS LONG-GRAIN
   GLUTINOUS RICE
1¾ CUPS WATER
1 WINE YEAST BALL (SEE
   INTRODUCTION ABOVE)

1. Rinse the rice in cold water until the water runs clear.
2. Place the rice in a steamer with the water and steam until just tender. Turn onto a large plate and spread out to cool.
3. Meanwhile, crush the wine yeast to a coarse powder with a mortar and pestle.
4. When the rice is lukewarm, scatter the crushed yeast over, and mix well. Next, put the rice mixture into a jar, preferably earthenware, and close the lid tightly. Do not fill the jar completely—you must leave a gap of a couple of inches above the rice. Wrap the jar in a warm cloth and leave to ferment for 3 days in a warm place. The wine can now be used, but it will keep indefinitely in the refrigerator.

HUNANESE LOTUS SEEDS WITH ROCK SUGAR
bing tang xiang lian

The lotus plant is part of the landscape of southern China, and its seeds are the most prized of its many edible parts. Their name in Chinese, *lian zi*, sounds the same as "successive sons," so they are a traditional symbol of fertility. They are most commonly sold when dried, but in the right season you may come across street vendors bearing basketsful of green lotus seed pods. You pluck the young green seeds from a nest of spongy green, ease off their skins, and eat them for their juicy crispness.

Lotus seeds grown in the Dongting Lake area of Hunan province (*xiang lian*) are renowned across China for their roundness, whiteness, and deliciously glutinous texture, and historically they were sent in tribute to the imperial court. They are used in various sweetmeats and tonic dishes, but it is with the following sweet soup that they are most strongly associated. The seeds, as one of my sources puts it, float at the surface of the soup "like pearls bobbing in a jadelike pool." They have a taste and texture reminiscent of chestnuts.

1½ CUPS DRIED LOTUS SEEDS

A SMALL HANDFUL DRIED
    SILVER EAR FUNGUS

2 TBSP. CHINESE WOLFBERRIES

2½ CUPS CRUSHED YELLOW ROCK
    SUGAR

2 CUPS COLD WATER

1. Soak the lotus seeds in cold water for a couple of hours or overnight, then drain and place in a heatproof bowl with hot water from the kettle to cover. Place the bowl in a steamer and steam for about 45 minutes, until the seeds are tender, but still holding their shape; drain and set aside.

2. Meanwhile, soak the silver ear fungus and the wolfberries, separately, in hot water from the kettle for about 15 minutes until soft. When the fungus is soft, rinse it to remove any impurities and break it into small pieces with your fingers, discarding any hard bits from the base.

3. Place the yellow lump sugar in a pan with the water over a gentle flame, stirring from time to time as the sugar dissolves. If there is any residue from the sugar, strain the liquid and then return it to the pan. Add the lotus seeds, bring to a boil, and then simmer for a few minutes to allow the syrup to penetrate. Add the silver ear fungus and wolfberries and simmer for another 1–2 minutes. Ladle the soup into individual bowls to serve.

EIGHT-TREASURE GLUTINOUS RICE
ba bao guo fan

Glutinous rice steamed with candied fruits, nuts, and seeds is a traditional New Year sweetmeat. When I spent the Chinese New Year holiday in Hunan, I was offered this dish made both with the white glutinous rice of the recipe below, and, on another occasion, with black glutinous rice, which has a dramatic purple color. The Yuloudong restaurant in Changsha serves a delicious version in which the cooked rice is flattened into a pancake, fried, and served with a sprinkling of white sugar. Crisp and slightly golden on either side, it is so fantastically delicious that it won a gold medal at a national culinary contest.

Some people like to arrange the fruits and nuts in a pretty pattern on the base of the steaming bowl, and then gently add the rice. If you do this, it looks wonderful when you turn it out onto the serving dish.

1¼ CUPS GLUTINOUS RICE

SCANT ¼ CUP LOTUS SEEDS

3 TBSP. RAW, SHELLED PEANUTS

12 CHINESE DATES (*HONG ZAO*)

1 TBSP. CHINESE WOLFBERRIES
(*GOU QI*)

4 TBSP. DRIED LONGAN FRUIT OR
DRAGON-EYE FRUIT (*LONG
YAN*)

2 TBSP. GOLDEN RAISINS

1½ TBSP. PEANUT OIL OR MELTED
LARD, PLUS A LITTLE EXTRA
FOR THE BOWL

3 TBSP. TURBINADO SUGAR

3 TBSP. MIXED CANDIED
CHERRIES AND ANGELICA OR
CANDIED CITRUS PEEL,
CHOPPED

GRANULATED SUGAR TO SERVE

1. Soak the glutinous rice in cold water overnight, or in hot water for 2–3 hours. Soak the lotus seeds and peanuts, separately from the rice, in water overnight.

2. The following day, set the Chinese dates, wolfberries, longan fruits, and golden raisins to soak in hot water from the kettle for at least 30 minutes.

3. Bring a saucepan of water to a boil. Rinse the soaked rice and add it to the water. Bring to a boil and simmer for 2–3 minutes until just tender, but not mushy; drain the rice.

4. Add the peanut oil or lard and the sugar to the rice. Then drain the soaked fruits and nuts and add them to the rice with the candied fruit; mix well.

5. Rub a heatproof bowl lightly with oil and add the rice mixture. Place the bowl in the steamer and steam for about 40 minutes to fuse the flavors. Turn out onto a plate and sprinkle with sugar to serve

NOTE

The "eight treasures" can include lotus seeds, cooked chestnuts, peanuts, Chinese jujube dates, golden raisins, dried longan fruits or dragon-eyes, candied orange peel, candied rose petals, candied cherries, candied winter melon, Chinese wolfberries—or anything else you fancy. Larger pieces of "treasure" should be chopped.

IO

PRESERVES, STOCKS, AND OTHER ESSENTIALS

其它

★ PRESERVES, STOCKS AND OTHER ESSENTIALS

Homemade pickles and preserves are part of the fabric of Hunanese life. In the farmhouses, rows of clay pickle jars are packed with homemade preserves; blood-red salted chiles, mixed pickled vegetables, dry-salted mustard greens, fermented bean curd, and a spicy relish made from Asian radish (*daikon*) and chili. Even in the cities, many people make their own pickled vegetables and salted chiles.

Market stalls near the Changsha riverside offer sacks full of dried vegetables: yard-long beans, flame-colored chiles, strips of white radish, bamboo shoots, perilla leaves, fiddlehead ferns, bitter melon, sheets of kelp, and strips of eggplant. Pickle stands at the Mawangdui wholesale market display colorful pickles in bowls atop knee-high earthenware jars, each cradled by a woven shell of looping bamboo. There are languid bunches of pickled string beans; knobby heads of mustard tuber, their gray-green skins stained rusty by chili; small gray-green chiles with flashes of orange; dark chili paste; and brilliant-scarlet chopped chiles. Nearby, there's a dark forest of hanging smoked meats.

Aside from chopped salted chiles (see opposite), there are green "wild mountain chiles" (*ye shan jiao*) pickled in brine, and pale "white" chiles (*bai la jiao, pu la jiao*) that have been blanched, sun-dried and then brined. Most intriguingly, there is the Changde specialty, *zha la jiao*, a pickle of red chiles, ground rice, and salt whose origins some people trace back to the fish preserves of ancient China. Stir-fried with a few leaves of green garlic and other seasonings, it has a wonderful and unusual taste and fragrance.

Fermented bean curd (*dou fu ru*) is an essential relish with a pungent, cheesy flavor and a creamy texture. It is made by covering firm bean curd in dry rice straw and leaving it to mold for a couple of weeks. The molded curd is cut into cubes, mixed with strong liquor, salt, star anise, and chili flakes, and packed into pickling jars for at least a month to mature. And then there are the preserved meats and fish, which are brined, wind-dried, and then cold-smoked over sawdust and rice husks, after which they can be kept for many months. (See page 76 for more information.)

In the countryside, these traditional preserves are still a way of dealing with an abundant harvest, and tiding the family over the winter. In the cities, they are enjoyed for their tastes and textures, and certain preserves, such as chopped salted chiles and bacon, have become some of the hallmarks of Hunanese cuisine. A thorough account of Hunanese food preservation would require a separate book, but I've included a few basic recipes here, alongside some other useful bits and pieces.

Left: PICKLE STALL, LIUYANG

HUNANESE CHOPPED SALTED CHILES
duo la jiao

The brilliant red of this easy preserve is one of the most characteristic colors of Hunanese cooking. It is used in stir-fries and steamed dishes (steamed fish heads with chopped salted chiles is currently one of the best-known and most popular Hunanese dishes), and is also offered as a relish with noodles and other snacks. My friend Fan Qun's mother makes hers in the traditional dark-glazed earthenware jar, which has a deep lip for a water-seal and a rough terracotta bowl for a lid, but you can use an ordinary preserving jar.

1 LB. VERY FRESH RED CHILES

¼ CUP SALT

1. Wash the chiles and dry thoroughly. Cut off their stems and bottoms, and chop coarsely with the seeds. (You might wish to use rubber gloves to do this, because it can get very spicy.) Place the chopped chiles in a bowl.

2. Add 3½ tablespoons of the salt to the chiles and mix thoroughly. Place in a glass jar and cover with the remaining salt. Seal with a tight-fitting lid. Leave in a cool place for a couple of weeks before using, then store in the refrigerator once opened. The chiles will keep for months.

CHILI OIL
la jiao oil

In the Miao villages of western Hunan, the older women still wear traditional dress: wide-legged blue trousers with embroidered edging, embroidered crossover tops, and silver jewelry, with conical straw hats, or heads wrapped in swathes of dark cloth. The villages themselves are known as *zhai*, a word meaning stockaded village or military stronghold, and one we visited was a small, tightly walled maze of houses. Outside it, an ancient stone bridge, now overgrown with weeds, arched over a stream, and water buffalo wallowed in muddy pools. An old lady pointed out the large house that had served as the village canteen during the Cultural Revolution—one of the most loathed institutions of the era, remembered mainly for the provision of disgusting food, and the temporary strangulation of one of the great pleasures of Chinese life, home cooking.

The old wooden houses in the Miao *zhai* are not divided into rooms, but have large living spaces, with an open hearth in the middle and curtained, four-poster beds tucked away at the sides. The kitchen areas have great arc-shaped ranges built of brick and clay, with several openings for woks, and winter meats are smoked over the main fire. We also saw the traditional tools for preparing food: wooden mortars for crushing glutinous rice for the New Year rice cakes, rows of pottery pickle jars, stone mills for grinding rice or soybeans, and stone mortars and pestles for pulverizing chiles.

As in other parts of Hunan, chili is an essential seasoning, and the coarsely ground chili flakes are added to many dishes. They can also be made into chili oil, which is used mainly for dressing cold dishes, but can also be added to cooked food to boost color and hotness. This condiment is easy to make, and keeps for ages. I make mine in large quantities, using dried chili flakes that are not too overpoweringly hot. Some people use the traditional camellia oil: one recipe I've seen suggests steeping the ground chiles in soy sauce and salt overnight, and then adding camellia oil that has been heated for an hour or two to 200°F.

1 CUP DRIED CHILI FLAKES,
    WITH SEEDS
2¼ CUPS PEANUT OIL

1. Place the chiles in a glass preserving jar.
2. Heat the oil over a high flame to about 350°F. Remove the wok from the heat and allow the oil to cool for about 10 minutes, to 225–250°F. Pour onto the chillies, stir once or twice, and then leave to cool in a shady place. Leave to settle for at least a day before using.

SIMPLE HUNANESE PICKLED VEGETABLES
hu nan pao cai

湖南泡菜

★

Mao Zedong's family home in Shaoshan has been turned into a shrine to the revolution. People still come here to pay their respects, and the middle of the village has a market selling Mao memorabilia: statues, good-luck charms, badges, and little red books. Mao's house is a modest farmhouse, built of adobe bricks, which has been spruced up and lovingly preserved in every detail—ironic for a man who did so much to destroy China's cultural heritage. Little plaques on the walls are inscribed with dubious propaganda: "It was by the side of the kitchen fire that Mao Zedong gathered the whole family together for meetings, where he encouraged them to devote themselves to the cause of the liberation of the Chinese people." Aside from these details, the house looks much like some of the older houses just up the road, with its wood-burning kitchen range, smoking rack above the fire for the winter bacon, and clay jar for making pickled vegetables.

Pickled vegetables are one of the staple relishes in every rural Hunanese home, and are still made by many urban people, too.

4 TSP. SALT

4 TSP. CRUSHED YELLOW ROCK
    SUGAR

1½ TBSP. Chinese clear grain
    SPIRIT OR VODKA (PAGE 24)

3 PICKLED JALAPENOS AND

    2 TBSP. BRINE FROM THE JAR

Wrap in a piece of cheesecloth:

¾-IN. PIECE FRESH GINGER,
    UNPEELED AND SLICED

2 SCALLIONS, CUT INTO PIECES

A SMALL HANDFUL DRIED
    CHILES

½ TSP. GROUND Sichuan PEPPER

¼ TSP. FENNEL SEEDS

3 STAR ANISE

A COUPLE PIECES CASSIA

1 *CAO GUO*, SLIGHTLY CRUSHED

5 GARLIC CLOVES, PEELED

Any or all of the following pickling vegetables:

YARD-LONG BEANS	CHILES
ASIAN RADISH (*DAIKON*)	BELL PEPPER STRIPS
ROUND WHITE CABBAGE	CARROT

1. Place the salt, sugar, and 2 cups water in a clean pickle jar with a tight-fitting lid and stir to dissolve. Add the rice wine, pickled jalapenos and brine and the bundle of spices.

2. Fill the jar with crisp, fresh vegetables cut into bite-size strips, then seal and leave in a cool place for at least 24 hours before eating. The vegetables can be eaten on their own as an appetizer or a relish, or they can be stir-fried with ground pork and chili. Keep replenishing the vegetables in the jar as you eat them, adding more salt, sugar, and wine as you go, and replacing the spices occasionally. The flavor of the pickles will improve as the brine develops over time. If you are not eating and replenishing the pickles on a daily basis, they are best kept in the refrigerator.

SALTED DUCK EGGS
xian dan

In the past, salting eggs was simply a way to preserve them: these days, it's as much about gastronomy. The salting alters the texture of the eggs as well as their taste: the whites become denser and less jelly-like, the yolks more granular. Hard-boiled, they can be simply halved or quartered and eaten off the shell as an appetizer or nibble, especially on the fifth day of the fifth lunar month, the Dragon Boat Festival. The raw whites are good drizzled into a broth with mustard greens, but it's the yolks that are most versatile as a cooking ingredient. (See recipe and variations on page 213.)

The sixth-century agricultural treatise *Essential Skills for the Life of the Common People (qi min yao shu)* mentions the salt-preservation of chicken eggs, but in modern China it's rare to see anything but duck eggs treated in this way. There are several salting methods: the eggs can be caked in a paste made from salt and mud, or salt and wood ash, or simply steeped in a very salty brine, as in the following recipe. Salted duck eggs are widely available in Chinese food stores.

You will need a 2-quart jar with a tight-fitting lid to make this recipe.

9 FRESH DUCK EGGS

⅔ CUP SALT

1. Give the duck eggs a good wash and a scrub with a vegetable brush to remove any dirt; discard any cracked eggs.
2. Bring 3⅓ pints water to a boil in a wok over a high flame. Add the salt and stir to dissolve, then leave the water to cool completely.
3. Place the eggs carefully in your preserving jar. Pour the salt solution over. Place a small ceramic dish or glass at the top of the jar to keep the top eggs completely covered by the water. Close the lid tightly and leave in a cool place for 2–3 weeks. (If you leave them longer, they can taste too salty.)
4. When the eggs are ready, remove them from the brine and hard-boil them. Allow them to cool completely before eating.

EVERYDAY STOCK
xian tang

★

This kind of stock is the base of most everyday soups and is also added to sauces for a richer flavor. The most common is simply pork-bone stock (*gu tou tang*), which is widely used in peasant cookery, although some recipes require chicken stock (*ji tang*). I tend to make a big potful of stock with either chicken carcasses and wings, or a mixture of chicken and pork bones, from time to time, depending on what my butcher has available, and freeze it in useful quantities. The basic method is as follows.

ANY OR ALL OF THE FOLLOWING:
CHICKEN CARCASSES,
CHICKEN WINGS, CHICKEN
BONES, PORK RIBS, PORK
BONES
FRESH GINGER, UNPEELED
SCALLIONS

1. Cover the chicken and/or pork bones generously with cold water and bring to a boil, skimming the surface as necessary. Crush a piece of ginger and a couple of scallions with the wide blade of your cleaver or a heavy object.
2. When the foam stops rising from the bones, add the ginger and scallions. Partially cover the pan and simmer over a gentle heat for 2–3 hours. Strain before using or storing.

QING QING'S VEGETARIAN BLACK BEAN STOCK
dou chi tang

★

The rich *umami* tastes of black fermented beans and winter-sacrifice beans mean they can be boiled into an easy and delicious vegetarian stock a little reminiscent of Japanese miso. Qing Qing Liu showed me how to make this.

1 QT. WATER
⅓ OZ. BLACK FERMENTED BEANS,
RINSED

1. Bring the water to a boil with the black fermented beans, then simmer for about 20 minutes. Strain out the whole beans, if desired, although it is not essential.

FINE STOCK
qing tang

Grander soups and banquet dishes require a fine stock, made from richer ingredients, such as chicken, duck, and pork knuckle or picnic, simmered over a very gentle heat for 3–4 hours. The following recipe is based on the one published in my earlier book, *Land of Plenty*.

1 LB. CHICKEN PIECES
    (DRUMSTICKS, WINGS,
    THIGHS, NECKS, ETC.)

1 LB. DUCK PIECES

14 OZ. PORK SPARE RIBS

14 OZ. MILD CURED HAM, SUCH
    AS SMITHFIELD, WITHOUT
    RIND

5 QT. WATER

¾-IN. PIECE FRESH GINGER,
    UNPEELED

1 SCALLION

1. For best results, begin by blanching all the meats and poultry pieces, except the ham, in boiling water until the water returns to a vigorous boil again, to remove any remaining blood and impurities, then rinse them under cold running water; discard the blanching water.

2. Place all the meats and poultry pieces in a large saucepan, add the water, and bring to a boil over a high flame, skimming any scum that rises to the surface. Crush the ginger and scallion slightly with the wide side of a cleaver or a heavy object, and add them to the stockpot.

3. Partially cover the pan and simmer very gently, over a low flame, for about 3 hours. Skim off any fat that gathers on the surface from time to time.

4. When the stock is ready, strain it into a clean saucepan, using cheesecloth or a very fine sieve.

LARD
zhu you

猪
油

In the Hunanese countryside, many households still make their own lard, and use it as an everyday cooking fat, where it adds a rich taste and a silky moistness to all kinds of otherwise vegetarian dishes. It's used less these days in the cities, although you can still find lard-making workshops in the backstreets of Changsha. I find bought lard fairly unsavory, but if you make it yourself it will have a subtle and delicious flavor. You can use it as a substitute for peanut oil as a cooking fat in many recipes in this book, or add a little to soups just before you serve them in the same way that Italians add olive oil. I first learned to make lard from Bruce Cost's *Foods from the Far East*, from which this recipe is derived.

Cut pork fatback into chunks and put into a saucepan with a generous covering of water. Bring to a boil and then simmer over a medium flame to allow the water to evaporate. When the water has almost disappeared, the liquid will start to spit and crackle. When the noise has subsided, remove the pan from the stove and strain the molten lard. It will keep for a week or so in the refrigerator. (The same method can be used to render chicken fat, which is often added to banquet dishes just before serving, adding a wonderful *umami* flavor.)

CARAMEL COLOR
tang se

糖
色

Chinese chefs make their own caramel to give a lustrous red-brown color to aromatic broth and red-braised dishes. Dark soy sauce can be used instead, but it does not give such an appetizing color.

½ CUP GRANULATED SUGAR

WATER

1. Heat the sugar gently with 4 tablespoons water in a wok, stirring as it dissolves. Continue to stir over a gentle flame for some time, scraping the sugar from the bottom of the wok—the sugar will dry out and become fudgy, and then it will melt again.

2. When the liquid has become dark brown, with large bubbles, add 1 cup cold water around the edge of the wok. Mix well and simmer for a while to reduce the liquid to a heavy, dark caramel. Store and use as required; it will keep indefinitely at room temperature.

"FLOWER" BEAN CURD
dou hua

★

This light bean curd is unpressed, so it retains a texture a little like that of crème caramel. It is usually eaten very fresh and still warm. Street vendors make it early in the morning and offer it with a sprinkling of white sugar. It is can also be eaten in soups, like the one on page 241.

Gypsum, the coagulant, can be found in good Chinese supermarkets.

¾ CUP DRIED YELLOW SOYBEANS

WATER

2 TSP. GYPSUM (SEE
    INTRODUCTION ABOVE)

1. Leave the soybeans to soak overnight in plenty of cold water, changing the water a few times, if possible. The following day, rinse the beans very well under cold running water, and then put them into a blender with 1 quart water (do this in 2 batches, if necessary). Whiz them for a few minutes until you can no longer see any bits of bean and there is a good head of froth on the liquid. Line a sieve or colander with a piece of cheesecloth and strain the soybean liquid into a saucepan. Squeeze the cheesecloth very tightly to extract as much soymilk as possible.

2. Dissolve the gypsum in 1 cup hot water. Place the strained soy milk into a saucepan and bring to a boil over a high flame. Skim off the surface foam with a slotted spoon and discard.

3. Pour the boiling milk into a bowl, and allow it to cool to about 185°F. Stir the gypsum mixture and scatter it over the soy milk. Give the milk a quick stir and then leave to set for 20 minutes. As it sets, gently press the surface of the curd with a slotted spoon to firm up the mixture and let any excess water escape.

4. If you don't wish to eat the bean curd immediately, cover it in hot water and set it over an extremely low flame to keep warm. If you are using bought soft bean curd, warm it up in a saucepan of gently simmering, lightly salted water.

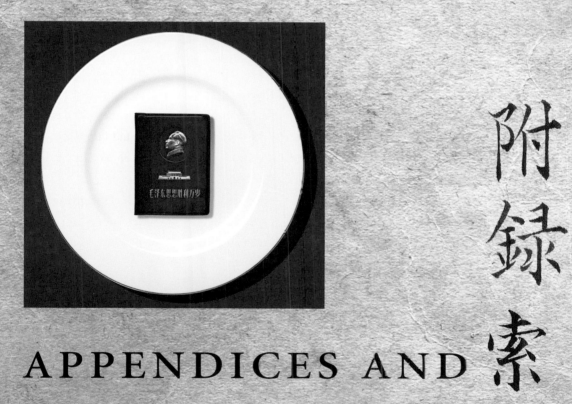

APPENDICES AND
INDEX

附錄 索引

★ GLOSSARY OF CHINESE CHARACTERS

爱群 *ai qun*—"Love the Masses"

安息茴香 *an xi hui xiang*—literally "Parthian fennel," Chinese scholarly name for cumin

白菜苔 *bai cai tai*—"white" baby cabbages (probably *Brassica campestris ssp. chinensis* var. *utilis*)

百叶 *bai ye*—"hundred leaves", sheets of pressed bean curd

板子 *ban zi*— wooden serving boards used in noodle restaurants

包菜 *bao cai*— literally "wrapped vegetable," round white cabbage with a tight heart (Brassica oleracea var. capitata)

煸炒 *bian chao*— simple stir-frying

病从口入 *bing cong kou ru*— "sickness enters through the mouth"

不吃辣椒不革命 *bu chi la jiao bu ge ming*— "if you don't eat chillies, you won't be a revolutionary"

菜藕 *cai'ou*— "vegetable lotus", a type of lotus

才鱼 *cai yu*— snakehead fish (*Ophiocephalus argus*)

蚕豆 *can dou*— fava beans (*Vicia faba*)

茶树菇 *cha shu gu*— a delicious mushroom (*Agrocybe aegerita*), often sold in its dried form. It has long stems and pale brown caps, and can be found packaged in good Chinese supermarkets

吃饱，吃好，吃巧 *chi bao, chi hao, chi qiao*— "eating your fill, eating well, eating skilfully"

吃苦 *chi ku*— "eat bitterness", metaphor for suffering

臭豆腐 *chou dou fu*— stinking bean curd

楚 *chu*— name for the ancient Chu state that once embraced Hunan

厨子的汤，戏子的腔 *chu zi de tang, xi zi de qiang* — "stock is to the cook what pitch is to the opera singer"

葱 *cong* — scallions (*Allium fistulosum*)

大蒜 *da suan* — Hunanese name for green garlic leaves

丁 *ding* — small cube

冬瓜 *dong gua* — winter melon (*Benincasa hispida*)

冬苋菜 *dong han cai* — leafy vegetable used mainly in soups (*Malva verticillata*)

豆腐脑 *dou fu nao* — alternative name for "flower" bean curd

豆腐乳 *dou fu ru* — fermented bean curd

豆角 *dou jiao* — yard-long beans (*Vigna unguiculata* var. *sesquipedalis*)

肥而不腻 *fei er bu ni* — "richly fat without being greasy"

粉丝 *fen si* — beanthread noodles

佛豆 *fo dou* — Buddha beans, alternative name for can dou

釜 *fu* — ancient cooking cauldron

割烹 *ge peng* — "to cut and to cook", an ancient Chinese name for cooking

刮子 *gua zi* — scraper for making scraped jelly ribbons

苋菜 *han cai* — purple amaranth (*Amaranthus tricolor*)

寒菌 *han jun* — "winter-cold mushroom" (*Lactarius deliciosus*) known in English as the saffron milk cap

黑山羊 *hei shan yang* — black goat

红菜苔 *hong cai tai* — "red' baby cabbages (probably *Brassica campestris ssp. chinensis* var. *utilis*)

红曲鱼 *hong qu yu* — fish pickled in red wine lees

红薯粉 *hong shu fen* — sweet potato starch jelly or

noodles

胡豆 *hu dou* — "foreign" or "barbarian" beans, another name for *can dou*

湖藕 *hu'ou* — "lake lotus", a kind of lotus root

滑 *hua* — slippery

黄花菜 *huang hua cai* — day-lily flowers (*Hemerocallis fulva*)

黄鸭叫 *huang ya jiao* — "yellow quack", a type of catfish (possibly *Pseudobagrus fulvidraco*)

鮰鱼 *hui yu* — a kind of catfish (*Leiocassius longirostris*)

火宫殿 *huo gong dian* — the Fire Temple Restaurant in Changsha

火辣辣 *huo la la* — literally "fire-hot-hot", an epithet for Hunanese women

荠菜 *ji cai* — shepherd's purse (*Capsella bursapastoris*; di cai in Hunan dialect)

酱板鸭 *jiang ban ya* — Yueyang pressed duck

酱辣椒 *jiang la jiao* — pickled chillies

焦 *jiao* — crisp

茭瓜 *jiao gua or jiao bai* — wild rice stem or water bamboo (*Zizania caduciflora* or *Zizania latifolia*)

金沙 *jin sha* — "golden sand", name for dishes made with salted duck egg yolk

金针菜 *jin zhen cai* — day-lily flowers (alternative name for *huang hua cai*)

蕨菜 *jue cai* — fiddlehead fern

开花 *kai hua* — "burst into flower", used to describe what happens to grains when they burst after long cooking

口蘑 *ko mo* — delicious wild mushrooms

空心菜 *kong xin cai* — water spinach, literally "hollowheart vegetable", also known as *weng cai* and *tong cai* in Mandarin, and *ong choy* and *tong choy* in Cantonese (*Ipomoea aquatica*)

口感 *kou gan* — mouthfeel

苦瓜 *ku gua* — bitter melon or bitter gourd (*Momordica charantia*)

块 *kuai* — chunk

脍残鱼 *kuai can yu* — "leftovers fish", alternative name for silver fish

捆鸡 *kun ji* — "bound chickens", vegetarian "chicken" made from bean curd

辣酱 *la jiang* — pickled chilli paste

腊月 *la yue* — the twelfth lunar month, or month of sacrifices

兰花干 *lan hua gan* — a kind of deep-fried bean curd

擂 *lei* — pounded or mashed

莲藕 *lian ou* — lotus (*Nelumbo nucifera*)

灵根 *ling gen* — "root of the soul", poetic name for the lotus

蒌蒿 *lou hao* — a kind of artemisia whose young stems are stir-fried with bacon (Chinese sources identify it as *Artemisia vulgaris* var. *vulgatissima*, see also *ti hao*)

萝卜 *luo bu* — Asian white radish, *daikon, mooli* (*Raphanus sativus*)

罗汉豆 *luo han dou* — Arhat beans, another name for *can dou*

毛红兵 *mao hong bing* — "Red Soldier Mao"

毛家菜 *mao jia cai* — "Mao's home-style cooking"

毛笋 *mao sun* — "hairy bamboo shoot", a type of edible bamboo (*Phyllostachys pubescens*)

没有辣椒，吃不下饭 *mei you la jiao, chi bu xia fan* — "can't get the rice down without chillies"

苗 *miao* — young shoots of a vegetable, for example peas

魔芋 *mo yu* — konnyaku yam jelly

糯米大烧卖 *nuo mi da shao mai* — steamed dumplings filled with glutinous rice

牌坊 *pai fang* — memorial archway

片 *pian* — slice

瓢子 *piao zi* — long-handled ladle

扑辣椒 *pu la jiao* — a kind of pickled chilli

青皮豆 *qing pi dou* — "green-skin beans", fresh
    green soybeans

肉食者 *rou shi zhe* — "meat-eaters", ancient
    Chinese term for the rich

入味 *ru wei* — "sending the flavours in"

箬叶 *ruo ye* — indocalamus or giant bamboo leaves
    (*Indocalamus tessellatus*)

馓子 *san zi* — deep-fried dough strands

臊 *sao* — foul (taste or odour)

涩 *se* — astringent (taste)

膻 *shan* — muttony (taste or odour)

石蜜 *shi mi* — rock honey

熟炒 *shu chao* — "cooked" stir-frying

涮羊肉 *shuan yang rou* — "scalded mutton", the
    "Mongolian hotpot" of Beijing

水芹菜 *shui qin cai* — water celery (*Oenanthe
    javanica*)

丝 *si* — "silken thread", a sliver of food

四季豆 *si ji dou* — "four-season beans", thin green
    beans (Phaseolus vulgaris)

酥 *su* — crisp

酸辣椒 *suan la jiao* — pickled chillies

蒜苗 *suan miao* — Hunanese name for garlic stems

酸肉 *suan rou* — sour pickled pork

蒜子 *suan zi* — garlic cloves

糖油粑粑 *tang you ba ba* — squidgy glutinous rice
    balls coated in golden toffee

提蒿 *ti hao or ni hao* in Hunan dialect — see *lou hao*

天麻 *tian ma* — Chinese medicinal tuber
    (*Gastrodia elata*)

甜藕 *tian"ou* — "sweet lotus", a type of lotus

条 *tiao* — strip

旺火 *wang huo* — hot flame

王墓豆 *wang mu dou* — "King"s grave beans",
    another name for *can dou*

微火 *wei huo* — tiny flame

文火 *wen huo* — small flame

闻起来臭，吃起来香 *wen qi lai chou, chi qi lai
    xiang* — "Smell it and it's stinky; eat it and it's
    deliciously fragrant" (a description of stinking
    bean curd)

莴笋 *wo sun* — a type of lettuce with a swollen
    stem (*Latuca sativa* var. *angustata*), both the stem
    and leaves are used in Hunanese cookery

武火 *wu huo* — moderate flame

下饭 *xia fan* — "send the rice down"

鲜 *xian* — delicious and savoury, the Chinese
    equivalent of *umami*

仙豆 *xian dou* — "fairy beans", another name for
    can dou

湘莲 *xiang lian* — Hunanese lotus seeds

小葱 *xiao cong* — "small scallions"

新军 *xin jun* — new army

腥味 *xing wei* — "fishy" taste or odour

血粑鸭 *xue ba ya* — blood-pudding duck

烟花之乡 *yan hua zhi xiang* — "the home of smoke
    flowers", poetic name for the city of Liuyang,
    a centre of firework production

野山椒 *ye shan jiao* — "wild mountain chillies"

异味 *yi wei* — peculiar smell

一月提，二月好，三月四月作柴烧 *yi yue ti, er
    yue hao, san yue si yue zuo chai shao* — "grows in
    the first month, tastes good in the second, but by
    the third and fourth months it"s only good for
    firewood", popular Yueyang rhyme about the
    seasonal wild vegetable *ti hao* (q.v)

银丝卷 *yin si juan* — "silver-silk rolls", steamed buns

银针茶 *yin zhen cha* — silver-needle tea, a tea
    produced on Junshan, near Yueyang

鳙鱼 *yong yu* — bighead carp (*Aristichthys nobilis*; *xiong* yu in Hunan dialect)

鱼米之乡 *yu mi zhi xiang* — "The home of fish and rice", poetic name for Hunan

芋头 *yu tou* — taro (*Colocasia spp.*)

原汁原味 *yuan zhi yuan wei* — "plain, original juices and flavours"

咋鱼 *zha yu* — fish pickled in red wine lees

寨 *zhai* — stockaded village

笊篱 *zhao li* — wire mesh strainer with a bamboo handle

盅 *zhong* — little china soup pots with lids

竹刷 *zhu shua* — bamboo wok brush

茱萸 *zhu yu* — cornel (*Cornus officinalis*)

紫菜 *zi cai* — "purple vegetable", laver seaweed, *nori* in Japanese (*Porphyra tenera*)

★ THE MAIN CHINESE DYNASTIES

XIA	*c.* 21ST–16TH CENTURY BC
SHANG	*c.* 16TH–11TH CENTURY BC
ZHOU	*c.* 11TH CENTURY BC–221 BC
QIN DYNASTY	221 BC–206 BC
HAN DYNASTY	206 BC–AD 220
THREE KINGDOMS	220–280
JIN	265–420
NORTHERN AND SOUTHERN DYNASTIES	386–589
SUI	581–618
TANG	618–907
FIVE DYNASTIES AND TEN STATES	907–979
SONG	960–1279
YUAN	1279–1368
MING	1368–1644
QING	1644–1911
REPUBLIC OF CHINA (*Nationalist Party*)	1912–1949
PEOPLE'S REPUBLIC OF CHINA (*Communist Party*)	1949– ?

★ BIBLIOGRAPHY

All the following books have been useful in my research, but I owe a particular debt to Liu Guochu's recent work on Hunanese culinary culture, *The Grand Banquet of Hunanese Cuisine*, and to the now out-of-print *A Collection of Traditional Hunanese Foods* edited by Yu Jinglin.

IN CHINESE

A Portrait of Ancient and Modern Changsha (*gu jin chang sha da xie zhen*), a magazine produced to commemorate the sixtieth anniversary of the Great Fire of Changsha, 1998.

Changde Shi Difang Zhibian Weihui, *The Magnificent Scenery of Changde* (*chang de feng wu da guan*), *bei jing chu ban she*, Beijing, 1988.

Huang Zhenlin (ed.), *A Guide to Hunan's Specialty Local Products* (*hu nan te chan feng wei zhi nan*), *hu nan mei shu chu ban she*, Changsha, 1983.

Jiang Zhiquan, *Famous Snacks of Hunan* (*hu nan ming dian xiao chi*), *hu nan ke xue ji shu chu ban she*, Changsha, 1989.

Jin Xing (ed.), *Make Your Own Preserves and Pickles* (*zi ji zuo jiang shi pao cai*), *hu nan wen yi chu ban she*, Changsha, 1999.

Li Jianguo, *Homestyle Dishes* (*jia chang cai*), *hu nan ke xue ji shu chu ban she*, Changsha, 2002.

Lin Shide, *Local Dishes* (*di fang cai*), *hu nan ke xue ji shu chu ban she*, Changsha, 2000.

Lin Shide, Yang Zhangyou (eds), *Hunanese Cuisine* (*xiang cai*), *hua xia chu ban she*, Beijing, 1997.

Liu Guochu, *The Grand Banquet of Hunanese Cuisine* (*xiang cai sheng yan*), *yue lu shu she*, Changsha, 2004.

Liu Hongwei, Wang Qingsong (eds), *Hunan Cookbook* (*hu nan cai pu*), *hu nan ke xue ji shu chu ban she*, Changsha, 2002.

Liu Jian'an, *The Spirit of the Hunanese* (*hu nan ren de jing shen*), *zhong guo she hui ke xue chu ban she*, Beijing, 2002.

Lu Baochun, *Eating All Over China—Hunanese Dishes* (*chi bian zhong guo, hu nan cai*), *zhong guo min zu she ying yi shu chu ban she*, Beijing, 2004.

Luo Jixiang, *Jixiang Delicacies* (*ji xiang mei shi*), *hu nan ren min chu ban she*, Changsha, 2000.

Mao Zedong, *Report on an Investigation of the Peasant Movement in Hunan*, 1927, available online at http://www.marxists.org

Nie Fengqiao, Zhao Lian (eds), *Dictionary of Chinese Cooking Ingredients* (*zhong guo peng ren yuan liao da dian*), *qing dao chu ban she*, Qingdao, 2004.

Qing Siren (ed.), *The Famous Historical and Cultural City of Yueyang* (*li shi wen hua ming cheng yue yang*), 1996.

Ren Baizun (ed.), *The Chinese Classic of Food* (*zhong guo shi jing*), *shang hai wen hua chu ban she*, Shanghai, 1999.

Shi Yinxiang, *Hunanese Cuisine Collection* (*xiang cai ji jin*), *hu nan ke xue ji shu chu ban she*, Changsha, 2001.

Sun Jinyun, Wang Ronghua (eds), *Eating in Republican China* (*chi zai min guo*), *jiang su wen yi chu ban she*, Nanjing, 2004.

Tan Tiansan, *Traditional Dishes (chuan tong cai)*, hu nan ke xue ji shu chu ban she, Changsha, 2000.

Wang Xingguo, Nie Ronghua (eds), *An Easy Chat About Hunan Culture (hu xiang wen hua zong heng tan)*, hu nan da xue chu ban she, Changsha, 1996.

Wu Xiwen, *Yueyang, The Bright Pearl of Dongting (dong ting ming zhu yue yang)*, zhong guo hua qiao chu ban she, Beijing, 1992.

Xiao Fan (ed.), *Chinese Culinary Dictionary (zhong guo peng ren ci dian)*, zhong guo shang ye chu ban she, Beijing, 1992.

Xu Juyun, *The Art of Cooking by Famous Chinese Cooks—Xu Juyun (zhong hua ming chu xu ju yun peng ren ji shu)*, liao ning ke xue ji shu chu ban she, Shenyang, 2001.

Xu Juyun, *Specialty Snacks (feng wei xiao chi)*, hu nan ke xue ji shu chu ban she, Changsha, 2001.

Yu Jinglin (ed.), *A Collection of Traditional Hunanese Foods (hu nan chuan tong shi pin hui cui)*, zhong guo shang ye chu ban she, 1992.

Zhang Chixiang, Gui Xiuwen (eds.), *Annals of Hunan Local Scenery (hu nan feng wu zhi)*, hu nan ren min chu ban she, Changsha, 1985.

Zhang Lixing, *Pastry Snacks (mian dian)*, hu nan ke xue ji shu chu ban she, Changsha, 2001.

IN ENGLISH

Boorman, Howard L. (ed.), *Biographical Dictionary of Republican China*, Columbia University Press, New York and London, 1970.

Chang, Jung and Halliday, Jon, *Mao: The Unknown Story*, Jonathan Cape, London, 2005.

Chang, K. C. (ed.), *Food in Chinese Culture*, Yale University Press, New Haven, 1977.

Chung, Henry W.S., *Henry Chung's Hunan Style Chinese Cookbook*, Harmony Books, New York, 1978.

Cost, Bruce, *Foods from the Far East*, Century, London, 1990.

Davidson, Alan, *Oxford Companion to Food*, Oxford University Press, Oxford, 1999.

Dunlop, Fuchsia, "The Strange Tale of General Tso's Chicken" in Hosking, Richard (ed.), *Proceedings of the Oxford Food Symposium 2005: Authenticity* (forthcoming).

Hosking, Richard, *A Dictionary of Japanese Food*, Charles E. Tuttle Company, Rutland, Vermont and Tokyo, 1996.

Hummel, Arthur W., *Eminent Chinese of the Ch'ing Period*, United States Government Printing Office, Washington, 1944.

Hunan Museum (ed.), *The Han Tombs of Mawangdui Changsha*, Hunan People's Publishing House, Changsha, 1987.

Larkcom, Joy, *Oriental Vegetables*, John Murray, London, 1991.

Li Zhisui, *The Private Life of Chairman Mao*, Arrow Books, London, 1996.

McGee, Harold, *McGee on Food and Cooking*, Hodder and Stoughton, London, 2004.

Roberts, J. A. G., *China to Chinatown: Chinese Food in the West*, Reaktion Books, London, 2002.

So, Yan-kit, *Classic Chinese Cookbook*, Dorling Kindersley, London, 1984.

So, Yan-kit, *Classic Food of China*, Macmillan, London, 1992

Wilkinson, Endymion, *Chinese History: A Manual*, Harvard University Asia Center, Harvard University Press, Cambridge and London, 1998.

★ ACKNOWLEDGMENTS

A HEARTFELT THANK-YOU TO:-

Liu Wei and Sansan, for their inspiring friendship and boundless hospitality, and for welcoming me into their family from the beginning. (As we've said many times, our meeting must have been some kind of *yuan fen*);

Tian Zhengqian and Fan Qun, with whom I have spent so many happy times in Yueyang, and in Fan Qun's idyllic home village, Ba Jing Dong;

Li Rui, Li Xiaorong, Chen Wenming, Xu Shikeng, Tong Huiru, Liu Xuzhang, and Liu Xutai, for being like a family to me in Changsha;

The communist model soldier Lei Feng, for introducing me, in a manner of speaking, to all my best friends in Changsha;

The editor of the *Sichuan Pengren* magazine, Wang Xudong, for encouraging me to write about Hunanese food, and for his unstinting help and friendship;

Professors Xiong Sizhi and Du Li of the Sichuan Institute of Higher Cuisine for paving my way to Changsha with letters of introduction;

Professor Feng Quanxin, Qiu Rongzhen, Feng Xiaoning, Liu Yaochun, Xu Jun, Lai Wu, Yu Bo, and Dai Shuang for their great friendship and constant support from my old Chinese HQ, Chengdu;

George Dong, and Deng Zhiyuan and his family, for finding me a flat to live in, and helping me take my first tentative steps into Changsha life;

Qin Lingzhi, the manager of the Xihulou restaurant company, for allowing me to study in her kitchens, and for her great kindness and hospitality;

Liu Guochu for his generous support and invaluable teaching, and his daughter Liu Qingqing for her cooking tips and enthusiasm;

Yang Zhangyou, the founder of the Hunan Culinary Association, for several fascinating and informative conversations, and for introducing me to some vital written sources;

Leading chefs Xu Juyun and Wu Tao at Yuloudong, and Luo Jixiang, for help in many culinary matters;

Tang Huaping in Yueyang, for sharing with me his passionate interest in food and for introducing me to the delicious flavors of his hometown;

Mr. Zhao, the owner of the Everyone Restaurant (*ren ren cai guan*) in Yueyang, for allowing me into the hectic kitchen of his popular restaurant, and for answering a million questions;

Li Peitian, Yueyang food expert and writer, for helping me on my way;

Fan Renhe and Zhu Yinglan for teaching me much of what I know about rural Hunanese food and cooking and Chinese New Year celebrations;

Tao Yanfang and Tao Damin, for so generously having me to stay in their farmhouse;

Tan Xinming and Yan Manying of the *Xiangcai* magazine, Wang Taozhen of the Hunan Culinary Association, food writers Lao Tao and Jason Wang, and Su Congjian of the Hunan Commercial and Technical College for a great deal of useful information;

Tan Fei, Zhou Houchang, and Li Jiahua for introducing me to the history and specialties of Huogongdian;

Mao Anping, for teaching me his favorite recipe, and telling me about the food habits of his uncle, Mao Zedong;

Xiong Aiqun, the manager of Guchengge restaurant, for allowing me to spend days of study in his kitchen, and Tao Jianqing, the head waitress, for her great kindness;

Veteran chef Shi Yinxiang, for giving me several books and telling me many fascinating tales;

Peng Chang-kuei and his son Peng T'ieh-cheng at the Peng Yuan restaurant in Taipei, for being so generous with their time and for allowing me into their kitchen;

Davide Quadrio, Stephanie Chauvel, Rob Gifford, Nancy Fraser, Gwen Chesnais, Nick Porter, Louise Beynon, Rob Kenny, and Leslie Kenny for being such wonderful, supportive, and hospitable friends in various parts of China;

My fantastic agent Zoe Waldie, and Nick Wilson, for their constant encouragement and enthusiasm;

My family, Bede, Carolyn, Merlin, Charlotte, Leonie, Poppy, and Thea Dunlop, for their love and support, and, in particular, to my mother for her invaluable help with recipe testing and for many useful comments on the manuscript;

Ren Jianjun of the Shangri-La Hunan Cuisine Restaurant in London, Shao Wei, Zhang Xiaozhong, Fu Bing, and Wu Xiaoming for helping me with some last-minute queries;

My dear friends Mara Baughman, Penny Bell, Patrizia Benvenuti, Bess Frimodig, Seema Merchant, Lipika Pelham, Yu-lan Su, and Francesca Tarocco for many things, and in particular to Mara for some early readings of the manuscript and Francesca for her expert advice and help with final readings;

Gillian Riley and Richard Hosking for their stimulating company, support, and camaraderie;

Liliane Landor at the BBC World Service for enabling me to spend time in China for my research;

Sarah Lavelle, Carey Smith, and Natalie Hunt at Ebury Press for putting so much into this book, and Beverly LeBlanc for her meticulous editing;

Maria Guarnaschelli at W. W. Norton for her great support and her enthusiasm for this and my previous book;

Georgia Glynn Smith for her stunning photographs, Alice Hart for her help, Qu Lei Lei for his calligraphy, and David Fordham for his beautiful design.

I also want to say thank you to Hugo Martin, who, in an extraordinary act of generosity, gave me the collection of books on Chinese food and cooking that belonged to his late mother, Yan-kit So Martin. Yan-kit was a treasured friend and mentor to me, and her books are a constant source of personal pleasure. They have also been more valuable to my work than I can adequately express.

I should like to point out that any errors in this book are, of course, my own. F.D.

★ INDEX